Contents

Complementary Feeding

A research-based guide

CLAIRE TUCK

PhD

Registered Nutritionist

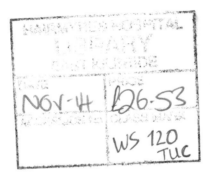

Radcliffe Publishing

London • New York

Radcliffe Publishing Ltd
33–41 Dallington Street
London
EC1V 0BB
United Kingdom

www.radcliffehealth.com

British Library Cataloguing in Publication Data

A catalogue record for this book is available from the British Library.

ISBN-13: 978 190891 193 3

The paper used for the text pages of this book
is FSC® certified. FSC (The Forest Stewardship
Council®) is an international network to promote
responsible management of the world's forests.

Typeset by Darkriver Design, Auckland, New Zealand
Printed and bound by TJI Digital. Padstow, Cornwall, UK

Preface

This book clearly describes current research, recommendations from government and advice from other valid sources regarding the introduction of solids to an infant's diet. Discrepancies between research and recommendations are related to the dilemmas faced by health professionals when giving advice to parents on introducing solids.

Current research is interpreted to provide up-to-date advice on the introduction of solids and continued dietary intake up to the age of 12 months. This is the first book on complementary feeding to illustrate a suggested balance of different foods and food groups needed to provide a healthy diet for infants.

A book such as this is timely; current practice appears to focus heavily on a poor balance of food, relying too heavily on fruits, vegetables and cereals in the initial months of complementary feeding. In addition, information for parents on complementary feeding is vague in terms of the proportion of different food groups that should be provided for the infant. The Food Standards Agency has commissioned a new study on infants aged 4–18 months, which will update the 1992 dietary intake data for UK infants. This study is being undertaken by the National Infant Diet and Health Study research team (see www.mrc-hnr.cam.ac.uk/NIDHS), and will assist the Scientific Advisory Committee on Nutrition in their examination of recommendations and advice on complementary feeding.

Understandably, government advice can only be developed when there is sufficient research. However, current government advice is based on research from over 20 years ago; new research indicates that updated advice is now required, to assist parents in the provision of a healthy infant diet. This book will assist the provision of new guidance on complementary feeding and is essential reading for all health professionals involved in infant feeding.

Claire Tuck
January 2013

About the author

Claire is a Registered Nutritionist, currently working as a nutrition lecturer and freelance nutrition writer. She has a PhD on dietary behaviour change and has worked for the past 20 years in the area of nutrition, covering research, health promotion and nutrition policy. Claire was previously nutrition advisor to the Welsh Government and the Food Standards Agency (Wales) and co-director of an institute of food at Bangor University.

Acknowledgement

Thanks go to Justin Allen Davies (www.gringodesign.co.uk) for his design input on Figure 5.3.

To my lovely family,
and especially Ella and Matt – thank you.

List of tables and figures

Tables

Figures

List of symbols and abbreviations

<	less than
≤	less than or equal to
>	more than
µg	microgram(s)
BLW	baby-led weaning
COMA	Committee on Medical Aspects of Food Policy
COT	Committee on Toxicity of Chemicals in Food, Consumer Products and the Environment
DH	Department of Health
DRV	Dietary Reference Value
EAR	Estimated Average Requirement
EFSA	European Food Safety Authority
ESPGHAN	European Society for Paediatric Gastroenterology, Hepatology and Nutrition
FAO	Food and Agriculture Organization of the United Nations
FSA	Food Standards Agency
g	gram(s)
ID	iron deficiency
IDA	iron deficiency anaemia
infant	from birth to 1 year of age
kcal	kilocalorie(s)
kg	kilogram(s)
kJ	kilojoule(s)
L	litre(s)
LDL	low-density lipoprotein
LRNI	Lower Reference Nutrient Intake
m^2	meter(s) squared
MAFF	Ministry of Agriculture, Fisheries and Food
mg	milligram(s)

MJ	megajoule(s) (1000 joules)
mmol	millimole(s)
NDNS	National Diet and Nutrition Survey
NHS	National Health Service
NMES	non-milk extrinsic sugars
NSP	non-starch polysaccharides
oz	ounce(s)
RE	Retinol Equivalent
RNI	Reference Nutrient Intake
SACN	Scientific Advisory Committee on Nutrition
WHO	World Health Organization

Summary of key facts

1. Complementary feeding means introducing solids to an infant's milk diet.
2. The current UK recommendation is to start introducing solids at 6 months but there is flexibility to start earlier, dependent upon the individual needs of each infant.
3. While research unequivocally shows that solids should not be introduced until after 4 months of age, debate continues regarding the ideal recommended age of introduction of solids, due to the limited evidence of benefits of exclusive breastfeeding to 6 months, relative to 4–6 months, in developed countries.
4. Breastfeeding has been shown to provide sufficient energy for normal growth and to meet recommended energy requirements for most infants at 6 months of age.
5. Breastfeeding is associated with a reduced risk of gastrointestinal infection in both developing and developed countries.
6. There is currently insufficient evidence to support recommendations on the appropriate age of introduction of gluten to the diet beyond 3 months of age. The current UK recommendation is to introduce gluten after 6 months of age.
7. There is insufficient evidence on the timing of introduction of other solids to minimise the risk of developing allergies.
8. While breastfeeding has been shown to be protective against overweight and obesity, there appears to be no association between the timing of introduction of solids and overweight or obesity in infancy.
9. While iron deficiency anaemia appears to be a cause of poor motor development in the first 3 years of life and iron deficiency may exist in the brain in the absence of iron deficiency anaemia, the effect of iron deficiency and iron deficiency anaemia on preschool children's motor, cognitive and behavioural development remains controversial.
10. Limited findings indicate that in developed countries, rates of iron

deficiency appear to be between 0% and 24% at 9–12 months, while rates of iron deficiency anaemia appear to be between 0% and 7% at 8–12 months.

11. An infant's iron stores at birth are positively related to maternal iron stores. Infants with low iron stores at birth appear to have a greater risk of iron deficiency anaemia at 6 and 12 months than infants whose iron stores are replete at birth.

12. Based on a limited number of studies, exclusive breastfeeding to 6 months is associated with a low risk of iron deficiency anaemia in developed countries, but a higher risk of iron deficiency anaemia in developing countries.

13. Meat and fish have been shown to be positively associated with iron status in infants, meat being well accepted as a first food in addition to most new foods.

14. The consumption of a wide variety of foods should help meet iron requirements; however, without fortified cereals and meat, these requirements will be difficult to attain. The best sources of iron for infants are tinned sardines and meat (beef). Good sources of iron include fortified infant cereals and fortified breakfast cereals.

15. Poor complementary feeding, in terms of low iron status, appears to reflect a low intake of meat and fish and a displacement of iron-containing foods with sweet foods, while six breast milk feeds or more a day and 600 mL of formula milk or more a day is related to a low iron intake from solids.

16. The guideline minimum intake of milk at 7–12 months is 500 mL; however, this guideline was suggested before the 2012 lower energy intake recommendations.

17. Many early complementary fruit, vegetable and cereal purees, mashes and finger foods contain less energy than breast milk. Most contain little or no fat.

18. Vitamin D is recommended as a supplement from 6 months of age if <500 mL per day of infant formula is consumed (all breastfed infants from 6 months; from 1 month if the vitamin D status of the mother is questionable). Health professional advice to parents on vitamin D supplements appears to be infrequent.

19. Current guidelines on how to introduce solids are largely based on tradition rather than research, while there is little evidence for the introduction of solids in any specific order or at any specific rate.

20. There are inconsistencies in current advice on complementary feeding from reputable sources, including the Department of Health, other UK health departments and the Food Standards Agency.

21. Responsive feeding is where a mother feeds an infant in response to his cues, allowing the infant to decide whether to eat and how much to eat. UK health departments currently recommend responsive feeding.

22. Baby-led weaning follows responsive feeding; there is no spoon-feeding by the parent, the infant feeding himself and being offered solid family foods rather than traditional purees (as at 4–6 months). Baby-led weaning appears feasible for many infants around 6 months of age who have developed the appropriate feeding skills.

23. Revised Estimated Average Requirements for energy for infants are lower than previous recommendations, with separate values now being given for breastfed, formula-fed and breastfed/formula-fed infants.

24. There is no recommendation for total fat intake for infants in the United Kingdom, other than not to restrict fat intake. Recommendations for total fat intake for infants elsewhere range from above 25% to 40%, while 30%–45% has been suggested to prevent restrictive and excessive intakes. Usual mean fat intakes appear to vary from 28% to 42% energy from fat at 6–12 months, being higher at a younger age; recent UK data is lacking but has been commissioned.

25. Lower saturated fat and trans fat and higher polyunsaturated fats appear to be more important than total fat intake from infancy in terms of later cardiovascular health. There is no recommendation for saturated fat intake in infants in the United Kingdom or elsewhere. The UK recommendation for children over 5 years of age and adults is to obtain no more than 10% of total daily energy intake from saturated fat.

26. There are no recommendations for intake of omega-3 and omega-6 polyunsaturated fatty acids among UK infants, with UK adult recommendations of 1% of daily energy as linoleic acid (omega-6), 0.2% as linolenic acid (omega-3) and 0.45 g per day of long chain omega-3 polyunsaturated fatty acids. Other countries and organisations recommend from 3.5% to 9% of daily energy intake from omega-6 polyunsaturated fatty acids, from 0.5% to at least 1% of daily energy intake from omega-3 polyunsaturated fatty acids and from 0.2% to 0.35% of total fat as long chain omega-3 polyunsaturated fatty acids for infants over 6 months of age.

27. There are no dietary fibre recommendations for infants in the United Kingdom. While there is insufficient data to make conclusive recommendations, data suggests that an intake of 7.6 g of non-starch polysaccharides (NSP) per 1000 kcal (7.3 g of NSP per day) at 13 months leads to later health benefits compared with lower fibre intakes; such levels do not lead

to growth faltering as long as energy intake is maintained, iron levels being positively associated with fibre intake.

28. While further research is needed, it is suggested that in the interim infants obtain >35% of energy from fat, boys have 5.8 g of NSP per day and girls have 5.3 g of NSP per day at 12 months, increasing from 6 months.

29. At 6–9 months, for an average weight infant to obtain >35% of energy from fat, he could consume 70–175 kcal or 3–7 tablespoons of solids per day before solids containing fat were needed (with 500 mL of milk per day).

30. Between ½ and 4 tablespoons of solids will provide 0.5 g of NSP (one fibre serving).

31. Four to nine fibre servings are suggested at 6–9 months, and five to eleven servings at 10–12 months. It is suggested that after 6 months of age, one or two servings a day of wheat cereals are given.

32. There are limited nutritional guidelines for infants both in the United Kingdom and elsewhere. There appears to be no pictorial representation of food intake by food group for infants.

33. While the Committee on Medical Aspects of Food Policy (COMA) guidelines give five food groups for infants, four are suggested, 'occasional foods' (salty and sugary foods) being excluded. The four food groups are (1) milk, dairy products and alternatives; (2) cereals (bread, rice, potatoes and other starchy foods); (3) fruit and vegetables; and (4) meat and alternatives (fish, eggs, beans and other non-dairy sources of protein).

34. COMA food group frequency guidelines (number of daily servings), which were based on 'pragmatic decisions', at 9–12 months are (1) no advice on dairy other than milk (minimum of 600 mL of breast milk or formula milk at 4–6 months and 500 mL at 7–12 months); (2) three to four servings of starchy foods; (3) three to four servings of fruit and vegetables; and (4) one serving of meat, fish or eggs or two of non-meat sources of protein. No portion size was defined.

35. Suggested food group–based dietary guidelines formulated to meet current government recommendations for energy intake, iron, zinc, calcium, iodine and vitamin D and suggested recommendations for fat and fibre intake are similar to COMA guidelines, except for meat and alternatives, portion size being defined. Where one portion is defined as a tablespoon (20 g) for most foods, the suggested number of portions a day are three to five cereals and fruit and vegetables, two to five meat and alternatives, and one to two portions of dairy products and alternatives, with 500–600 mL of milk.

36. A suggested pictorial representation of the suggested food group–based dietary guidelines is a simple pie chart divided into five sections, called the Balanced Infant Guide. There are two equally sized sections for cereals and for fruit and vegetables, a slightly smaller section for meat and alternatives, a smaller section for dairy products, plus the largest section for breast milk or formula milk. The pictorial representation can be used to show daily food intake by food group (number of portions) or average intake over several days or a week.

Further key facts are highlighted throughout the text.

CHAPTER 1

When to introduce solids

Key facts

1. Complementary feeding means introducing solids to an infant's milk diet.

2. The current recommendation is to start introducing solids at 6 months but there is flexibility to start earlier, dependent upon the individual needs of each infant.

3. While research unequivocally shows that solids should not be introduced until after 4 months of age, debate continues regarding the ideal recommended age of introduction of solids, because of the limited evidence of benefits of exclusive breastfeeding to 6 months, relative to 4–6 months, in developed countries.

4. Breastfeeding has been shown to provide sufficient energy for normal growth and to meet recommended energy requirements for most infants at 6 months of age.

5. Breastfeeding is associated with a reduced risk of gastrointestinal infection in both developing and developed countries.

6. There is currently a lack of data regarding the most appropriate time to introduce solids, including gluten, in terms of minimising the risk of development of allergies and coeliac disease.

7. While breastfeeding has been shown to be protective against overweight and obesity, there appears to be no association between the timing of introduction of solids and overweight or obesity in infancy.

8. An infant's iron stores at birth are positively related to maternal iron stores. Infants with low iron stores at birth appear to have a greater risk of iron deficiency anaemia at 6 and 12 months than infants whose iron stores are replete at birth.

9. Based on a limited number of studies, exclusive breastfeeding to 6 months is associated with a low risk of iron deficiency anaemia in developed countries, but a higher risk of iron deficiency anaemia in developing countries.
10. Vitamin D is recommended as a supplement from 6 months of age if <500 mL per day of infant formula is consumed (all breastfed infants from 6 months; from 1 month if the vitamin D status of the mother is questionable).

WEANING AND COMPLEMENTARY FEEDING

Weaning, in its true sense, is the cessation of breastfeeding, while complementary feeding means introducing solid food to an infant's milk diet while still giving milk.[1] These two terms are often incorrectly interchanged. Initially, complementary feeding involves getting the infant used to different tastes and textures, food being given on a spoon or by allowing the infant to self-feed.

THE UK RECOMMENDATION FOR INTRODUCING SOLID FOODS

The Department of Health (DH)[2] recommends that solid foods are introduced *at 6 months* of age, later than the previous DH recommendation of between 4 and 6 months.[3] This 6 months (26 weeks) recommendation followed new guidance from the World Health Assembly[4] and a new global strategy on infant feeding by the World Health Organization (WHO).[5]

The DH recommendation[2] is for all infants, whether breastfed or formula-fed, exclusive breastfeeding being recommended until the introduction of solids. This 6 months recommendation does, however, suggest a flexible approach to the timing of introduction of solids: 'all babies are individuals and will require a flexible approach to optimise nutritional needs',[2] and 'if an infant is showing signs of being ready to start eating solids (taking an interest in what the family is eating, picking up and tasting food) then they should be encouraged'.[2] Interestingly, these signs are no longer included as signs that an infant is ready for solids (*see* Chapter 2).

EVIDENCE RELATING TO THE 6-MONTH EXCLUSIVE BREASTFEEDING RECOMMENDATION

Evidence relating to the 6-month exclusive breastfeeding recommendation[2] focuses largely on energy and growth, risk of gastrointestinal infection, overweight and obesity, and the development of allergies.

Energy and growth

A WHO-commissioned Cochrane review[6] compared exclusive breastfeeding for 3–4 months versus 6 months. Only two of the 20 studies were randomised intervention trials, both of which were carried out in developing countries. One study in Belarus found less morbidity from gastrointestinal infection in infants exclusively breastfed for 6 months than in those exclusively breastfed for 3 months. The review concluded that there was no difference in growth between infants exclusively breastfed for 3–4 months versus 6 months.[6] That is, breast milk provided enough energy for growth for 6 months in infants from a developing country, where birthweight and thus energy requirements are less than those in the United Kingdom.

An update of this review,[7] which included 11 studies from developed countries, found no difference in weight or length gain between infants exclusively breastfed for 6 months versus 3–4 months, larger sample sizes being required to confirm these findings. A small UK study[8] found that breast milk production at 6 months provided adequate energy intake[9] and enabled normal infant growth.

> It therefore appears that breastfeeding to 6 months provides adequate energy intake for most infants in developing and developed countries.

Risk of gastrointestinal infection

The WHO-commissioned Cochrane review[6] showed that only one study in Belarus found less morbidity from gastrointestinal infection in infants exclusively breastfed for 6 months than for 3–4 months. A later study conducted in Mexico[10] found that infants predominantly breastfed for 6 months had a significantly lower incidence of gastrointestinal infection at 6 months than non-predominantly breastfed infants (partially breastfed and formula-fed combined). Similarly, a reduced risk of gastrointestinal infection was found from 6 months of exclusive breastfeeding versus 3–4 months among infants from Belarus, Nigeria and Iran.[7] These studies support the protective effect of

6 months of exclusive breastfeeding on risk of gastrointestinal infection in developing countries.

A further review by Duijts *et al.*[11] found that a longer duration of exclusive breastfeeding had a protective effect on risk of gastrointestinal infection in industrialised countries, the authors concluding that further research was needed to determine the optimum duration of exclusive breastfeeding on protection from infectious diseases.

> While it is recommended to introduce solids at 6 months because of a reduced risk of gastrointestinal disease, there is limited evidence for a reduced risk in developed countries.

Overweight and obesity

A meta-analysis of 33 studies[12] found that breastfeeding appeared to protect against overweight and obesity in children and adolescents, but not in adults; however, most studies were observational and therefore were prone to bias. Several studies have found a greater protective effect against overweight and obesity associated with a longer duration of non-exclusive breastfeeding,[13] while others have found no protective effect of a longer duration (average of 3 months) of breastfeeding.[14] These studies do not appear to have compared the effect of 6 months of exclusive breastfeeding relative to 4–6 months of exclusive breastfeeding on later risk of overweight and obesity.

De Kroon *et al.*[15] found a significant inverse relationship between duration of exclusive breastfeeding (zero to 6 or more months) and body mass index, waist circumference and waist-to-hip ratio among Dutch adults aged 18–28 years. While body mass index decreased by $0.14\,\text{kg/m}^2$ per month of exclusive breastfeeding,[15] it is unclear whether this decrease was significant each month, and whether the decrease following 6 months of exclusive breastfeeding was significantly greater than that following 4–5 months of exclusive breastfeeding.

A recent systematic review found no association between the timing of introduction of solids and obesity in infancy and childhood,[16] supporting previous findings.[17–19]

> Breastfeeding appears to protect against later obesity in childhood and adolescence, the protective effect of duration of breastfeeding being unclear. Further research is required.

Development of allergies

Recent meta-analyses indicate a protective effect of at least 4 months of exclusive breastfeeding on atopic dermatitis, wheezing and asthma in infancy and early childhood.[20,21] There is a lack of data on the most appropriate time to introduce solids, including gluten, in terms of minimising the risk of development of allergies and coeliac disease [22,23] (*see* Introduction of solids and potential allergens, p. 28). The current recommendation in the United Kingdom is to introduce gluten after 6 months of age,[3] while evidence suggests that breastfeeding at the time of introduction of gluten reduces the risk of developing coeliac disease.[22]

> There is a lack of data on the most appropriate time to introduce solids, including gluten, in terms of minimising the risk of development of allergies and coeliac disease.[22,23]

IRON STATUS

Since there appear to be no studies from developed countries comparing iron deficiency anaemia (IDA) and iron deficiency (ID) occurrence at 6 months of age with 4–6 months of exclusive breastfeeding compared with 6 months of exclusive breastfeeding, it is difficult to discuss iron status in terms of the ideal timing of exclusive breastfeeding. A Cochrane review[7] stated that exclusive breastfeeding for 6 months may compromise iron status in developing countries, where the infant's iron stores at birth may be suboptimal (*see* Chapter 3 for effect of IDA and ID upon the infant).

> Exclusive breastfeeding for 6 months may compromise iron status in developing countries, where the infant's iron stores at birth may be suboptimal.

Iron status in developed and developing countries

IDA levels in developed countries appear to be low, with levels of 1% IDA being found among a small sample of exclusively breastfed Australian infants[24] and 3% among Norwegian breastfed and formula-fed infants, introduced to solids before or at 6 months.[25] Levels of IDA at 6 months following 6 months of exclusive breastfeeding are higher in developing countries than in developed countries, with IDA levels of 3.6% being found among Chilean infants predominantly breastfed for 5–6 months,[26] 4% among Mexican low-income infants predominantly breastfed for 5–6 months,[10] and 5% among a pooled sample of infants exclusively breastfed for 6 months from Mexico (4%), Honduras (5%–11%), Ghana (8%–16%) and Sweden (2%).[27]

Levels of ID at 6 months following 6 months of exclusive breastfeeding appear to be high in developing countries (20%,[27] 22%[10]). Data on levels of ID at 6 months in developed countries following 6 months of exclusive breast-feeding is limited; ID levels of 6% were found in a small study from Sweden.[27]

Thus, while the majority of infants exclusively breastfed for 6 months or less from developed countries appear to have sufficient iron at 6 months, a minority appear to have insufficient iron. However, it should be noted that studies on ID and IDA in infants are often difficult to interpret because of small sample sizes and assessment of ID and IDA (often poor or varied cut-off points.[28]

UK infant iron levels at 6 months

A review by Butte *et al.*[29] found that an infant's iron stores at birth were suffi-cient to meet iron requirements at 6 months; however, this finding was based on only three small studies of infants from developed countries, levels of ID ranging from 7% to 17%.[30,31] The Scientific Advisory Committee on Nutrition (SACN)[28] stated that healthy UK term infants are born with sufficient iron stores to meet their needs for 6 months, based on requirements.[9] However, there is no recent UK national data on iron levels at 6 months; the Food Standards Agency-funded National Infant Diet and Health Study[32] should rectify this situation.

> It appears that the majority of infants from developed countries who are breastfed for 6 months have sufficient iron, whereas a minority have insuffi-cient iron.

Maternal iron supplementation

While Honduran infants, whose birthweights were greater than 3 kg, were not iron deficient following 6 months of exclusive breastfeeding,[33] over half the sample of mothers received iron prenatally; this has been shown to lead to greater maternal iron status at term than with non-supplementation with iron.[34] Infants born to women with low iron stores have been shown to have 30%–60% lower iron stores (as measured by cord ferritin) than infants born to women with higher iron stores.[35,36] Further, 30% of pregnant women in UK studies have been found to have low iron stores at the end of pregnancy, despite iron supplementation.[37,38]

The National Institute for Health and Clinical Excellence[39] recommended that iron supplementation should be considered only for women with hae-moglobin iron concentration <110 g/L in the first trimester and <105 g/L at 28 weeks; the Scientific Advisory Committee on Nutrition[28] supports this recommendation. However, not all pregnant women requiring iron appear to be prescribed iron; while 24% of over 2000 pregnant women across 11 UK maternity units were found to be anaemic at some stage during the antenatal period, there was considerable variation by maternity unit in the administration of iron.[38]

Since maternal iron status is the key factor determining the iron status of the term infant at birth,[3,35,36] maternal iron status thus determines the appropriateness of 6 months of exclusive breastfeeding in terms of iron requirements. Between 5% and 9% of women of childbearing age in the United Kingdom are anaemic, while 8%–21% have low iron stores, iron status being poorer among women from lower socio-economic groups (*see* Chapter 3).[40,41] This implies that a sizeable proportion of women have a compromised iron status at the start of pregnancy. Antenatal iron supplementation where required therefore appears paramount to enable breastfeeding to 6 months in the absence of infant iron deficiency.

> Maternal iron status is the key factor determining the iron status of the infant at birth and thus the appropriateness of 6 months of exclusive breastfeeding in terms of iron requirements. Poor iron status is evident among a significant proportion of UK women of childbearing age.

Infant iron supplementation

The American Academy of Pediatrics Committee on Nutrition[42] recommended that exclusively breastfed term infants and partially breastfed infants (who receive more than half their milk intake as breast milk and no solids) received an iron supplement of 1 mg/kg per day from 4 months of age until appropriate iron-containing complementary foods had been introduced. This recommendation was based on a study showing higher haemoglobin concentration at 6 months of age and better visual and developmental indices at 13 months for infants exclusively breastfed for 6 months and supplemented with iron from 1 month of age, compared with unsupplemented infants,[43] and on six additional studies indicating that breastfed infants are at risk of ID and IDA, or that iron supplementation improved iron status.[44] However, all of these additional studies measured iron status post 6 months of age (hence, part of this difference in iron status could be explained by complementary feeding practices), while several studies were small and were carried out in low-income areas.

Friel[45] stated that infants from low socio-economic groups, in addition to low-birthweight infants, who are exclusively breastfed for 6 months are at risk of IDA and ID and should receive supplemental iron.

In 2012, the American Academy of Pediatrics[46] recommended exclusive breastfeeding for about 6 months, based on evidence of benefits of 6 months of exclusive breastfeeding versus 4–6 months for otitis media (ear infection) and respiratory infections. In addition, it was stated that supplemental iron drops before 6 months may be needed to support iron stores, while complementary foods rich in iron should be introduced at about 6 months.[46]

> While the American Academy of Pediatrics[46] recommends exclusive breast-feeding for about 6 months, it also states that supplemental iron drops may be needed before 6 months. Further research on iron supplementation in infants is needed, particularly in developed countries and among low socio-economic-group infants at 6 months of age.

VITAMIN D

While vitamin D status in infants is not discussed in relation to the optimal duration of exclusive breastfeeding, it is important when considering the effect of the length of exclusive breastfeeding on the nutritional status of the infant. Vitamin D status of an infant at birth is determined by maternal vitamin D status during pregnancy.[47] The UK National Diet and Nutrition Survey for 2008–10 identified low vitamin D status among females,[48] while intake of vitamin D supplements among pregnant and breastfeeding women and their infants appears to be low.[49]

In addition, the vitamin D content of breast milk is typically low, containing approximately 1 µg/L.[50] Thus, exclusive breastfeeding can be seen as a predisposing factor to vitamin D deficiency.[51,52] The European Society for Paediatric Gastroenterology, Hepatology and Nutrition (ESPGHAN)[53] states that all breastfed infants in Europe should receive vitamin D supplements regardless of maternal vitamin D status, although infant age at initiation of supplementation is not specified. The American Academy of Pediatrics[46] recommends that all breastfed infants should receive an oral vitamin D supplement of 10 µg per day, beginning at time of hospital discharge.

In the United Kingdom, breastfed infants and infants not drinking 500 mL or more a day of infant formula are recommended to take a vitamin D supplement of 7 µg a day from 6 months, a 7 µg a day supplement also being recommended for breastfed infants from 1 month of age if the mother is not taking a supplement (10 µg a day) or did not do so when pregnant (*see* The recommendation for Vitamin D, p. 79).[54]

> The vitamin D status of an infant at birth is dependent upon the vitamin D status of the mother; breast milk is low in vitamin D. Exclusive breastfeeding is a predisposing factor to vitamin D deficiency and supplementation is recommended.

THE RECOMMENDED AGE FOR INTRODUCTION OF SOLIDS IN DIFFERENT COUNTRIES

The WHO[5] recommendation for 6 months of exclusive breastfeeding was based on limited scientific evidence from developed countries; this has led to much debate about the appropriate age of introduction of solids, many countries adopting the 6-month recommendation and others maintaining the 4- to 6-month recommendation. Some countries, such as the UK, have recommended that solids are introduced *at 6 months*,[2] while others, such as Australia, have recommended that solids are introduced at *around 6 months*.[55] As already mentioned (*see* Infant iron supplementation, p. 7), the American Academy of Pediatrics[46] recommends exclusive breastfeeding for about 6 months, while stating that supplemental iron drops may be needed before 6 months to support iron stores. ESPGHAN[53] took a mixed standing, stating that exclusive breastfeeding for *about 6 months* was a desirable goal while also stating that complementary feeding should not start before 17 weeks and should not be later than 26 weeks.

> Many countries have adopted the WHO 6-month recommendation for exclusive breastfeeding, while others have maintained the 4- to 6-month recommendation.

ESPGHAN: NO DISADVANTAGE OF INTRODUCING SOLIDS AT 4–6 MONTHS

ESPGHAN[56] stated that for breastfed infants in developed countries, there was currently no scientific evidence that introducing complementary foods between 4 and 6 months was disadvantageous compared with introducing complementary foods after 6 months. ESPGHAN[56] also concluded that while exclusive breastfeeding for around 6 months was a desirable goal, partial breastfeeding and a shorter duration of breastfeeding were also of value.

> For breastfed infants in developed countries, there appears to be little scientific evidence of benefits from introducing complementary foods after 6 months versus introducing complementary foods at 4–6 months.[53] However, the American Academy of Pediatrics[46] recommends exclusive breastfeeding for about 6 months, based on evidence of reduced otitis media (ear infection) and respiratory infection with 6 months of exclusive breastfeeding versus 4–6 months of exclusive breastfeeding.

REFERENCES

1. Humphrey LT. Weaning behaviour in human evolution. *Semin Cell Dev Biol.* 2010; **21**(4): 453–61.
2. Department of Health. *Infant Feeding Recommendation.* London: Department of Health; 2003. Available at: www.dh.gov.uk/assetRoot/04/09/69/99/04096999.pdf (accessed 17 March 2011).
3. Department of Health. *Weaning and the Weaning Diet: Report of the Working Group on the Weaning Diet of the Committee on Medical Aspects of Food Policy.* Report on Health and Social Subjects, 45. London: The Stationery Office; 1994.
4. World Health Assembly. *Infant and Young Child Nutrition.* WHA55.25. Geneva, Switzerland: World Health Organization; 2002. Available at: www.who.int/nutrition/publications/infantfeeding/gs_infant_feeding_eng.pdf (accessed 12 June 2011).
5. World Health Organization. *Global Strategy for Infant and Young Child Feeding.* Geneva, Switzerland: World Health Organization; 2003. Available at: www.who.int/nutrition/publications/gs_infant_feeding_text_eng.pdf (accessed 10 June 2011).
6. Kramer MS, Kakuma R. Optimal duration of exclusive breastfeeding. *Cochrane Database Syst Rev.* 2002; **1**: CD003517.
7. Kramer MS, Kakuma R. Optimal duration of exclusive breastfeeding. *Cochrane Database Syst Rev.* 2012; **8**: CD003517.
8. Nielsen SB, Reilly JJ, Fewtrell MS, *et al.* Adequacy of milk intake during exclusive breastfeeding: a longitudinal study. *Pediatrics.* 2011; **128**(4): e907–14.
9. Department of Health. *Dietary Reference Values for Energy and Nutrients for the UK: Report of the Committee on Medical Aspects of Food Policy.* Report on Health and Social Subjects, 41. London: HMSO; 1991.

10. Monterrosa EC, Frongillo EA, Vásquez-Garibay EM, *et al*. Predominant breast-feeding from birth to six months is associated with fewer gastrointestinal infections and increased risk for iron deficiency among infants. *J Nutr.* 2008; **138**(8): 1499–504.

11. Duijts L, Ramadhani MK, Moll HA. Breastfeeding protects against infectious diseases during infancy in industrialized countries: a systematic review. *Matern Child Nutr.* 2009; **5**(3): 199–210.

12. Horta BL, Bahl R, Martines JC, *et al*. *Evidence on the Long-Term Effects of Breastfeeding: systematic review and meta-analyses.* Geneva, Switzerland: World Health Organization; 2007. Available at: http://whqlibdoc.who.int/publications/2007/9789241595230_eng.pdf (accessed 12 June 2011).

13. Harder T, Bergmann R, Kallischnigg G, *et al*. Duration of breastfeeding and the risk of overweight: a meta-analysis. *Am J Epidemiol.* 2005; **162**(5): 397–403.

14. Kramer MS, Matush L, Vanilovich I, *et al*. Effects of prolonged and exclusive breast-feeding on child height, weight, adiposity, and blood pressure at age 6.5 y: evidence from a large randomized trial. *Am J Clin Nutr.* 2007; **86**(6): 1717–21.

15. De Kroon ML, Renders CM, Buskermolen MP, *et al*. The Terneusen Birth Cohort: longer exclusive breastfeeding duration is associated with leaner body mass and a healthier diet in young adulthood. *BMC Pediatr.* 2011; **11**(33).

16. Moorcroft KE, Marshall JL, McCormick FM. Association between timing of introducing solid foods and obesity in infancy and childhood: a systematic review. *Matern Child Nutr.* 2011; **7**(1): 3–26.

17. Cohen RJ, Brown KH, Canahuati J, *et al*. Effects of age of introduction of complementary foods on infant breast milk intake, total energy intake, and growth: a randomised intervention study in Honduras. *Lancet.* 1994; **344**(8918): 288–93.

18. Dewey KG, Cohen RJ, Brown KH, *et al*. Age of introduction of complementary foods and growth of term, low-birth-weight, breast-fed infants: a randomized intervention study in Honduras. *Am J Clin Nutr.* 1999; **69**(4): 679–86.

19. Morgan JB, Lucas A, Fewtrell MS. Does weaning influence growth and health up to 18 months? *Arch Dis Child.* 2004; **89**(8): 728–33.

20. Dutch State Institute for Nutrition and Health.Van Rossum CMT, Buchner FL, Hoekstra J. *Quantification of Health Effects of Breastfeeding: review of the literature and model situation. RIVM Report 350040001/2005.* Available at: www.rivm.nl/biblio theek/rapporten/350040001.pdf (accessed 17 April 2011).

21. Agency for Healthcare Research and Quality. *Breastfeeding and Maternal and Infant Outcomes in Developed Countries.* AHRQ Publication No. 07-E007. Rockville, MD: Agency for Healthcare Research and Quality; 2007. Available at: http://archive.ahrq. gov/downloads/pub/evidence/pdf/brfout/brfout.pdf (accessed 2 April 2011).

22. Scientific Advisory Committee on Nutrition; Committee on Toxicity. *Joint Statement: timing of introduction of gluten into the infant diet.* London: The Stationery Office; 2011. Available at: http://cot.food.gov.uk/pdfs/cotsacnstatementgluten201101.pdf (accessed 10 June 2011).

23. European Food Safety Authority Panel on Dietetic Products, Nutrition and Allergies. Scientific opinion on the appropriate age for introduction of complementary feeding of infants. *EFSA Journal.* 2009; **7**(12): 1423–42.

24. Makrides M, Leeson R, Gibson RA, *et al*. A randomized controlled clinical trial of increased dietary iron in breast-fed infants. *J Pediatr.* 1998; **133**(4): 559–62.

25. Hay G, Sandstad B, Whitelaw A, *et al*. Iron status in a group of Norwegian children aged 6–24 months. *Acta Paediatr*. 2004; **93**(5): 592–98.

26. Lozoff B, De Andraca I, Castillo M, *et al*. Behavioural and developmental effects of preventing iron-deficiency anemia in healthy full-term infants. *Pediatrics*. 2003; **112**(4): 846–54.

27. Yang Z, Lönnerdal B, Adu-Afarwuah S, *et al*. Prevalence and predictors of iron deficiency in fully breastfed infants at 6 mo of age: comparison of data from 6 studies. *Am J Clin Nutr*. 2009; **89**(5): 1433–40.

28. Scientific Advisory Committee on Nutrition. *Breast Milk Composition Literature Review*. London: The Stationery Office; 2010. Available at: www.sacn.gov.uk/pdfs/smcn1106_annex_2a_nutrient_composition_of_breast_milk_re_.pdf (accessed 12 June 2011).

29. Butte NF, Lopez-Alarcon MG, Garza C. *Nutrient Adequacy of Exclusive Breast Feeding for the Term Infant during the First Six Months of Life*. Geneva, Switzerland: World Health Organization; 2002.

30. Duncan B, Schifman RB, Corrigan JJ, *et al*. Iron and the exclusively breast-fed infant from birth to six months. *J Pediatr Gastroenterol Nutr*. 1985; **4**(3): 421–25.

31. Siimes MA, Salmenpera L, Perheentupa J. Exclusive breast-feeding for 9 months: risk of iron deficiency. *J Pediatr*. 1984; **104**(2): 196–9.

32. Food Standards Agency-funded National Infant Diet and Health Study. Available at: www.mrc-hnr.cam.ac.uk/NIDHS (accessed 17 September 2011).

33. Dewey KG, Cohen RJ, Rivera LL, *et al*. Effects of age of introduction of complementary foods on iron status of breastfed infants in Honduras. *Am J Clin Nutr*. 1998; **67**(5): 878–84.

34. Pena-Rosas JP, Viteri FE. Effects and safety of preventive oral iron or iron+folic acid supplementation for women during pregnancy. *Cochrane Database Syst Rev*. 2009; 4: CD004736.

35. Ilyés I, Jezerniczky J, Kovács J, *et al*. Relationship of maternal and newborn (cord) serum ferritin concentrations measured by immunoradiometry. *Acta Paediatr Hung*. 1985; **26**(4): 317–21.

36. Jaime-Perez JC, Herrera-Garza JL, Gomez-Almaguer D. Sub-optimal fetal iron acquisition under a maternal environment. *Arch Med Res*. 2005; **36**(5): 598–602.

37. Kelly AM, MacDonald DJ, McDougall AN. Observations on maternal and fetal ferritin concentrations at term. *Brit J Obstet Gynaecol*. 1978; **85**(5): 338–43.

38. Barroso F, Allard S, Kahan BC, *et al*. Prevalence of maternal anaemia and its predictors: a multi-centre study. *Eur J Obstet Gynecol Reprod Biol*. 2011; **159**(1): 99–105.

39. National Institute for Health and Clinical Excellence. *Antenatal Care: routine care for the healthy pregnant woman*. London: NICE; 2008. Available at: www.nice.org.uk/nicemedia/pdf/CG062NICEguideline.pdf (accessed 28 May 2011).

40. Ruston D, Hoare J, Henderson L, *et al*. *The National Diet and Nutrition Survey: adults aged 19 to 64 years. Volume 4: Nutritional Status (anthropometry and blood analytes), blood pressure and physical activity*. London: HMSO; 2004. Available at: www.food.gov.uk/multimedia/pdfs/ndns5full.pdf (accessed 12 June 2011).

41. Nelson M, Erens B, Bates B, *et al*. *Low Income Diet and Nutrition Survey. Volume 3: Nutrition status, physical activity and economic, social and other factors*. London: The Stationery Office; 2007. Available at: www.food.gov.uk/multimedia/pdfs/lidnsvol03.pdf (accessed 28 May 2011).

42. Baker RD, Greer FR; for Committee on Nutrition American Academy of Pediatrics. Diagnosis and prevention of iron deficiency and iron deficiency anaemia in infants and young children (0–3 years of age). *Pediatrics*. 2010; **126**(5): 1040–50.

43. Friel JK, Aziz K, Andrews WL, *et al.* A double-masked, randomized control trial of iron supplementation in early infancy in healthy term breast-fed infants. *J Pediatr*. 2003; **143**(5): 582–86.

44. Baker RD, Greer FR. Re: screening for iron deficiency [response]. *Pediatrics*. 2011. Available at: http://pediatrics.aappublications.org/content/126/5/1040.short/reply (accessed 3 March 2012).

45. Friel J. Iron supplementation of exclusively breast-fed infants. *Vitam Trace Elem*. 2012; **1**(2): e108–9.

46. American Academy of Pediatrics. Breastfeeding and the use of human milk. *Pediatrics*. 2012; **129**(3): e827–41.

47. Hollis BW, Wagner CL. Assessment of dietary vitamin D requirements during pregnancy and lactation. *Am J Clin Nutr*. 2004; **79**(5): 717–26.

48. Pot GK, Prynne CJ, Roberts C, *et al.* National Diet and Nutrition Survey: fat and fatty acid intake from the first year of the rolling programme and comparison with previous surveys. *Br J Nutr*. Epub 2011 Jul 18.

49. Scientific Advisory Committee on Nutrition. *Update on Vitamin D*. London: SACN; 2007. Available at: www.sacn.gov.uk/pdfs/sacn_position_vitamin_d_2007_05_07.pdf (accessed 12 June 2011).

50. Reeve LE, Chesney RW, DeLuca HF. Vitamin D deficiency of human milk: identification of biologically active forms. *Am J Clin Nutr*. 1982; **36**(1): 122–6.

51. Dawodu A, Agarwal M, Hossain M, *et al.* Hypovitaminosis D and vitamin D deficiency in exclusively breast-feeding infants and their mothers in summer: a justification for vitamin D supplementation of breast-feeding infants. *J Pediatr*. 2003; **142**(2): 169–73.

52. Thatcher TD, Fischer PR, Strand MA, *et al.* Nutritional rickets around the world: causes and future directions. *Ann Trop Paediatr*. 2006; **26**(1): 1–16.

53. Agostoni C, Braegger C, Decsi T, *et al.*; for ESPGHAN Committee on Nutrition. Breast-feeding: a commentary by the ESPGHAN Committee on Nutrition. *J Pediatr Gastroenterol Nutr*. 2009: **49**(1): 112–25.

54. Department of Health. *Nutrition and Bone Health: with particular reference to calcium and vitamin D. Report of the Subgroup on Bone Health, Working Group on the Nutritional Status of the Population, Committee on Medical Aspects of Food and Nutrition Policy*. London: The Stationery Office; 1998.

55. National Health and Medical Research Council. *Dietary Guidelines for Children and Adolescents in Australia incorporating the Infant Feeding Guidelines for Health Workers*. Canberra, Australia: National Health and Medical Research Council; 2003. Available at: www.nhmrc.gov.au/_files_nhmrc/publications/attachments/n34.pdf (accessed 10 March 2012).

56. Agostoni C, Decsi T, Fewtrell M, *et al.*; for ESPGHAN Committee on Nutrition. Complementary feeding: a commentary by the ESPGHAN Committee on Nutrition. *J Pediatr Gastroenterol Nutr*. 2008; **46**(1): 99–110.

CHAPTER 2

How to introduce solids

Key facts

1. Current guidelines on complementary feeding are largely based on tradition rather than research, while there is little evidence for the introduction of solids in any specific order or at any specific rate.
2. There are inconsistencies in current advice from reputable sources, including the Department of Health, other UK health departments and the Food Standards Agency.
3. Meat and fish have been shown to be positively associated with iron status in infants, meat being well accepted as a first food in addition to most new foods.
4. UK infants consuming fewer than six breast milk feeds a day or <600 mL per day of formula milk appear to be more likely to have satisfactory iron intakes than infants consuming higher quantities of milk.
5. There is insufficient evidence to support recommendations on the appropriate age of introduction of gluten to the diet beyond 3 months of age. The current UK recommendation is to introduce gluten after 6 months of age.
6. There is insufficient evidence on the timing of introduction of solids to minimise the risk of developing allergies.
7. The most favourable time to introduce different food textures is not accurately known.
8. Responsive feeding is where a mother feeds an infant in response to his cues, allowing the infant to decide whether to eat, and how much to eat. UK health departments currently recommend responsive feeding.
9. Baby-led weaning follows responsive feeding, the infant feeding himself

so there is no spoon-feeding by the parent, and the infant being offered solid family foods rather than traditional purees (as at 4–6 months). Baby-led weaning appears feasible for many infants around 6 months of age who have developed the appropriate feeding skills.

10. At about 6 months, infants can be given soft finger foods as well as mashes and purees at the start of complementary feeding, depending upon the infant's feeding skills. Responsive feeding is followed, the infant being assisted by the parent to feed and/or self-feeding. A variety of food should be given, including good sources of iron such as meat, fortified infant cereals and breakfast cereals.

CURRENT GUIDELINES

Current guidelines from both government and related agencies, including the Department of Health (DH),[1] the Food Standards Agency (FSA),[3] and the National Health Service (NHS),[2] on how to introduce solids – what to give and how – are largely based on tradition rather than research. This is because the number of studies on complementary feeding is limited. Variation in interpretation of this limited research together with differences in dietary intake patterns between countries are reflected in differences in complementary feeding advice between countries.[4]

> Current guidelines on complementary feeding are largely based on tradition rather than research.

While government advice is to breastfeed exclusively for 6 months[5] – that is, to introduce solids at 6 months – most parents in the United Kingdom introduce solids earlier.[6] Thus, in order to support all parents, health professionals need to be able to offer advice to parents on how to introduce solids before 6 months, as well as at 6 months.

Current guidelines are based on the report *Weaning and the Weaning Diet* by the Committee on Medical Aspects of Food Policy (COMA).[7] These guidelines were produced when the recommended age for introduction of solids was 4–6 months.

> Current guidelines on complementary feeding relate to the recommendation to introduce solids at 4–6 months.

First and early foods

COMA[7] recommended non-wheat cereals as first foods, along with fruit, vegetables and potatoes. Plain yoghurt and custard were also recommended as good first foods, while cheese sauce and meat were recommended as good early foods that could be introduced after 4 months when an infant was used to eating from a spoon.[7]

> Non-wheat cereals, fruit, vegetables, potatoes, yoghurt and custard were recommended by COMA[7] as good first complementary foods, cheese sauce and meat being recommended as good early foods.

Later foods

Wholegrain bread and cereals were recommended after 6 months of age, and encouraged after 9 months, while a 'moderate amount' of butter or margarine could be used after 9 months.[7]

> Wholegrain bread and cereals were recommended after 6 months of age.[7]

After 6 months, solid (not soft) eggs could be used, while after 12 months cow's milk as a drink and honey could be used. It was advised to limit salty and sugary foods, with no added salt and added sugar limited for use with sour fruits.[7]

> Solid eggs could be used after 6 months, cow's milk as a drink and honey after 12 months. It was advised to limit salty and sugary foods.[7]

Stages

The introduction of solids was traditionally divided into three stages: 4–6 months, 6–9 months and 9–12 months plus. These stages were related to age and development, to assist the appropriate introduction of solids; it was acknowledged that infants often do not match these stages since they develop at different rates.[7]

In the initial stage of complementary feeding at 4–6 months, the aim was seen as accustoming an infant to taking food from a spoon, foods being smooth and bland. Once a variety of foods were accepted from a spoon two to three times a day, an infant was ready for the second stage. This stage, at 6–9 months, involved giving food with different textures and stronger tastes, with family foods being mashed to give soft lumps, meat being coarsely pureed, and finger foods being introduced for the infant to self-feed. The third stage, at 9–12-plus months, saw progression to three main meals plus snacks and/or milk (with a minimum suggested intake of breast or formula milk of 600 mL a day at 4–6 months and 500 mL at 6–12 months).[7]

> Complementary feeding was traditionally divided into three stages, with smooth, bland foods at 4–6 months, to accustom the infant to taking food from a spoon, different textures and stronger tastes being introduced at 6–9 months, family foods being mashed and finger foods introduced for self-feeding. The minimum suggested intake of breast or formula milk was 600 mL a day at 4–6 months and 500 mL at 6–12 months.[7]

Meat could be minced or finely chopped, cooked vegetables could be chopped and finger foods given at each meal to encourage self-feeding. By the end of this third stage, the family diet could be offered to the infant, separately prepared foods no longer being necessary.[7]

Texture and finger foods

The texture of food should be matched to the feeding abilities of the infant; hence, smooth purees may be offered first when introducing solids before 6 months, moving to mashed food with soft lumps and then to chopped food, with meat being smoothly pureed at first, and then coarsely pureed, minced, finely chopped or given as soft cubes.[7]

Developmentally, infants usually put foods into their mouths from 6 months, and hence finger foods are advised from 6 months. As infants develop feeding skills at different rates, it was previously acknowledged that introduction of solids could begin at 5 or 6 months when 'the infant begins first by putting pieces of food into the mouth', rather than by consuming purees.[7]

> Solids could be introduced at 5–6 months with the infant self-feeding pieces of food, since infants develop feeding skills at different rates.[7]

Other developmental stages include taking a bolus of food from the front to the back of the mouth (3 months); reaching out for objects and taking them to the mouth (5½ months); making chewing movements and self-feeding handheld foods (6½ months); picking up raisin-sized food (9 months); and trying to spoon-feed but unable to stop the spoon rotating and losing food (12 months).[8]

Food groups

COMA[7] lists five food groups: (1) milk, dairy products and substitutes (including hard cheese, yoghurt, custard and cheese sauce); (2) 'the starchy foods' (e.g. rice, bread and cereals including breakfast cereals – including some wholemeal from 6 months); (3) vegetables and fruit; (4) meat and meat alternatives (including meat, fish, pulses, hard-cooked egg); and (5) occasional foods (salty, sugary foods and fat). The number of daily servings of food from these food groups at 6–9 months and 9–12 months are *suggestions* only, based on pragmatic decisions by COMA[7] (*see* Chapter 5).

> The five COMA food groups were (1) milk, dairy products and substitutes; (2) 'the starchy foods'; (3) vegetables and fruit; (4) meat and meat alternatives; and (5) occasional foods. The COMA number of daily servings of food from five food groups at 6–9 months and 9–12 months were *suggestions* only.[7]

CURRENT ADVICE ON INTRODUCING SOLIDS

Age-related stages are now rarely used in advice for parents on introducing solids, although infant food manufacturers commonly use them. Similar information to that found in *Weaning and the Weaning Diet*[7] is now given, in a less rigid format as it is not usually age or stage defined, the infant moving at his own pace, in terms of texture and frequency of food.

> Age-related stages are rarely used in UK publications on complementary feeding, but are used by infant food manufacturers.

The main publications on complementary feeding available in the UK are from the DH, the FSA and the NHS, in addition to publications from Wales, Scotland and Northern Ireland.[1–3,9–12]

Department of Health, National Health Service and Unicef *Weaning* booklet

The DH, NHS and Unicef[1] booklet on complementary feeding recommends introducing solids at *about* 6 months, when an infant can sit up, is putting objects in his mouth and can reach and grab objects accurately.

> The DH, NHS and Unicef[1] booklet on complementary feeding recommends introducing solids at *about* 6 months, when an infant can sit up, is putting objects in his mouth and can reach and grab objects accurately.

Advice is given on the foods to avoid if parents decide to introduce solids before 6 months, including wheat-based foods and other foods containing gluten, eggs, fish, shellfish, nuts, seeds and soft and unpasteurised cheeses.[1]

> Foods to avoid before 6 months include wheat-based foods and other foods containing gluten, eggs, fish, shellfish, nuts, seeds and soft and unpasteurised cheeses.[1]

Vegetables or fruit, mashed or as soft pieces, and cereal such as rice are recommended as first foods at about 6 months,[1] rather than the purees recommended at 4–6 months.[7] When the infant is used to eating these, additional foods are advised: namely, meat, fish and chicken; pasta and noodles; lentils or pulses; and full-fat dairy foods such as yoghurt, fromage frais or custard,[1] recommended as first foods by COMA.[7] Finger foods such as soft fruit and vegetables are encouraged from the start to encourage the infant to chew, later finger foods including toast and cheese cubes.[1] Mashed-up family foods are advised, without the addition of salt or sugar.[1] Responsive feeding (responding to the infant's signals of hunger or fullness) is suggested, the infant being seen as the best guide to how much food to give.[1] These recommendations reflect the COMA second-stage recommendations.[7]

> Vegetables or fruit, mashed or as soft pieces, and cereal such as rice are recommended as first foods at about 6 months,[1] rather than the purees recommended at 4–6 months.[7] Responsive feeding is suggested, the infant being seen as the best guide to how much food to give.

Parents are advised to offer solid foods once a day to start with, then twice and finally three times a day, offering food from three food groups: (1) starchy (such as potatoes, yams, rice or bread); (2) fruit and vegetables; and (3) protein (meat, fish, eggs, tofu or pulses).[1] Information on formula milk is specific – namely, to give 500 mL or 600 mL a day until at least 12 months – while the advice on breastfeeding is less specific, parents being advised to 'keep breastfeeding', a milk feed being dropped when the infant is 'eating plenty of solids several times a day'.[1]

Parents are advised to offer food from three food groups: (1) starchy (such as potatoes, yams, rice or bread); (2) fruit and vegetables; and (3) protein (meat, fish, eggs, tofu or pulses).[1]

From about 9 months, it is advised to offer three to four servings of starchy foods, three to four servings of fruit and vegetables, and two servings of meat, fish, eggs, dhal or other pulses a day[1] (a *minimum* of one daily serving of meat, fish or eggs or two 'from vegetable sources' being advocated by COMA).[7] Healthy snacks between meals (such as fruit or toast) are also suggested.[1] These recommendations reflect the COMA third-stage recommendations.[7]

From about 9 months, it is advised to offer three to four servings of starchy foods, three to four servings of fruit and vegetables, and two servings of meat, fish, eggs, dhal or other pulses a day.[1]

Parents are advised to avoid using salt, sugar, honey, nuts and low-fat foods, while red meat (beef, lamb or pork) is highlighted as an excellent source of iron.[1]

Parents are advised to avoid using salt, sugar, honey, nuts and low-fat foods.[1]

National Health Service *Birth to Five* book

The 2009 version of the NHS *Birth to Five* book[2] also recommends using fruit, vegetables and rice as first foods (pureed, mashed, or pieces for the infant to pick up), with additional foods as at the previous section, 'Department of Health, National Health Service and Unicef *Weaning* booklet' (plus small pieces of toast).

The infant is seen as the best guide to how much solid food to give, identical recommendations to the DH, NHS and Unicef[1] booklet being given on the number of feeds, variety of foods and frequency of foods from the different food groups after 9 months. The statement that the infant 'may still like some breast or formula milk . . . between meals'[2] is confusing, since COMA[7] suggested that infants have at least 500 mL of milk a day after 9 months. Red meat is given as an excellent source of protein, while its role as an excellent iron source is not mentioned.[2]

Food Standards Agency *Feeding Your Baby* booklet

In comparison with the DH, NHS and Unicef booklet[1] and the NHS book,[2] the 2010 FSA *Feeding Your Baby* booklet[3] advises that when introducing solids 'at around six months' any food that the parent feels comfortable with can be offered as first foods, or whatever food the infant seems most interested in, being mindful of the foods to avoid before 12 months of age (if introducing solids between 4 and 6 months, it is suggested that parents speak with their health visitor or general practitioner first, since they might suggest purees of fruit, vegetables and baby rice).

This broader 'first foods' advice[3] appears justified because of the lack of scientific evidence on which foods to give as first foods and the low nutrient content of popular first foods (*see* Chapter 4). First foods and later additional foods are similar to those in the DH, NHS and Unicef booklet[1] and the NHS book,[2] although cheese is not suggested as a finger food until 9 months.[3]

> In contrast with the DH, NHS and Unicef (2008) booklet,[1] the FSA booklet[3] advises offering any food that the parent feels comfortable with offering as first foods at around 6 months, or whatever food the infant seems most interested in, being mindful of the foods to avoid before 12 months of age.

From 9 months, parents are advised to give 'some iron-rich foods' every day, with meat and oily fish being highlighted as good sources of iron,[3] but unlike information from the DH, NHS and Unicef[1] and the NHS,[2] no advice is given on the number of servings, while two servings a day of beans, pulses and well-cooked eggs are advised if meat or fish is not given.[3] Three or four meals are advised by 12 months,[3] in addition to healthy snacks (three meals being advised by the previous publications[1,2]). From 9 months, it is advised to breastfeed as often as before the introduction of solids, letting the infant decide how much he needs.[3] While no information is given on the amount of formula milk required, cessation of one or two of the daily formula feeds is advised[3] (cessation of one breastfeed or formula feed being advised in the previous publications[1,2]).

National Health Service, Unicef and Department of Health *Introducing Solid Foods* booklet

The NHS, Unicef and DH booklet *Introducing Solid Foods*[9] contains similar information to the DH, NHS and Unicef booklet.[1] Feeding advice is skewed towards an infant self-feeding fruit and vegetables as first foods, either mashed or as finger foods, in addition to baby rice; it is advised that while an infant *can* be spoon-fed, he will soon be able to use a spoon himself.[9]

> Feeding advice is skewed towards an infant self-feeding fruit and vegetables as first foods, either mashed or as finger foods, in addition to baby rice.[9]

From 8–9 months, it is advised that an infant moves towards three meals a day, and at 12 months also has healthy snacks and milk (although no amount of milk is specified at any age), small portions of family foods being advised. There is no information on iron. Cheese is listed as a salty food, 'salt and salty food' to be limited, along with bacon, sausages, chips with added salt, gravy and meals made with stock cubes (*see* Salt, p. 26).[9] However, the DH, NHS and Unicef[1] booklet lists small cubes of cheese as a healthy snack, while the FSA booklet[3] advises giving milk products such as small amounts of cheese every day. The statement that infants who are big for their age do not need solid foods earlier than other infants is misleading[9]; it would be more accurate to state that it is unclear, research suggesting that an infant's weight affects the timing of introduction of first solids, in addition to birthweight and rate of growth, heavier infants being introduced to solids earlier than smaller infants (*see* Timing of introduction of solids, p. 29).[13,14]

Wales, Scotland and Northern Ireland

The NHS, Unicef and DH booklet[9] is also available bilingually in Wales from NHS Wales and the Welsh Government.[10] *Fun First Foods* from NHS Health Scotland and the Scottish Government[11] contains similar information to the DH, NHS and Unicef booklet,[1] mashed fruit and vegetables and baby rice being suggested as first foods as well as pieces of fruit and vegetables, toast, bread, rice cakes, cheese, slices of hard-boiled eggs, chunks of fish and mashed-up 'healthy family foods' – a slightly different list to those mentioned earlier.[1–3,9,10]

Vegetable oils such as olive or sunflower oil are suggested for cooking, with vegetable margarine (such as sunflower) for bread or toast fingers,[11] COMA[7] suggesting that small amounts of butter or margarine can be used. Parents are advised, rather vaguely, to give iron-rich foods 'regularly' (with liver a maximum of once a week), while in addition to the three food groups mentioned in the DH, NHS and Unicef booklet,[1] two to three servings a day of dairy products are also recommended from 9 months, in addition to 500–600 mL of milk.[11]

> Vegetable oils such as olive or sunflower oil are suggested for cooking and
> vegetable margarine (such as sunflower margarine) for bread or toast fingers;
> iron-rich foods are advised to be eaten regularly (with liver a maximum of once
> a week), while two to three servings a day of dairy products are recommended
> from 9 months.[11]

Weaning Made Easy from the Public Health Agency in Northern Ireland[12] also
contains similar information to the DH, NHS and Unicef booklet,[1] while
giving additional foods relatively high in fibre (smooth peanut butter and
Weetabix) as foods suitable to be given 'after the first couple of weeks'. Specific
advice to give foods rich in iron every day *from 6 months* is also given.[12] This
booklet gives slightly more age-related information than the other publications discussed[1–3,9–11] stating that from about 7 months an infant can have
three spoon-feeds a day, and that from 9 months an infant can have chopped
food.[12]

> Foods rich in iron are advised every day *from 6 months*, while smooth peanut
> butter and Weetabix, relatively high-fibre foods, are advised 'after the first
> couple of weeks'.[12]

Other information sources

Popular websites with information and forums on infant feeding include
Mumsnet,[15] with information similar to that already given here, plus Rapley
Weaning,[16] which gives information on baby-led weaning (BLW) (*see* Baby-led
weaning, p. 32). In addition, there are many other websites and books on infant
feeding, providing varying amounts and quality of information.

Eating Well: First Year of Life by The Caroline Walker Trust[17] gives clear,
practical advice on food intake in the form of a week's menu for infants at
7–9 months and at 10–12 months, including menu recipes. This resource is
novel in that the menus meet nutritional recommendations,[18] except for the
2011 energy recommendations.[19] While portion sizes are shown in the menu,
in the form of both text and pictures, portion size for some foods is variable
(which may reflect infant eating patterns), being based on the intake required
to meet nutritional recommendations. While there are no guidelines on the
number of daily portions from different food groups, this resource is the only
practical guide that meets nutritional recommendations.

Eating Well: First Year of Life by The Caroline Walker Trust[17] is the only practical guide that meets nutritional recommendations; guidelines on the number
of daily portions from different food groups are not included.

RESEARCH AND ADVICE ON INTRODUCING SOLIDS

The following 13 sections cover most of the current research and advice on
introducing solids to an infant's milk diet.

Meat as a first food

Beef and cereals have been found to be equally well accepted as first solids
among 5- to 7-month-old infants,[20,21] lamb, poultry and fish being as well
accepted as other solids by 8-month-old infants.[22] In fact, the reaction to most
new foods among 5- to 7-month-old infants appears to be positive, both bitter-
and sour-tasting foods being easily accepted.[4]

> Beef and cereals have been found to be equally well accepted as first solids,
> lamb, poultry and fish being as well accepted as other foods by 8-month-old
> infants.

Government advice relating to the introduction of solids at 4–6 months[7] is
to introduce meat when an infant is used to taking food from a spoon (usually within a few weeks of commencing complementary feeding), since this is
associated with better iron status in older infants. A 1992 UK survey of 6- to
12-month-old infants[23] found that after 12 weeks of complementary feeding,
<10% of infants were given meat. More recent data indicates that between 8
and 10 months of age (i.e. up to 6 months after the introduction of solids),
25% of UK infants were reported to have meat less than once a week (quantities not assessed) (*see* Chapter 3, Meat and fish, p. 74).[6]

> UK data indicates that between 8 and 10 months of age (i.e. up to 6 months
> after the introduction of solids), 25% of infants were reported to have meat
> less than once a week (quantities not assessed).[6]

In addition, a small sample of 7-month-old infants given pureed beef as a first
food daily from 6 months had increased zinc intake (but not zinc status) after
1 month compared with infants given fortified baby rice daily as a first food.[24]

Milk

Cow's milk is not recommended as a main drink until after 12 months of age,[7] as it contains very little iron (0.03 mg per 100 g)[25] in comparison with breast milk (0.07 mg per 100 g, very well absorbed)[25] and formula milk (0.5–0.8 mg per 100 mL for first infant milks and 1.0–1.3 mg per 100 mL for follow-on milks suitable from 6 months).[26] In addition, calcium and casein, present in high amounts in cow's milk, inhibit the absorption of non-haem iron.[27]

The amount of milk that should be consumed to meet an infant's nutritional needs after the introduction of solids is unclear, being dependent upon the complementary diet. COMA[7] suggests 500–600 mL of breast or formula milk a day from 6 to 12 months, based on pragmatic decisions rather than data analysis. The Caroline Walker Trust[17] produced a week's menu for infants aged 7–9 months and for infants aged 10–12 months, in line with government recommendations.[18] A complementary diet with 600 mL of breast or formula milk at 7–9 months, and 400 mL of breast or formula milk at 10–12 months (less than the COMA[7] minimum guideline of 500 mL of breast or formula milk) was used to formulate these nutritionally adequate diets.[17] *See* Chapter 3 (Milk intake, p. 75) for milk and iron intake.

> The amount of milk that should be consumed to meet an infant's nutritional needs after the introduction of solids is unclear, being dependent upon the complementary diet. COMA[7] suggests 500–600 mL of breast or formula milk a day from 6–12 months, while 400 mL at 10–12 months has been shown to meet nutritional requirements.[17]

Bread

Wholemeal, brown and granary bread all contain more available iron than white bread (2.4, 2.2, 1.9 and 1.6 mg of iron per 100 g of food, respectively).[25] Compared with white bread, granary and brown bread contain over twice as much fibre, while wholemeal bread contains over three times as much fibre (1.5, 3.3, 3.5 and 5 g per 100 g of food, respectively) (*see* Chapter 3, Fibre intake, p. 75).[25]

> Wholemeal, brown and granary bread all contain more iron and fibre than white bread.

Salt

The Recommended Nutrient Intake (RNI) for sodium is 320 mg per day at 7–9 months and 350 mg per day at 10–12 months, equating to an upper limit of 1 g of salt a day up to 12 months.[28] There is limited evidence relating salt intake with blood pressure and cardiovascular risk in children.[28] Sodium intake from complementary foods among 8-month-old UK infants was found to be higher than the RNI for 70% of infants, those with the highest intakes having a high intake of bread, cow's milk as a main drink, and salty flavourings such as yeast extract and gravy, based on data from 1991/92.[29] It is advised that salt intake will be moderated by not adding salt to an infant's food.[7]

> The RNI for sodium is 320 mg per day at 7–9 months and 350 mg per day at 10–12 months, equating to an upper limit of 1 g of salt a day up to 12 months. There is limited evidence relating salt intake with blood pressure and cardiovascular risk in children.[28]

Care should be taken with regard to limiting or removing specific foods from the infant diet because of their sodium or salt content, since their contribution to salt intake may be low when eaten in small quantities, but their contribution to the intake of other nutrients may be high. For example, kebabs, bacon, sausages and ham are high in sodium (860, 990, 1080 and 1200 mg per 100 g, respectively) in comparison with an average cut of beef (35 mg per 100 g) and with beefburgers (290 mg per 100 g).[25] Kebabs, bacon, sausages and ham have three times the sodium content of chips (fries) with added salt (310 mg per 100 g), twice the sodium content of recommended cereals such as white and wholemeal bread (461 and 487 mg per 100 g, respectively) and are higher in sodium than cheddar cheese (723 mg per 100 g) and crisps (800 mg per 100 g).[25]

However, ham, bacon and sausages contain a similar amount of iron per 100 g as beef (0.7, 0.8, 1.1 and 1.0 mg, respectively), beefburgers and kebabs containing approximately twice as much iron as beef (1.7, 2.1 and 1.0 mg, respectively, per 100 g), all these meats also being quite good sources of zinc.[25] Among UK children aged 2–10 years from low socio-economic groups, kebabs, bacon, sausages, ham and beefburgers provided a third of the haem iron intake and 5% of total iron intake (with a further 5% of total iron intake coming from chips and fried and roast potatoes.[30] Thus, advising parents to limit the intake of these foods because of their sodium content could detrimentally affect the iron intake of older infants from low socio-economic groups if lower sodium iron alternatives are not available.

Gluten

The European Society for Paediatric Gastroenterology, Hepatology and Nutrition Committee on Nutrition[31] recommended avoiding early (before 4 months) or late (7 months or later) introduction of gluten, to reduce the risk of coeliac disease and type 1 diabetes mellitus. In addition, the European Food Safety Authority[32] recommended the introduction of gluten between 4 and 6 months of age, no later than 6 months, while still breastfeeding, in order to reduce the risk of coeliac disease and type 1 diabetes mellitus.

Breastfeeding at the time of introduction of gluten has been found to lead to a reduced risk of coeliac disease,[33] while a longer duration of breastfeeding (greater than 6 months) has been associated with a reduced risk of coeliac disease in a small sample of infants.[34] Scientific Advisory Committee on Nutrition (SACN) and the Committee on Toxicity (COT)[35] surmised that there was insufficient evidence to support the European Food Safety Authority's recommendation, stating that there was insufficient evidence to support recommendations on the appropriate age of introduction of gluten into the diet beyond 3 completed months of age. The current recommendation in the UK is still to introduce gluten after 6 months of age.[7]

> SACN and COT[35] stated that there was insufficient evidence to support recommendations on the appropriate age of introduction of gluten into the diet beyond 3 completed months of age.

Introduction of solids and potential allergens

There is currently a lack of data regarding the most appropriate time to introduce solid foods (including allergenic foods) into the infant diet, in terms of minimising the risk of developing allergies.[32,35] A systematic review on behalf of COT[36] concluded that there was no consistent evidence to show that duration of breastfeeding or timing of introduction of solids was associated with development of food sensitisation or food allergy.

> There appears to be no consistent evidence relating the duration of breastfeeding and timing of introduction of solids with food sensitisation or food allergy.[32,35,36]

Food acceptance

There appear to be sensitive times or 'windows of opportunity' in terms of an infant's acceptance of tastes and textures; however, the most favourable times are not known accurately.[37] For example, compared with UK infants introduced to lumpy solids between 6 and 9 months, mothers reported that infants offered lumpy foods after 9 months consumed less food from several food groups, including fruit and vegetables, and had more feeding problems at 7 years of age.[38] The introduction of a wide variety of foods in the first 18 months of solids may lead to the acceptance of a wider variety of foods in later life,[39] while repeated exposure to a food (often 10–15 times) also appears to increase the acceptance of complementary foods. However, the long-term impact of these factors is not accurately known.[37]

> There appear to be sensitive times or 'windows of opportunity' in terms of an infant's acceptance of tastes and textures; however, the most favourable times are not known accurately.[37]

There appears to be little evidence for any beneficial effect of introducing solid foods in any specific order or at any specific rate.[39] Thus, there is no evidence of a benefit from introducing fruit, vegetables or unfortified rice as first foods, either before or after 6 months. However, as mentioned previously (*see* Meat as a first food, p. 25), beef appears to be as equally well accepted as baby rice as a first food, with meat and fish being positively associated with iron status and iron absorption, and also with zinc intake.[24,40]

> There appears to be little beneficial effect of introducing solids in any specific order or rate,[39] although meat and fish are positively associated with iron absorption and status and with zinc intake.

Timing of introduction of solids

The timing of introduction of first solids appears to be influenced by an infant's weight at this time, by birthweight and rate of growth, heavier infants being introduced to solids earlier than smaller infants.[13,14] This appears to be due to mothers responding, accurately or inaccurately, to cues from their infants, perceived hunger being the most common reason for introduction of solids, in addition to infant size (large infants being perceived as needing more energy overall, and small infants needing more energy to grow), and an infant showing an interest in food,[41] previously given as a sign of readiness in advice to parents.[1]

> The timing of introduction of first solids appears to be influenced by an infant's weight at this time, by birthweight and rate of growth, heavier infants being introduced to solids earlier than smaller infants.[13,14]

Home-made and commercial ready-made complementary foods

COMA[7] recommended home-made foods when introducing solid foods. The home preparation of food for infants has increased since the 1990s, although the 2005 Infant Feeding Survey[6] found that infants were more likely to be given commercial infant foods at 4–6 months, while the use of home-made foods increased at 8–10 months.

In the 1990s, many home-made foods for infants were found to be high in salt and low in fat compared with commercially available foods[42] and high in NSP fibre and sodium and low in energy, protein, fat, iron, calcium and zinc compared with European Commission directives for infant foods.[43] In the UK, 11% of tested commercial foods for infants did not comply with European Commission directives for calcium, sugar and salt; 34% of Hipp Organic products had added salt, 14% of Boots products and 11% of Cow & Gate products had added sugar, while Organix was the only brand, of six tested brands, to have all products within European Commission regulations.[44] The current nutritional value of home-made versus commercial complementary foods is unclear.

> The nutritional value of home-made versus commercial complementary foods is unclear; in the 1990s, many home-made foods for infants were found to be high in salt and fibre and low in energy, fat, protein, iron, calcium and zinc,[43] while in 2012, 11% of tested commercial foods for infants were found to have added salt or sugar.[44]

Some major infant cookbooks have been found to give inaccurate nutritional advice – for example, one advised mainly fruit and vegetable purees up to 9 months of age.[45] In addition, recipes in five major infant cookbooks have been found to promote low-fat foods and to suggest diets that were often low in energy, iron and vitamin D (*see* Chapter 3, Commercial infant foods, p. 75).[45]

Proportion of food from different food groups

Infants need a variety of foods to meet their nutrient requirements – the greater the diversity of the diet, the greater the chance of obtaining all the nutrients needed.[7,46] Food groups, and guidelines based on these groups, help ensure the inclusion of different types of food in the diet, in the correct proportions to meet nutritional needs.

COMA guidelines[7] on the number of daily servings of food for infants at 6–9 months and 9–12 months were two to three and three to four daily servings, respectively, for starchy foods, two, and three to four daily servings, respectively, for vegetables and fruit; one, and a minimum of one daily serving from animal sources or two from vegetable sources, respectively, for meat and meat alternatives; while no serving guidelines were given for dairy products or occasional foods (*see* Chapter 5). However, the scientific rationale used to formulate these values is unclear; the number of servings for each food group 'are based in some cases on pragmatic decisions', and 'are simply designed to act as a guide to meet the nutritional recommendations'.

> COMA[7] guidelines on the number of daily servings of food for infants at 6–9 months and 9–12 months were as follows: two to three and three to four daily servings, respectively, for starchy foods; two, and three to four daily servings, respectively, for vegetables and fruit; one, and a minimum of one daily serving from animal sources or two from vegetable sources, respectively, for meat and meat alternatives; while no serving guidelines were given for dairy products or occasional foods.

Perceptions of a healthy infant diet

A 1990 UK survey of 1000 mothers with infants found that over 80% believed that infants needed a low-fat, high-fibre diet, while most correctly perceived a wide variety of foods and a low intake of sugar and salt to be important.[47] More recently, most mothers were found to be aware of the need to avoid specific foods (such as undercooked eggs) and to introduce a variety of foods,[41] although a survey of ethnic minority mothers found that mothers often didn't know which foods were appropriate at different ages.[41] It is unclear whether previously reported beliefs regarding fat and fibre intake are still widely held.

Demonstrating feeding skills

Demonstrating feeding skills, as opposed to simply giving verbal prompts, appears to help children develop feeding skills.[48]

Responsive feeding

Responsive feeding is where an infant is fed in response to his cues and psychomotor abilities, the parent providing appropriate healthy foods and drinks and allowing the infant to decide whether and how much to eat and drink.[49] Theoretical frameworks for the effect of responsive feeding have been outlined,[50] yet there is a lack of research of the effect on an infant's food intake. Interventions to promote responsive feeding have, however, led to greater infant self-feeding and verbal response by the mother to an infant's food needs.[51] A lack of responsive feeding appears to have a role in the development of overweight in infants and children, although further research is needed.[52]

> Responsive feeding is where an infant is fed in response to his cues and psychomotor abilities, the parent providing appropriate healthy foods and drinks and allowing the infant to decide whether and how much to eat and drink.[49]

BABY-LED WEANING

BLW[53] is a method of introducing solids at about 6 months, where the infant is not persuaded to eat certain foods or to eat more, but is simply allowed to choose from the foods given, as in responsive feeding.[49] BLW differs from responsive feeding in that the infant feeds himself; this can only be achieved by infants who have developed the necessary skills of being able to take food to their mouths and chew. The major difference between BLW and recent popular practice is that the infant is offered solid family foods, not the traditional purees (although mashed foods and runny foods like yoghurt can be provided), and so there is no spoon-feeding by the parent.

> BLW[53] is a method of introducing solids at about 6 months, where the infant is not persuaded to eat certain foods or to eat more, but is simply allowed to choose from the foods provided. The infant feeds himself, and hence only infants who have developed the necessary feeding skills can achieve BLW.

This method of feeding warrants further investigation, particularly in terms of nutrient intake and status of BLW infants compared with spoon-fed infants in the first few months of complementary feeding. However, BLW does appear to be feasible for most infants, a UK study of 1029 infants (the majority of whom were introduced to solids before 6 months) finding that 56% of infants reached out for food before 6 months, while 6% had not reached out for food at 8 months.[54] This implies that as the majority of infants in the UK are introduced to solids before 6 months, many would not be able to self-feed initially, while BLW would not be appropriate for infants with 'developmental delays' until they were able to self-feed, as advised by Rapley.[53]

Brown and Lee[55] investigated the use of BLW among a large UK sample of mothers recruited over the Internet, the average age of infants being 8.3 months. BLW was practised by 51% of the sample (BLW being classified as spoon-feeding or giving purees ≤10% of the time, i.e. BLW was used with a minimum of purees and spoon-feeding), the remaining infants being spoon-fed (25%–75% of the time). BLW infants were more likely than spoon-fed infants to be involved in family meal times, fed family foods, offered home-made food as a first food (fruit or vegetables, compared with rice for traditional spoon-fed infants), and to have night milk feeds. BLW infants were introduced to solids later than spoon-fed infants, independent of socio-economic status (although the sample was skewed towards higher social class). BLW mothers also reported lower consumption of solids and higher milk intake, had fewer concerns about nutrient intake and mess during meal times, had higher levels of confidence in introducing solids, and sought less advice from health professionals (health visitors and general practitioners) than mothers using spoon-feeding.[55]

One of the most interesting points about BLW is that the infant is largely in control of his food intake, determining how much is eaten and what is eaten. This should reduce the risk of overfeeding and reduce parents' concerns about how much solids to give. However, appropriate proportions of foods from different food groups would still need to be *offered* to help ensure that intake of all nutrients was adequate, even though the infant may choose his own required balance of foods.

> One of the most interesting points about BLW is that the infant is largely in control of his food intake, determining how much is eaten and what is eaten. This should reduce the risk of overfeeding and reduce parents' concerns about how much solids to give.

INTRODUCING SOLIDS: SUMMARY

- At about 6 months, infants can be given soft finger foods, mashes and purees at the start of complementary feeding, depending upon the infant's feeding skills.
- Responsive feeding should be followed, the infant being assisted by the parent to feed and/or self-feeding.
- A variety of food should be given, in no particular order or rate, including good sources of iron such as meat, fortified infant cereals and breakfast cereals.
- The following foods should not be given before 6 months: wheat-based foods and other foods containing gluten, eggs, fish, shellfish, nuts, seeds, and soft and unpasteurised cheeses.
- The following should not be given before 12 months: cow's milk as a drink and honey.
- The amount of milk that should be consumed to meet an infant's nutritional needs after the introduction of solids is unclear, being dependent upon the complementary diet. COMA[7] suggests 500–600 mL of breast or formula milk a day from 6–12 months, while 400 mL at 10–12 months has been shown to meet nutritional requirements, dependent upon the complementary diet.[17]

REFERENCES

1. Department of Health (DH), National Health Service, Unicef. *Weaning: starting solid food*. London: DH; 2008 Available at: www.dh.gov.uk/prod_consum_dh/groups/dh_digitalassets/documents/digitalasset/dh_084164.pdf (accessed 16 March 2011).
2. National Health Service (NHS). *Birth to Five*. London: NHS; 2009. Available at: http://webarchive.nationalarchives.gov.uk/+/www.dh.gov.uk/prod_consum_dh/groups/dh_digitalassets/@dh/@en/@ps/@sta/@perf/documents/digitalasset/dh_117167.pdf (accessed 28 May 2011).
3. Food Standards Agency (FSA). *Your Baby*. London: FSA; 2010 Available at: www.food.gov.uk/multimedia/pdfs/publication/yourbaby0210.pdf (accessed 19 April 2011).
4. Schwartz C, Scholtens PA, Lalanne A, *et al*. Development of healthy eating habits early in life: review of recent evidence and selected guidelines. *Appetite*. 2011; 57(3): 796–807.
5. Department of Health (DH). *Infant Feeding Recommendation*. London: DH; 2003. Available at: www.dh.gov.uk/assetRoot/04/09/69/99/04096999.pdf (accessed 17 March 2011).
6. Department of Health (DH). *Infant Feeding Survey 2005*. London: DH; 2007. Available at: www.ic.nhs.uk/statistics-and-data-collections/health-and-lifestyles-related-surveys/infant-feeding-survey (accessed 16 March 2011).
7. Department of Health. *Weaning and the Weaning Diet. Report of the Working Group on*

the Weaning Diet of the Committee on Medical Aspects of Food Policy. Report on Health and Social Subjects, 45. London: The Stationery Office; 1994.

8. Poskitt E. Nutrition in childhood. In: Morgan JB, Dickerson JWT, editors. *Nutrition in Early Life*. Chichester: Wiley; 2003. pp. 298.

9. National Health Service; Unicef; Department of Health. *Introducing Solid Foods*. London: Department of Health; 2011 Available at: www.dh.gov.uk/prod_consum_dh/groups/dh_digitalassets/documents/digitalasset/dh_125828.pdf (accessed 8 March 2012).

10. NHS Wales; Welsh Government. *Introducing Solid Foods: giving your baby a better start in life*. Cardiff: NHS Wales; 2011. Available at: www.wales.gov.uk/docs/health challenge/publications/110920solidsen.pdf (accessed 28 May 2012).

11. NHS Health Scotland; Scottish Government. *Fun First Foods: an easy guide to introducing solid foods*. Edinburgh: NHS Health Scotland; 2011. Available at: www.child-smile.org.uk/documents/303.aspx (accessed 21 May 2012).

12. Public Health Agency. *Weaning Made Easy: moving from milk to family meals*. Belfast, Northern Ireland: Public Health Agency; 2012. Available at: www.publichealth.hscni.net/publications/weaning-made-easy-moving-milk-family-meals (accessed 12 June 2012).

13. Grote V, Schiess SA, Closa-Monasterolo R, *et al.*; for European Childhood Obesity Trial Study Group. The introduction of solid food and growth in the first 2 y of life in formula-fed children: analysis of data from a European cohort study. *Am J Clin Nutr*. 2011; **94**(6 Suppl.): S1785–93.

14. Van Rossem L, Kiefte-de Jong JC, Kleinman CWN, *et al.* Weight change before and after the introduction of solids: results from a longitudinal birth cohort. *Br J Nutr*. Epub 2012 Apr 5.

15. www.mumsnet.com

16. www.rapleyweaning.com

17. The Caroline Walker Trust. *Eating Well: first year of life; practical guide*. Abbots Langley: The Caroline Walker Trust; 2011. Available at: www.firststepsnutrition.org/pdfs/First year of Life Practical Guide.pdf (accessed 2 June 2012).

18. Department of Health. *Dietary Reference Values for Energy and Nutrients for the UK. Report of the Committee on Medical Aspects of Food Policy*. Report on Health and Social Subjects, 41. London: HMSO; 1991.

19. Royal College of Paediatrics and Child Health (RCPCH). UK-WHO growth charts: early years. London: RCPCH; 2011. Available at: www.rcpch.ac.uk/growthcharts (accessed 28 July 2011).

20. Westcott JL, Simon NB, Krebs NF. Growth, zinc and iron status, and development of exclusively breastfed infants fed meat vs cereal as a first weaning food. *Faseb J*. 1998; **12**(5): A847.

21. Jalla S, Westcott J, Steirn M, *et al.* Zinc absorption and exchangeable zinc pool sizes in breast-fed infants fed meat or cereal as first complementary food. *J Pediatr Gastroenterol Nutr*. 2002; **34**(1): 35–41.

22. Engelmann MD, Sandström B, Michaelsen KF. Meat intake and iron status in late infancy: an intervention study. *J Pediatr Gastroenterol Nutr*. 1998; **26**(1): 26–33.

23. Mills A, Tyler HA. *Food and Nutrient Intakes of British Infants Aged 6–12 Months*. London: HMSO; 1992.

24. Krebs NF, Westcott JE, Butler N, *et al.* Meat as a first complementary food for breast-fed infants: feasibility and impact on zinc intake and status. *J Pediatr Gastroenterol Nutr.* 2006; **42**(2): 207–14.

25. Food Standards Agency. *McCance and Widdowson's The Composition of Foods.* 6th summary ed. Cambridge: Royal Society of Chemistry; 2002.

26. Crawley H, Westland S. *Infant Milks in the UK.* Abbots Langley: The Caroline Walker Trust; 2011. Available at: www.cwt.org.uk/pdfs/infantsmilk_web.pdf (accessed 16 March 2012).

27. Ziegler EE. Consumption of cow's milk as a cause of iron deficiency in infants and toddlers. *Nutr Rev.* 2011; **69**(Suppl. 1): S37–42.

28. Scientific Advisory Committee on Nutrition. *Salt and Health.* London: The Stationery Office; 2003. Available at: www.sacn.gov.uk/pdfs/sacn_salt_final.pdf (accessed 12 June 2011).

29. Cribb VL, Warren JM, Emmett PM. Contribution of inappropriate complementary foods to the salt intake of 8-month-old infants. *Eur J Clin Nutr.* Epub 2011 July 20.

30. Nelson M, Erens B, Bates B, *et al.*; for Food Standards Agency. *Low Income Diet and Nutrition Survey. Volume 3: Nutrition status, physical activity and economic, social and other factors.* London: The Stationery Office; 2007. Available at: www.food.gov.uk/multimedia/pdfs/lidnsvol03.pdf (accessed 28 May 2011).

31. Agostoni C, Decsi T, Fewtrell M, *et al.*; for ESPGHAN Committee on Nutrition. Complementary feeding: a commentary by the ESPGHAN Committee on Nutrition. *J Pediatr Gastroenterol Nutr.* 2008; **46**(1): 99–110.

32. European Food Safety Authority Panel on Dietetic Products, Nutrition and Allergies. Scientific Opinion on the appropriate age for introduction of complementary feeding of infants. *EFSA Journal.* 2009; **7**(12): 1423–42.

33. Akobeng AK, Ramanan AV, Buchan I, *et al.* Effect of breast feeding on the risk of coeliac disease: a systematic review and meta-analysis of observational studies. *Arch Dis Child.* 2006; **91**(1): 39–43.

34. Norris JM, Barriga K, Klingensmith G, *et al.* Timing of initial cereal exposure in infancy and risk of islet autoimmunity. *JAMA.* 2003; **290**(13): 1713–20.

35. Scientific Advisory Committee on Nutrition; Committee on Toxicity. *Joint Statement: timing of introduction of gluten into the infant diet.* London: The Stationery Office; 2011. Available at: http://cot.food.gov.uk/pdfs/cotsacnstatementgluten201101.pdf (accessed 10 June 2011).

36. Thompson R, Miles L, Lunn J, *et al. Systematic review of literature on early life patterns of exposure to and avoidance of food allergens and later development of sensitisation and clinical food allergy, with particular reference to peanut allergy. Final Technical Report of FSA research project T07052.* London: Food Standards Agency; 2008. Available at: www.foodbase.org.uk/results.php?f_report_id=439 (accessed 15 April 2011).

37. Nicklaus S. Children's acceptance of new foods at weaning: role of practices of weaning and of food sensory properties. *Appetite.* 2011; **57**(3): 812–15.

38. Coulthard H, Harris G, Emmett P. Delayed introduction of lumpy foods to children during the complementary feeding period affects child's food acceptance and feeding at 7 years of age. *Matern Child Nutr.* 2009; **5**(1): 75–85.

39. Butte N, Cobb K, Dwyer J, *et al.*; for American Dietetic Association; Gerber Products

Company. The Start Healthy Feeding Guidelines for Infants and Toddlers. *J Am Diet Assoc*. 2004; **104**(3): 442–54.

40. Thorsdottir I, Gunnarsson BS, Atladottir H, *et al.* Iron status at 12 months of age: effects of body size, growth and diet in a population with high birth weight. *Eur J Clin Nutr*. 2003; **57**(4): 505–13.

41. Department of Health. *Breastfeeding and Introducing Solid Foods: consumer insight summary*. London: Department of Health; 2008. Available at: www.dh.gov.uk/en/Publicationsandstatistics/Publications/PublicationsPolicyAndGuidance/DH_116885 (accessed 16 March 2011).

42. Wharton BA. Weaning in Britain: practice, policy and problems. *Proc Nutr Soc*. 1997; **56**(1A): 105–19.

43. Stordy BJ, Redfern AM, Morgan JB. Healthy eating for infants: mothers' actions. *Acta Paediatr*. 1995; **84**(7): 733–41.

44. Raza S, Parrett A, Garcia AL. Are infant/toddler commercial ready to eat foods in the UK market meeting the European Commission Directives for relevant nutrients? *Proc Nutr Soc*. 2012; **71**(OCE1): E16.

45. Sritharan N, Morgan J. Complementary feeding for the full-term infant. In: Morgan JB, Dickerson JWT, editors. *Nutrition in Early Life*. Chichester: Wiley; 2003. pp.233-56.

46. World Health Organization (WHO). *Iron Deficiency Anaemia: assessment, prevention, and control; a guide for programme managers*. Geneva, Switzerland: WHO; 2001. Available at: www.who.int/nutrition/publications/en/ida_assessment_prevention_control.pdf (accessed 9 September 2011).

47. Morgan JB, Kimber AC, Redfern AM, *et al.* Healthy eating for infants: mothers' attitudes. *Acta Paediatr*. 1995; **84**(5): 512–15.

48. Bober SJ, Humphry R, Carswell HW, *et al.* Toddlers' persistence in the emerging occupations of functional play and self-feeding. *Am J Occup Ther*. 2001; **55**(4): 369–76.

49. Satter E. Feeding dynamics: helping children to eat well. *J Pediatr Health Care*. 1995; **9**(4): 178–84.

50. Hurley KM, Black MM. Introduction to a supplement on responsive feeding: promoting healthy growth and development for infants and toddlers. *J Nutr*. 2011; **141**(3): 489.

51. Aboud FE, Shafique S, Akhter S. A responsive feeding intervention increases children's self-feeding and maternal responsiveness but not weight gain. *J Nutr*. 2009; **139**(9): 1738–43.

52. DiSantis KI, Hodges EA, Johnson SL, *et al.* The role of responsive feeding in overweight during infancy and toddlerhood: a systematic review. *Int J Obes (Lond)*. 2011; **35**(4): 480–92.

53. Rapley G. Baby-led weaning: transitioning to solid foods at the baby's own pace. *Community Pract*. 2011; **84**(6): 20–3.

54. Wright CM, Cameron K, Tsiaka M, *et al.* Is baby-led weaning feasible? When do babies first reach out for and eat finger foods? *Matern Child Nutr*. 2011; **7**(1): 27–33.

55. Brown A, Lee M. A descriptive study investigating the use and nature of baby-led weaning in a UK sample of mothers. *Matern Child Nutr*. 2011; **7**(1): 34–47.

CHAPTER 3

The dietary requirements of infants

Key facts

1. Revised Estimated Average Requirements for energy for infants are lower than previous recommendations, with separate values now being given for breastfed, formula-fed and breastfed/formula-fed infants.

2. New weight-for-age recommendations for infants are lower for girls than for boys.

3. The guideline for minimum intake of milk at 7–12 months is 500 mL; however, this guideline was suggested before the lower energy intake recommendations, when the recommended age for introducing solids was 4–6 months (rather than at 6 months).

4. There is no recommendation for total fat intake for infants in the United Kingdom, other than not to restrict fat intake. Recommendations for total fat intake for infants elsewhere range from above 25%–40%, while 30%–45% has been suggested to prevent restrictive and excessive intakes. Usual mean fat intakes appear to vary from 28% to 42% energy from fat at 6–12 months, being higher at a younger age; recent UK data is lacking but has been commissioned.

5. Lower saturated fat and trans fat and higher polyunsaturated fats appear to be more important than total fat intake from late infancy in terms of later cardiovascular health.

6. There is no recommendation for saturated fat intake in infants in the United Kingdom or elsewhere. The UK recommendation for children over 5 years of age and adults is to obtain no more than 10% of total daily energy intake from saturated fat.

7. There are no recommendations for intake of omega-3 and omega-6

polyunsaturated fatty acids among UK infants, with UK adult recommendations of 1% of daily energy as linoleic acid (omega-6), 0.2% as linolenic acid (omega-3) and 0.45 g per day of long-chain omega-3 polyunsaturated fatty acids. For infants over 6 months of age, other countries and organisations recommend from 3.5% to 9% of daily energy intake from omega-6 polyunsaturated fatty acids, from 0.5% to at least 1% of daily energy intake from omega-3 polyunsaturated fatty acids, and from 0.2% to 0.35% of total fat as long-chain omega-3 polyunsaturated fatty acids.

8. There are no dietary fibre recommendations for infants in the United Kingdom. While there is insufficient data to make conclusive recommendations, data suggests that an intake of 7.6 g non-starch polysaccharides (NSP) per 1000 kcal (7.3 g NSP per day) at 13 months leads to later health benefits compared with lower fibre intakes; such levels do not lead to growth faltering as long as energy intake is maintained, iron levels being positively associated with fibre intake.

9. Health professional advice to parents on vitamin D supplements appears to be infrequent.

10. While further research is needed, it is suggested that in the interim, infants obtain >35% energy from fat at 6–12 months; boys have 5.8 g of NSP per day, and girls have 5.3 g of NSP per day at 12 months, increasing from 6 months.

CHANGES IN INFANTS' NUTRITIONAL NEEDS DURING GROWTH

Infants need more energy, iron and zinc as they grow, while requirements for protein and most vitamins and other minerals hardly change over this period.[1,2] Between 4 and 7 months, energy, zinc and iron requirements increase by about 20%,[2] 25% and 75%, respectively.[1] From 7 to 12 months, energy requirements increase by about 20%,[2] while zinc and iron requirements remain constant.[1] Boys on average require more energy than girls, because of their higher body weight.[3]

Energy requirements increase by approximately 20% at 4–7 months and also at 7–12 months, zinc requirements increase by 25% and iron requirements increase by 75% between 4 and 7 months.

No recommendations for fat intake or fibre intake for infants were made by COMA,[4] because of a lack of scientific evidence at that time.

> No recommendations for fat intake or fibre intake for infants were made by the Committee on the Medical Aspects of Food Policy (COMA),[4] because of a lack of scientific evidence at that time.

ENERGY RECOMMENDATIONS

A good indicator of how much energy an infant needs may be how much solid food and milk he wants. If he is in control of how much he eats and drinks, as in responsive feeding and baby-led weaning, he will stop when he is no longer hungry.[5,6]

The Estimated Average Requirement (EAR) for energy for infants is the amount of energy that is estimated to be sufficient to meet the energy needs of half the infant population, but insufficient for the other half.[1]

> The EAR for energy for infants is the amount of energy that is estimated to be sufficient to meet the energy needs of half the infant population, but insufficient for the other half.[1]

Revised EARs for energy[2] were calculated using the UK-World Health Organization (WHO) Growth Standard[3] based on breastfed and formula-fed infants, calculated as total daily energy expenditure plus energy deposition. These revised EARs[2] are 7%–19% lower after 3 months of age than previous values.[1] Revised EARs for energy for infants[2] are given in Table 3.1.

> Revised EARs for energy[2] are 7%–18% lower after 3 months of age than previous values.[1]

While grouped EARs for energy are given in Table 3.1, EARs for energy (kilocalories per day) per month for breastfed boys are as follows: 620 at 6 months, 634 at 7 months, 659 at 8 months, 685 at 9 months, 718 at 10 months, 740 at 11 months and 762 at 12 months.[2] Similarly, for breastfed girls, EARs for energy (kilocalories per day) per month are as follows: 572 at 6 months, 574 at 7 months, 601 at 8 months, 624 at 9 months, 652 at 10 months, 673 at 11 months and 693 at 12 months.[2]

TABLE 3.1 Revised Estimated Average Requirements for energy for infants aged 3–12 months[2]

Age (months)	Breastfed		Breast milk substitute fed		Mixed feeding or unknown	
	MJ (kcal)/ kg/day	MJ (kcal)/ day	MJ (kcal)/ kg/day	MJ (kcal)/ day	MJ (kcal)/ kg/day	MJ (kcal)/ day
Boys						
3–4	0.4 (96)	2.4 (574)	0.4 (96)	2.6 (622)	0.4 (91)	2.5 (598)
5–6	0.3 (72)	2.5 (598)	0.4 (96)	2.7 (646)	0.3 (72)	2.6 (622)
7–12	0.3 (72)	2.9 (694)	0.3 (72)	3.1 (742)	0.3 (72)	3.0 (718)
Girls						
3–4	0.4 (96)	2.2 (526)	0.4 (96)	2.5 (598)	0.4 (96)	2.3 (550)
5–6	0.3 (72)	2.3 (550)	0.4 (96)	2.6 (622)	0.3 (72)	2.4 (574)
7–12	0.3 (72)	2.7 (646)	0.3 (72)	2.8 (670)	0.3 (72)	2.7 (646)

The average growth rates for boys and girls are as follows: 145 and 134 g a week, respectively, at 4 months; 97 and 92 g a week, respectively, at 6 months; 67 and 62 g a week, respectively, at 9 months; and 55 and 53 g a week, respectively, at 12 months of age, based on growth rates for both breastfed and formula-fed infants.[3] A Ministry of Agriculture, Fisheries and Food survey of infants aged 6–12 months[7] found that average daily energy intakes increased by almost 15% between the younger 6- to 9-months age group and the older 9- to 12-months age group, the majority of infants having been introduced to solids at around 4 months.

Role of milk in energy provision following the introduction of solids

Milk intake should decrease gradually following the introduction of solids; for an infant introduced to solids before 6 months, the COMA guideline minimum intake of milk is 600 mL at 4–6 months and 500 mL at 7–12 months.[4] These minimum guidelines may change, as they were set before the recommendation to introduce solids at 6 months[8] and before the new lower energy requirements for infants.[2]

> Minimum guidelines for milk intake (600 mL at 4–6 months and 500 mL at 7–12 months)[4] may change, as they were set before the recommendation to introduce solids at 6 months[8] and before the new energy requirements for infants.[2]

While there are no new guidelines for minimum milk intake based on the introduction of complementary foods at 6 months rather than at 4–6 months, it seems logical that milk may have a greater role in energy provision at 6–9 months for infants introduced to solids at 5 months than for those introduced to solids almost 2 months earlier. This would appear to be the case even if complementary feeding proceeded more quickly when started at 6 months, since guidelines suggest that milk provides just over 60% of energy intake by 6 months for infants introduced to solids between 4 and 6 months – that is, just over 60% of energy intake up to 2 months post-introduction of solids.[4] It is therefore feasible that milk provides approximately 60% of energy intake by 8 months for infants introduced to solids at 6 months, assuming the same rate of introduction of solids at 6 months as at 4–6 months, or a slightly faster rate. Rapley[9] suggests that historically, milk intake has been reduced too quickly.

> Guidelines[4] suggest that milk provides just over 60% of energy intake up to 2 months after the introduction of solids at 4–6 months, and it is feasible that this also applies to the introduction of solids at 6 months.

FAT INTAKE

Infant nutrition surveys have shown that average fat intake is approximately 50% of energy intake in the first 4 months, prior to the introduction of solids.[10,11] For example, among British breastfed infants[10] and American breastfed and formula-fed infants,[11] average fat intake was 50% of energy intake at 2–4 months. Total fat intake decreases upon the introduction of complementary food, with studies carried out in developed countries since 1990 indicating that fat intake ranges from 43% to 31% of energy from fat at 4–12 months.

- At 4 months: 43% of energy from fat among British breastfed and formula-fed infants.[12]
- At 6 months: 42% of energy from fat among American infants[11]; 37.4% among German non-breastfed infants[13]; 37% among British 6- to 12-month-old infants, mainly formula fed.[7]
- At 8 months: 35% among British infants, mainly formula fed[14]; 34% among American infants, mainly formula fed,[11] majority formula fed.
- At 9 months: 37.9% among Danish infants, 39.5% for partially breastfed infants, 36% for infants no longer breastfed[15]; 36% for Australian infants[16]; 35% for American 9- to 12-month-old infants[17]; 32% for Danish partially breastfed infants, 31% for non-breastfed infants.[18]

- At 12 months: 35.7% for German non-breastfed infants[13]; 34% for British infants, mainly formula fed[10]; 32% for American infants, mainly formula fed.[11]

It is evident from these studies that fat intake tends to be higher at a younger age (e.g. at 4 or 6 months compared with 12 months); this is as expected, because of higher intakes of milk at younger ages.[7]

Fat intake in infants following the introduction of solids may reflect maternal fat intake, since infant diet has been shown to reflect maternal diet[19,20] and may be partly influenced by the dietary guidelines for a given country[19] and the importance placed on those guidelines by health professionals and government. For example, Robinson et al.[19] found that among UK infants at both 6 and 12 months, the infant diet was dependent upon the maternal diet, following either infant guidelines or a diet characterised by a high intake of white bread, chips, crisps and sweets. Further, Gondolf et al.[15] found that fat intake in Denmark was higher than a previous study by Michaelsen,[18] the authors commenting that this may have been due to a greater focus in infant dietary guidelines on the importance of fat intake, due to concerns regarding the previously low fat intake. Differences in fat intake between the various studies may also be partly due to the sample characteristics and the dietary measurement tool.

> Fat intake in infants following the introduction of solids may reflect maternal fat intake, since infant diet has been shown to reflect maternal diet[19,20] and may be partly influenced by the dietary guidelines for a given country.

While not indicative of optimum fat intake, these studies indicate that mean fat intake appears to vary between 43% and 31% of energy from fat in developed countries following the introduction of solids. While there is limited data on infant fat intake in developing countries, intake appears to be similar to that in developed countries. For example, Prentice and Paul[21] found that among 7- to 12-month-old infants from the Gambia, fat intake was 34.4% of total energy intake. Total fat supply, as opposed to fat intake, has been found to vary from 16% to 36% of total energy intake in developing countries, with the least developed countries such as Bangladesh, Ethiopia and Malawi having the lowest fat supply (12%–16% of total energy intake); this could adversely affect the fat content of the complementary feeding diet.[22]

Current fat intakes appear to range from 31% to 43% of energy from fat among 6- to 12-month-old infants in developed countries.

Dietary fat recommendations in the United Kingdom

The current UK government recommendation on fat intake for infants is simply not to restrict fat in children under 2 years old, fat intake being gradually reduced from 2 years of age to meet the adult fat recommendation (of no more than 35% of energy from fat) at 5 years of age.[1] COMA[4] made no recommendation for total fat intake for UK infants because of a lack of studies at that time looking at the optimum quality and quantity of dietary fat needed during infancy.

> The current UK government recommendation on fat intake for infants is simply not to restrict fat in children under 2 years old.[1]

Dietary fat recommendations in other countries

Several countries and organisations have made recommendations for total fat intake for infants, with most recent recommendations being lower than previous recommendations from the 1980s and 1990s.[23–25] Current recommendations for infants include:

- 40% energy from fat (Adequate Intake) at more than 6–12 months, United States[26]
- 40% energy from fat at 6–11 months (Adequate Intake), the Netherlands[27]
- 40% of energy from fat, 30 g of fat per day, at 7–12 months (Adequate Intake), United States/Canada[28]
- 35%–45% energy from fat at 4 months to less than 12 months, German-Austrian-Swiss recommendations, 2008[29]
- 30%–45% at 6–11 months, Nordic countries[30]
- 30%–40% energy from fat at 6–9 months, Food and Agriculture Organization of the United Nations (FAO)[31]
- at least 30% of energy as fat at 6–24 months, WHO[32]
- above 25% energy from fat from 6 months, European Society for Paediatric Gastroenterology, Hepatology and Nutrition (ESPGHAN).[33]

> Recommendations for total fat intake for infants from 6 months of age vary from an Adequate Intake of 40% energy from fat[26] to above 25% energy from fat.[33]

New Australian infant feeding guidelines were consulted on in 2011; these were food based and did not include nutrient recommendations.[34] Canadian recommendations[35] are not to restrict fat intake during the first 2 years of life.

US recommendations are for 30%–40% of energy as fat between 1 and 3 years of age,[36] while the German-Austrian-Swiss recommendations[26] are for 30%–40% of energy from fat from 1 to less than 4 years of age. The Nordic Nutrition Recommendations are for 30%–35% of energy from fat between 12 and 23 months of age,[37] and the Health Council of the Netherlands[38] recommendations are for 25%–40% of energy from fat from 12 months.

From 2 years of age, most European countries recommend 30%–35% energy from fat, including Denmark, Finland, Iceland, Norway, Sweden and Latvia, the Netherlands having the lowest minimum level at 25%–40% energy from fat.[39]

These recommendations from different countries and organisations for fat intake for infants and children can be confusing, since some are 'average daily intake' or 'adequate intake' population recommendations while others are recommendations for individuals. The EURRECA (EURopean micronutrient RECommendations Aligned) network has been working toward alignment of reference values for fat intake among infants (and also for other reference values) in European Union countries, and has found that clear evidence for differing recommendations between countries is often lacking.[29]

An 'Adequate Intake' recommendation for infants, as used by the European Food Safety Authority,[26] the Health Council of the Netherlands,[27] and the Institute of Medicine,[28] is the average observed daily level of intake of a population group of apparently healthy infants that is assumed to be adequate, set when an average requirement cannot be determined. Thus in the United Kingdom, the Adequate Intake recommendation for total fat (the average observed daily level of fat intake among UK infants), would be 37% based on the Ministry of Agriculture, Fisheries and Food survey of 6- to 12-month-old UK infants.[7] However, more recent intake data will be available from the National Infant Diet and Health Study.[40]

Fat intake, growth and development

Consumption of <22% energy from fat has been shown to lead to failure to thrive in infants.[41] Intakes of 30% of energy from fat have been shown to have no effect on growth during infancy if energy and protein intakes remained at acceptable levels.[18,42] In terms of later growth and development, a diet of 25%–30% of energy from fat from 7 months did not lead to compromised growth to 14 years of age[43] or sub-normal neurological development at 5 years of age.[44] Further, there have been no reports of impaired growth in infancy and early childhood with low-saturated fat diets, at 12 months,[45,46] at 3 years,[47] and at 5 years.[44]

> Infant diets with <22% energy from fat have been shown to lead to failure to thrive, while diets of 30% energy from fat have not compromised growth during infancy if energy and protein levels remained acceptable. A diet of 25%–30% of energy from fat from 7 months of age did not compromise neurological development at 5 years of age or growth to 14 years of age. Low saturated fat diets have not led to impaired growth during infancy or early childhood.

While breastfed infants receive long-chain omega-3 polyunsaturated fatty acids in breast milk, the supply of long-chain omega-3 polyunsaturated fatty acids in formula-fed infants is dependent upon the formula used and the consumption of fish in the complementary diet. A meta-analysis of fourteen studies looking at the effect of long-chain omega-3 polyunsaturated fatty acid supplementation on growth in term formula-fed infants up to 12 months of age found no effect on infant weight or length.[48] In terms of neurological development, the Scientific Advisory Committee on Nutrition (SACN) and the Committee on Toxicity (COT)[49] concluded that long chain omega-3 polyunsaturated fatty acids supplementation studies consistently demonstrated short-term beneficial effects on visual function in preterm infants, and while there were less consistent findings in term infants, the majority of studies also demonstrated a beneficial effect on visual function. ESPGHAN[33] advised the inclusion of good sources of long-chain polyunsaturated fatty acids such as oily fish in the infant diet, while recognising that there was not strong evidence linking a low intake of long-chain polyunsaturated fatty acids with poor neurodevelopment.

> Long-chain omega-3 polyunsaturated fatty acids appear to have a beneficial effect on visual function.

A meta-analysis by Makrides et al.[50] found no effect of long-chain omega-3 polyunsaturated fatty acids supplementation on behavioural development among formula-fed infants. Further, Makrides et al.[51] commented that it would not be surprising if long-chain polyunsaturated fatty acid supplementation among breastfed and formula-fed infants resulted in small, inconsistent effects, since most term infants in developed countries would have had a supply of long-chain polyunsaturated fatty acids in utero (when brain growth was at its maximum) and been born with a fat reserve. This suggests that infants who did not have a sufficient supply of long-chain polyunsaturated fatty acids in utero may benefit from supplementation.

Fat intake and later obesity

While a reduction of total fat intake (to 25%–30% of energy from fat) and of saturated fat intake from 7 months of age has been shown to reduce obesity risk 10 years later in girls,[52] there appears to be insufficient data to support restriction of fat intake in the first 2 years of life with regard to later obesity risk.[53] Similarly, ESPGHAN[54] concluded that while it is likely that total fat intake and saturated fat play a role in the development of childhood obesity, no recommendations on dietary fat intake in infancy could be made, owing to insufficient data.

> While high total fat intake and high saturated fat intake from infancy may play a role in the development of childhood obesity, further research is needed.

Quality of fat intake and cardiovascular health

In terms of future cardiovascular health, it appears that lower intakes of trans fats and saturated fats in relation to higher intakes of polyunsaturated fats and monounsaturated fats during late infancy are more important than the total amount of fat in the diet.[43,46,55–57] For example, Ohlund et al.[57] found that increased polyunsaturated fat and reduced saturated fat intake in Swedish infants from 6 to 12 months led to reduced total cholesterol and low-density lipoprotein (LDL) cholesterol at 12 months, *independent* of total fat consumption. The resulting reduction in risk of coronary heart disease in adulthood is unknown but is likely to be high.[58,59] A reduction in saturated fat by repeated dietary counselling has been shown to reduce serum LDL cholesterol to 19 years of age.[60] Replacing saturated fat intake with polyunsaturated fats appears to lead to a greater reduction in risk of coronary heart disease than replacing saturated fat with monounsaturated fats, both omega-3 and omega-6 polyunsaturated fats appearing to be beneficial.[61] In addition, replacing saturated fat with simple carbohydrates may increase the risk of coronary heart disease.[61,62]

> While a reduced intake of saturated and trans fats and a corresponding increase in polyunsaturated and monounsaturated fats in late infancy may reduce future cardiovascular risk, replacing saturated fat with polyunsaturated

fat, rather than monounsaturated fat, appears to be more important than the total amount of fat in the diet in terms of future cardiovascular health.

Essential fatty acids

The 18-carbon chain polyunsaturated fatty acids linoleic acid (omega-6) and alpha-linolenic acid (omega-3) are essential fatty acids, in that they cannot be synthesised by the body and must be obtained from the diet. Linoleic acid can be obtained from many plant, seed and nut oils such as corn, soybean, sesame and sunflower, while alpha-linolenic acid can be obtained from soybeans, walnuts, wheatgerm, rapeseed oil, linseeds and their oils. The longer carbon chain omega-3s, eicosapentaenoic acid (20 carbons) and docosahexaenoic acid (22 carbons), found in fatty fish and shellfish (such as herring, fresh tuna, salmon and mackerel) are seen as conditionally essential, since they can only be formed to a limited extent in the body from alpha-linolenic acid.[63] Docosahexaenoic acid is important in the development of the brain and retina, and together with eicosapentaenoic acid, is important in the prevention of cardiovascular disease.[63]

While excess omega-6 linoleic acid (well above 10% of total energy intake) appears to reduce the formation of docosahexaenoic acid and eicosapentaenoic acid from omega-3 alpha-linolenic acid in adults[63,64] and infants,[65] the current average intake of omega-6 polyunsaturated fatty acids is 5.3% of food energy (1.1% of food energy for omega-3 polyunsaturated fatty acids.[66]

High omega-6 linoleic acid levels together with a low intake of fish or seafood lead to populations with a poor docosahexaenoic acid status.[67] Oily fish is not a major contributor to omega-3 polyunsaturated fatty acid intake in the United Kingdom, making up only 2% of daily fat intake in adults and only 1% of total fat intake among 1½ to 3-year-old children.[66] Similarly, UK infants have been shown to have low intakes of fish, with a median intake of 8 g per day, only 45% of infants consuming fish.[7]

Docosahexaenoic acid concentration in breast milk appears to be dependent upon the fatty acid status of the mother[68]; data from developing countries suggests that fish intake is the most important determinant of docosahexaenoic acid concentration in breast milk.[22] Docosahexaenoic acid levels in breast milk in the United States appear to be lower than in developing African countries[69]; levels may be so low in some populations that even breastfed infants may be at risk of insufficient intake.[68]

> The long-chain omega-3 fatty acid docosahexaenoic acid is important in the development of the brain and retina. Fish intake appears to be the most important determinant of docosahexaenoic acid concentration in breast milk, fish intake being low among UK adults.

Breast and formula milk have been found to be important sources of omega-3 and omega-6 polyunsaturated fatty acids during complementary feeding among German infants having a high intake of commercial foods.[70]

Suggestions for total fat intake

It has been suggested that 30%–45% of total energy intake as fat is an advisable range for infants aged 6–12 months, preventing restrictive and excessive intakes.[71,72] More recently, a gradual reduction of fat intake from 6 months to a level of 30%–35% of energy from fat by 3 years of age has been proposed by Uauy and Dangour,[41] based on new standards for acceptable weight for infants and children,[73] which could be compatible with the 2012 UK revised energy recommendations[2]; findings of failure to thrive among infants consuming <22% of energy as fat,[41] and findings of no adverse effect on growth or neurodevelopment with intakes of 30% energy from fat, where energy intake was sufficient.[18,41,44,47] Uauy and Dangour[41] state that there is insufficient data to establish lower and upper mean values for fat intake.

> It has been suggested that 30%–45% of total energy as fat is an advisable range for infants aged 6–12 months.[71,72] Uauy and Dangour[41] state that there is insufficient data to establish lower and upper mean values for fat intake.

Interestingly, these research-based suggestions are in line with recommendations from various countries such as the Netherlands[27] and Norway,[30] and the European Food Safety Authority[26] but higher than recommendations from organisations such as WHO[32] and ESPGHAN.[33]

A conservative suggestion for fat intake in the United Kingdom

In order to advise parents on the proportion of foods from different food groups needed by an infant, a suggested fat intake is required (to calculate these food group proportions, along with fibre intake). It seems reasonable to advise parents that infants need more fat than adults, in order to prevent parents giving a low-fat diet.

As described in the previous section, Suggestions for total fat intake, there is evidence for a lower level of fat intake (30% of energy from fat) but not an upper level.[41,71,72] However, 30% energy from fat is lower than the COMA[1] Dietary Reference Value (DRV) of no more than 35% energy from fat. If we suggest that infants should have a higher fat intake than adults, then 'more than 35% energy from fat' may be appropriate.

> 'More than 35% energy from fat' may be an appropriate conservative suggestion for fat intake for 6- to 12-month-old infants, being higher than the recommended fat intake for adults.[1]

Breast milk contains approximately 50% of energy from fat,[1] while the legal requirements for formula milk are between 30% and 56.6% of energy from fat.[74] We would expect fat intake to decrease during complementary feeding, and thus while it is difficult to suggest an upper fat limit, owing to a lack of research, a conservative upper limit for percentage of energy from fat for infants after the introduction of solids could be <50% energy from fat. Based on the total fat content of breast milk (50%), the expectation that fat intake would decrease during complementary feeding and the advisable upper limit of 45% of total energy intake from fat for infants at 6–12 months,[71,72] a reasonable upper limit for fat for infants after the initial introduction of complementary foods could be 45% of total energy intake.

> A reasonable upper limit for fat for infants after the initial introduction of complementary foods could be 45% of total energy intake.

As shown earlier (*see* Dietary fat recommendations in other countries, p. 45), a suitable Adequate Intake for fat could be 40% of energy from fat for infants aged older than 6–12 months, as proposed by the European Food Safety Authority[26]; this proposal was based on both experimentally derived estimates of Adequate Intake, based on current fat intake levels among infants,[75] which correspond to 37% of energy from fat in the United Kingdom,[7] and a consensus statement from ESPGHAN[33] of >25% of energy from fat.

Recommended intake of omega-3 and omega-6 fatty acids

Previous COMA[1] recommendations for polyunsaturated fat intake for adults of 1.2% of total dietary energy, 1% as linoleic acid (omega-6) and 0.2% as linolenic acid (omega-3), were amended by SACN and COT[49] to include 0.45 g per day of long-chain polyunsaturated fatty acids, omega-3 polyunsaturated fatty acids with 20 or 22 carbon atoms, as found in oily fish (eicosapentaenoic acid (20 carbon atoms), docosapentaenoic acid (22 carbon atoms), and docosahexaenoic acid (22 carbon atoms)). However, no recommendations have been made in the United Kingdom for intake of omega-3 and omega-6 polyunsaturated fats for infants or children under 5 years of age.

The recommended intake of omega-3 polyunsaturated fats for infants from 6 months of age from other countries and organisations ranges from:

- 0.4% of daily energy intake[76]
- 0.5% of daily energy intake[28,29,77]
- 1% of daily energy intake[27]
- at least 1% of daily energy intake.[30]

Similarly, the recommended intake of omega-6 polyunsaturated fats for infants from 6 months of age ranges from:

- 2% of daily energy intake[27]
- 3%–4.5% of daily energy intake[76]
- 3.5% of daily energy intake[29]
- 4.5% of daily energy intake[77]
- 6% of daily energy intake[28]
- 9% of daily energy intake (4%–9% of daily energy intake).[30]

The criteria used to determine these omega-3 and omega-6 recommendations by the FAO,[76] Institute of Medicine[28] and the Health Council of the Netherlands[27] are based on average intakes from breast milk; the Health Council of the Netherlands[27] also using a gradual reduction of fat intake due to reduced breast milk intake at 6–12 months,[78] while the FAO recommendations[76] assume breast milk intake provides half of daily energy needs.

> While there are no UK recommendations for intake of omega-3 and omega-6 polyunsaturated fatty acids in infants from 6 months of age, recommendations in other countries range from 0.4% to at least 1% of daily energy intake for omega-3 polyunsaturated fatty acids and from 2% to 9% of daily energy intake for omega-6 polyunsaturated fatty acids.

Research-based suggestions by Uauy and Castillo[56] for omega-3 and omega-6 polyunsaturated fatty acids are that infants should have at least 3%–4.5% of total energy from omega-6 linoleic acid and at least 0.5% energy from omega-3 linolenic acid to meet essential fatty acid requirements.

Research-based suggestions for omega-3 and omega-6 polyunsaturated fatty acids intake for infants are at least 3%–4.5% of total energy from omega-6 linoleic acid and at least 0.5% energy from omega-3 linolenic acid to meet essential fatty acid requirements.[56]

Uauy and Dangour[41] concluded that optimal amounts of long-chain polyunsaturated fatty acids could not be specified. However, 20 mg of docosahexaenoic acid per kilogram body weight have been recommended for infants from 6 months of age,[31] while Adequate Intake levels have been proposed by the European Food Safety Authority Panel on Dietetic Products, Nutrition, and Allergies[26] of 100 mg per day of docosahexaenoic acid for infants over 6 months of age, in addition to 4% of total daily energy intake from omega-6 linolenic acid and 0.5% of total daily energy intake from omega-3 linoleic acid (based on lowest estimated mean intakes in the European Union where deficiency symptoms are not present), higher levels than currently recommended for UK adults.[1,49]

For infants over 6 months of age, the European Food Safety Authority Panel[26] has proposed adequate intake levels of 0.5% of total daily energy intake for omega-3 linoleic acid, 4% of total daily energy intake for omega-6 linolenic acid and 100 mg per day of docosahexaenoic acid. These levels are higher than currently recommended for UK adults.

Recommended and suggested saturated fat intake

There is no UK recommendation for saturated fat intake in infants, while the recommendation for children over 5 years of age and adults is to obtain no more than 10% of total daily energy intake from saturated fat.[1] Uauy and Dangour[41] suggest that saturated fats should provide 10% or less of total energy intake for infants over 6 months (at high risk of cardiovascular disease and living in a clean environment with a low prevalence of infection, which presumably includes most Western infants), and that total polyunsaturated fatty acids should provide <15% of total daily energy intake; these suggestions were based on beneficial effects of reduced saturated fat on LDL cholesterol in adults rather than in children.[79] However, as shown in Chapter 4, such a level of saturated fat intake is not feasible for infants consuming 500 mL of breast or formula milk a day.

While there is no UK recommendation for saturated fat intake in infants, it has been suggested that saturated fats should be reduced slightly to provide 10% or less of total energy intake for infants over 6 months of age.

BODY WEIGHT

Following the publication of the FAO, WHO and United Nations University updated recommendations for energy intake,[31] SACN re-evaluated the COMA DRVs for food energy.[1] The resulting UK-WHO growth standards[3] give separate average weights for boys and girls and are based on both breastfed and formula-fed infants. These new growth standards are generally lower than previous values,[4] which were based on formula-fed infants, indicating that infants should be longer and leaner than previously thought. Table 3.2 gives 2011 and 1994 weight for age values.

TABLE 3.2 Weight for age by year (2011[a] and 1994[b])

Age (months)	Weight (kg)		
	Boys (2011)	Girls (2011)	Boys and girls (1994)
4	7	6.4	7.7
5	7.5	6.9	7.7
6	7.9	7.3	7.7
7	8.3	7.6	8.9
8	8.6	8.0	8.9
9	8.9	8.2	8.9
10	9.2	8.5	9.8
11	9.4	8.7	9.8
12	9.7	9.0	9.8

Notes: [a]Fiftieth percentile weight for age UK-World Health Organization growth standards[3]; [b]Department of Health.[4]

Overweight and obesity

As outlined earlier (*see* Fat intake and later obesity, p. 48), there appears to be insufficient data to link fat intake in the first 2 years of life with later obesity risk.[53,54] Similarly, breastfeeding does not appear to be an important determinant of body weight[79,80,81] although it has been found to lead to slightly lower mean body mass index during childhood and adulthood than formula-feeding,[81] SACN[82] stating that the type of milk feeding in infancy may affect body composition. The effect of breastfeeding on fat mass during childhood is debatable, with a seemingly lower fat mass at 4 years of age[19] but conversely not at 5 years of age,[79] 6½ years of age,[83] or 9–10 years of age.[84]

Higher birthweight is associated with higher body mass index in later life, although higher birthweight may also be associated with greater lean body mass.[3] Obesity in infancy appears to be a risk factor for later obesity as does rapid infant growth.[85,86]

> Obesity and rapid infant growth appear to be important risk factors for later obesity.

In terms of complementary feeding, age at introduction of complementary foods has not been found to be associated with obesity at 5 years of age[79] or later.[87] Interestingly, a complementary feeding diet in line with UK infant feeding guidelines in terms of fruit, vegetables, home-prepared food and breast milk, measured at 6 and 12 months, appears to lead to significantly greater lean body mass in children at 4 years of age than a diet less in line with the guidelines (higher in processed foods and bread), with diet not being related to mean body mass index.[19]

> Compared with a diet higher in processed foods and bread, a complementary feeding diet in line with UK guidelines at 6 and 12 months of age appears to lead to a significant increase in lean body mass at 4 years of age, while not being related to body mass index.

DIETARY FIBRE

Dietary fibre may be defined as non-starch polysaccharides (NSP),[1] which are the main constituents of fibre (consisting of soluble and insoluble non-cellulose polysaccharide and cellulose) or as non-digestible carbohydrates plus lignin (total dietary fibre), including NSP, resistant oligosaccharides, resistant starch and lignin, as defined by the European Food Safety Authority Panel on Dietetic Products, Nutrition and Allergies.[26] This total dietary fibre definition is in accordance with the Codex Alimentarius.[88]

Measurement of dietary fibre and recommendations

In the United Kingdom, dietary fibre recommendations[1] are based on NSP, measured by the Englyst method, while an alternative method used by the

Association of Official Analytical Chemists (the AOAC method) measures non-digestible food components other than NSP and is used across Europe, America and Canada and also by the food industry.[89] The AOAC method gives mean fibre values 1.33 times greater than the Englyst method.[90] The use of different measurement methods complicates interpretation of research on which to base recommendations and comparisons of recommendations between countries.

In addition to different methods of measuring dietary fibre, the comparison of recommendations and of dietary fibre measurements in different countries is further complicated by differing units of measurement – namely, grams per day and grams per 1000 kcal (or kilojoules). Comparisons of fibre intakes in infants and children, expressed as dietary fibre density (grams per 1000 kcal), appear to show that fibre intakes increase during infancy, reaching a maximum intake at 12 months of age[91] or at 2 years of age[92] and then remaining constant throughout childhood and adolescence. Fibre intake, measured as grams of fibre per kilogram body weight, does not show this stable pattern, and hence it has been suggested that dietary fibre density is the most appropriate measure for establishing a reference value for dietary fibre for children and adolescents.[91] This could potentially also be the case for infants aged 6–12 months, although fibre intake would be increasing over this period.

> Dietary fibre density reaches a maximum intake at 12 months of age[91] or 2 years of age[92] and may be the most appropriate measure for establishing a reference value for dietary fibre for children and adolescents, and potentially for infants aged 6–12 months.

Fibre intake

In the United Kingdom, a representative study of infants aged 6–12 months[7] found that boys and girls aged 6–9 months had intakes of 4 g of NSP per day and 3 g of NSP per day (4.8 g of NSP per 1000 kcal and 3.8 g of NSP per 1000 kcal), respectively, while fat intake at 6–9 months was 36.7% of energy intake for boys and 34.6% for girls.[7]

Similarly, a 1992 study of 8-month-old infants in the United Kingdom[14] found that boys and girls had intakes of 4 g of NSP per day (5.0 g of NSP per 1000 kcal, 5.1 g of NSP per 1000 kcal for girls, and 4.8 g of NSP per 1000 kcal for boys). Fat intakes were similar to the previous UK study, at 35.4% of energy intake.[14] Almost a quarter of infants were anaemic; haem iron intakes were low, while levels of anaemia were not associated with fibre intake, only with high milk intake.[93]

Fibre intake among UK children aged 1½ to 3 years[94] was 8.2 g of NSP per day, while the average energy intake was 1137 kcal per day, giving 7.2 g of NSP per 1000 kcal. Such a fibre density may correspond to intake at 12 months.[91] However, it should be noted that solids commenced largely before 6 months in all of the previous studies, which could lead to higher fibre intakes than if solids commenced at 6 months.

A longitudinal study of over 900 German infants[91] found that fibre intake at 6 months was 4.5 g of AOAC per day (3.4 g of NSP per day, 7.2 g of AOAC per 1000 kcal, 5.4 g of NSP per 1000 kcal), doubling by 9 months to 8.9 g of AOAC per day (6.7 g of NSP per day, 12.4 g of AOAC per 1000 kcal, 9.3 g of NSP per 1000 kcal), and at 12 months was 10.2 g of AOAC per day (7.7 g of NSP per day, 12.8 g of AOAC per 1000 kcal, 9.6 g of NSP per 1000 kcal). Fat intake at 12 months was 33% of total energy for boys and 36% of total energy for girls.[95] Again, solids commenced largely prior to 6 months of age.

While not indicative of usual fibre intake, a longitudinal intervention study investigating the health effects of reducing saturated fat intake among over 500 Finnish children followed from 8 months of age found that the mean fibre intake at 8 months (pre-intervention) was 3.9 g of AOAC per day for boys and 3.4 g of AOAC per day for girls, equivalent to 2.9 and 2.6 g of NSP per day, respectively.[92] At 13 months, the mean intake for a high fibre group was 2.4 g of AOAC per 1000 J (7.6 g of NSP per 1000 kcal), 7.3 g of NSP per day.[92] Fat intake was 29.5% of total energy intake at 8 months, and 26.6% at 13 months.[96] Later health benefits were associated with this high level of fibre intake (*see* Benefits of fibre intake, p. 59).

Fibre intake in UK studies among infants aged 6–9 months was up to 5.1 g of NSP per 1000 kcal, with fat intake approximately 35% of energy intake or higher. At 12 and 13 months, fibre intakes were higher in a German study than in a Finnish study (9.6 g of NSP per 1000 kcal and 7.6 g of NSP per 1000 kcal, respectively), as was fat intake (33% of energy from fat among boys, 36% of energy from fat among girls and 26% of energy from fat, respectively). Later health benefits were associated with these fibre intakes in Finnish children.[92]

Fibre recommendations and suggestions

The UK recommendation for adult average fibre intake is 18 g of NSP a day, while the recommendation for individuals is 12–24 g a day.[1] This is comparable with the recommendations for average adult fibre intake in other European countries, which range from 25 to 45 g of AOAC per day, equivalent to 18.8–33.8 g of NSP per day.[26,89] No UK fibre recommendations for infants were made in 1991, owing to a lack of research at that time.[1]

> Advice from COMA[1,4] for children under 2 years of age is that their intake of NSP rich foods (especially those with high phytate levels) should not compromise energy intake or the bioavailability of micronutrients, while fibre intake in those over 2 years of age should be proportionately lower than in adults and related to body size.

Fibre recommendations[1] have not been revisited, although a limited amount of recent research on the benefits and concerns regarding fibre intake in infants is now available, as described in the following two sections (*see* Benefits of fibre intake, p. 59, and Concerns regarding a high fibre diet, p. 61). Recommendations for infants in other countries are based on data extrapolated from adult studies. Hermoso *et al.*[29] found no viable reason for the variation in recommendations between countries. Suggestions and recommendations for fibre intake from 6 months of age include:

- a gradual increase in fibre intake *from 6 months* to 5 g of AOAC (3.8 g of NSP) per day at 12 months for American infants by increasing intake of fruit and vegetables[97]
- an Adequate Intake for dietary fibre of 10 g of AOAC (7.5 g of NSP) per day *at 1–3 years*, based on the 25 g per day recommendation for adults, adjusted for energy intake[26]
- 19 g of AOAC (14.3 g of NSP) per day or 14 g of AOAC (10.5 g of NSP) per 1000 kcal for American children *at 1–3 years* of age[28]
- the identical recommendation of 14 g of AOAC (10.5 g of NSP) per 1000 kcal for children *over 1 year old* and adults[38]
- the suggested levels of fibre intake of age + 5 g per day,[98] age + 5 g per day as a minimum intake and age + 10 g per day as a maximum[99] for American children *over 2 years of age*
- the UK food industry body, the Institute of Grocery Distribution, Guideline Daily Amounts for fibre of 12 g of AOAC (9 g of NSP) per day for *4- to 6-year-olds*.[100]

Recommendations and suggestions for fibre intake for infants include an increased intake from 6 months to 3.8 g of NSP per day at 12 months, plus 7.5 g of NSP or 14.3 g of NSP per day and 10.5 g of NSP per 1000 kcal at 1–3 years.

Benefits of fibre intake

The longitudinal study of Finnish children described earlier (*see* Fibre intake, p. 56)[92] found that serum total and LDL cholesterol concentration at 9 years of age decreased with increasing fibre intake, being lowest among children with a high fibre intake at 13 months (2.4 g of AOAC per 1000 kJ, equivalent to 10.1 g of AOAC per 1000 kcal and *7.6 g of NSP per 1000 kcal*). An increase of 1 g of AOAC a day reduced serum cholesterol by 0.001 mmol/L, independent of fatty acid intake, an interaction effect between fibre and saturated fatty acid leading to a stronger effect of fibre on serum cholesterol at lower saturated fat intakes.[92] A high fibre intake was associated with lower saturated fat intake among boys but not girls; the authors comment that this could have been due to a greater difference in fibre intake between intervention and control boys than between girls, since saturated fat intakes were similar in both intervention and control groups.[92]

Fibre intake was positively associated with weight gain from 8 months to 2 years of age, showing that growth was not compromised by fibre intake.[92] Finnish children with a high fibre intake at 13 months had a higher intake of vitamins and minerals, including iron and zinc, than children with lower fibre intakes; this was also the case at 5 and 9 years of age.[92]

> Finnish children with a high fibre intake at 13 months (7.6 g of NSP per 1000 kcal) had the lowest serum total and LDL cholesterol concentration at 9 years of age.[92] Growth was not compromised by fibre intake, while a high fibre intake at 13 months, 5 and 9 years was associated with a higher intake of vitamins and minerals, including iron and zinc.[92]

These dietary and health benefits suggest that 7.6 g of NSP per 1000 kcal could be a suitable fibre recommendation for infants at 12 months, since intake appears to peak at 12 months[91] or at 2 years,[92] and remains constant thereafter.

> A maximum intake of 7.6 g of NSP per 1000 kcal among 12-month-old infants may not compromise energy or micronutrient intake, and would therefore be in line with advice from COMA.[4]

However, we do not know whether a mean fibre intake greater than 7.6 g of NSP per 1000 kcal[92] would also give health benefits, neither do we know the most advantageous fibre levels in terms of later health benefits for infants *under* 12 months. Fat intake among infants put on a reduced saturated fat diet was lower at 13 months than recommended for adults in the United Kingdom (26% of energy from fat in the high fibre group), with per cent energy from fat being significantly inversely related to fibre intake, an increase in fibre of 0.08 g being associated with a 1% reduction in energy from fat.[92] However, infants at 12 months of age in a German study, discussed earlier in this section,[91] had a higher fibre intake (9.6 g of NSP per 1000 kcal) and a higher fat intake (33% of energy from fat in boys and 36% of energy from fat in girls) than in the study by Ruottinen *et al.*,[92] inferring that a high fibre intake of 7.6 g of NSP per 1000 kcal at 12 months could be associated with approximately 35% of energy from fat or more.

> A high fibre intake of 7.6 g of NSP per 1000 kcal at 12 months could be associated with approximately 35% of energy from fat or more.

A higher fibre intake among 13-month-old Finnish children[92] (7.6 g of NSP per 1000 kcal) was achieved by a higher intake of cereals, vegetables and fruit compared with children with lower fibre intakes; the consumption of meat and fish, was similar among fibre groups, even though a high fibre intake was associated with a higher intake of iron compared with children with a lower fibre intake, iron intakes being almost three times those in a UK study of 6- to 12-month-old infants.[7] In addition, while the intake of cereals (a source of phytates) was highest among children consuming the most fibre, their intake of fruit and vegetables was also the highest,[92] the vitamin C from these fruits and vegetables feasibly counteracting any reduction in non-haem iron absorption because of phytates. The main sources of phytates in the UK diet are cereals and cereal products (such as breakfast cereals and breads), followed by vegetables, potatoes and savoury snacks (such as chips and crisps) and fruits and nuts.[101]

SACN[102] stated that dietary fibre can help reduce the risk of coronary heart disease, while there is insufficient evidence for a health effect in relation to colorectal cancer, obesity, diabetes, blood pressure lowering and prebiotic effects.

> SACN[102] stated that dietary fibre can help reduce the risk of coronary heart disease.

Concerns regarding a high-fibre diet

Fears that a high-fibre diet among children under 5 years of age leads to growth faltering and mineral imbalance are not well supported in the literature except for children on a macrobiotic diet and among vegans.[103]

A high-fibre diet may not necessarily infer a low fat diet; while fat intake among 13-month-old Finnish children consuming a high fibre diet of 7.6 g of NSP per 1000 kcal[92] was low (26% of energy from fat), these infants had purposely been put on a reduced saturated fat diet, which could result in a reduction in total fat intake, but not if there was a corresponding increase in polyunsaturated or monounsaturated fat intake. German infants have been found to have higher fibre intakes (9.6 g of NSP per 1000 kcal) and also higher fat intakes (33% of energy from fat in boys and 36% of energy from fat in girls),[95] demonstrating that a high-fibre diet can contain around 35% of energy from fat.

> A high-fat diet among children under 5 years of age only appears to lead to growth faltering and mineral imbalance in children on a macrobiotic diet and among vegans,[103] while a high-fibre diet can contain around 35% of energy from fat.

Suggested fibre recommendations for infants in the United Kingdom

Based on the UK mean adult fibre recommendation of 18 g of NSP a day,[1] adjusted for an infant's weight using the 2011 UK-WHO values,[3] an appropriate suggested fibre intake for a 6-month-old boy may be 2.0 g of NSP per day (based on 18 g of NSP per day for a 70 kg adult and 7.9 kg body weight for a 6-month-old boy – that is, [(7.9/70) × 18 g per day]). Using the range of UK adult fibre recommendations for an individual (12–24 g of NSP a day)[1] gives 1.4–2.9 g of NSP a day for a 6-month-old boy. Additional values are shown in Table 3.3.

While ESPGHAN considered extrapolation of fibre guidelines for children from adult guidelines impossible, due to differences in recommendations based on body weight and on energy intake, recommendations based on adult energy intake possibly leading to excessive fibre intakes in children,[104] the European Food Safety Authority Panel on Dietetic Products, Nutrition and Allergies[26] states that fibre calculations for children from 1 year of age should be based on adult recommendations, adjusted for energy intake. Calculating fibre density (grams of NSP per 1000 kcal) based on the UK adult fibre recommendation and UK adult male energy recommendation of 2500 kcal per day,[1] rather than revised EARs for energy[3] gives *7.2 g of NSP per 1000 kcal* [(18/2500) × 1000].

Based on a fibre intake of 7.2 g of NSP per 1000 kcal and revised EARs for energy for infants (*see* Table 3.1), the mean fibre intake for a breastfed boy of 6 months would be:

$$= (EAR/1000\,kcal) \times 7.2\,g\,NSP$$
$$= (620/1000) \times 7.2\,g\,NSP$$
$$= 4.5\,g\,NSP\,a\,day.$$

Similarly, the mean fibre intake for a breastfed boy of 8 months would be 4.7 g of NSP a day, 5.2 g of NSP a day at 10 months and 5.5 g of NSP a day at 12 months. Values for girls are shown in Table 3.3.

> The suggested fibre density for infants based on the UK adult fibre recommendation would be 7.2 g of NSP per 1000 kcal.

Note that the mean fibre intake for a breastfed boy at 8 months using these values would give <5 g of NSP per 1000 kcal for boys and girls, the level observed in a UK study where fat intake was 35.4% of energy from fat, slightly above the UK recommended adult level.[14] Similarly, the mean fibre intake at 8 months would be identical for boys (but slightly higher for girls) to another UK study where fat intake at 6–9 months was above the UK adult recommendation for boys (36.7% of energy from fat) but not for girls (34.6% of energy from fat[7]). This indicates that the suggested grams of NSP per 1000 kcal is achievable.

> Based on weight-adjusted UK mean adult fibre recommendations and the range of UK adult fibre recommendations, the suggested fibre intake for a 6-month-old boy would be 2.0 g of NSP per day and 1.4–2.9 g of NSP per day, respectively. Similarly, based on fibre density, calculated using weight-adjusted UK mean adult fibre recommendations and revised EARs for energy, the suggested fibre intake for a 6–month-old boy would be 4.5 g of NSP per day. The calculated fibre density corresponds to fibre intake among UK infants where fat intake was approximately 35% of energy intake.

However, in these UK studies,[7,14] complementary feeding had largely commenced well before 6 months, and hence fibre intakes may be higher than if complementary feeding had started at 6 months, as currently recommended.[8]

This suggested fibre intake (7.2 g of NSP per 1000 kcal and 5.5 g of NSP a day at 12 months) is higher than the US suggestion of 3.8 g of NSP per day at 12 months,[9] similar to the fibre intake of Finnish 13-month-old infants discussed earlier (*see* Benefits of fibre intake, p. 59) (7.6 g of NSP per 1000 kcal[92]), but lower than the recommendations from the European Food Safety Authority Panel on Dietetic Products, Nutrition and Allergies,[26] and recommendations from the United States[28] and the Netherlands[38] at 1 year of age.

We would expect fibre intake to increase from 6 to 12 months as infants consume more complementary foods (*see* Table 3.3). This may be a gradual increase, as suggested by Agastoni *et al.*[97]; however, among German infants, fibre intake almost doubled between 6 and 9 months, and then hardly increased to 12 months.[91] It should be noted that the rate at which fibre intake should increase to 13 months to produce the observed diet and health outcomes[60,92] is not known.

Using the mean high fibre intake among Finnish infants[92] of 7.6 g of NSP per 1000 kcal and revised EARs for energy for infants,[2] the mean fibre intake for a 12-month-old breastfed boy would be:

$$= (EAR/1000 \, kcal) \times 7.6 \, g \, NSP$$
$$= (762/1000) \times 7.6 \, g \, NSP$$
$$= 5.8 \, g \, NSP \, per \, day.$$

Similarly, using the mean fibre intake among UK children aged 1½ to 3 years[66] of 8.2 g of NSP per day or 7.2 g of NSP per 1000 kcal, identical to the fibre density calculated from the adult DRV for fibre,[1] the mean fibre intake for a 12-month-old breastfed boy would be:

$$= (EAR/1000 \, kcal) \times 7.2 \, g \, NSP$$
$$= (762/1000) \times 7.1 \, g \, NSP$$
$$= 5.4 \, g \, NSP \, per \, day \, at \, 12 \, months.$$

> The fibre density among UK children aged 1½ to 3 years[94] is identical to the fibre density calculated from the adult DRV for fibre.[1]

The suggested mean grams of NSP and grams of AOAC (using a conversion factor of 1.33[90]) per day and per 1000 kcal for 12-month-old boys and girls, breastfed and formula fed, are shown in Table 3.3. Further research is needed to determine whether suggested fibre intakes based on fibre recommendations for UK adults and on fibre density at 13 months in Finnish infants[92] is appropriate for infants. Basing suggestions on a single study appears questionable; however, slightly lower fibre intakes have been found among 8-month-old UK infants[14] and among young children in the UK.[1] In the interim, it would seem more appropriate to base suggested mean fibre intakes on intakes for a similar age group where dietary and health benefits have been shown[60,92] than to base suggested mean fibre intakes on adult fibre intake.

It may be inappropriate to give suggestions for fibre intake for 6- and 7-month-old infants based on an intervention with infants from 8 months of age.[92] Since it is recommended that complementary feeding commences at 6 months,[8] low solid intake (and hence low fibre intake) may be expected at 6 and 7 months. It is therefore suggested that at 6 and 7 months, fibre intake should increase, while from 8 months, fibre intakes are based on intakes among 13-month-old Finnish infants.[92]

> It is suggested that at 6 and 7 months, fibre intake should increase, while from 8 months, fibre intakes are based on intakes among 13-month-old Finnish infants.[92]

As shown in Table 3.3, suggested fibre intakes at 12 months based on 13-month-old Finnish children[92] are more than double those extrapolated from the UK adult DRV of 18 g of NSP per day[1] and close to the calculated fibre density based on the UK adult DRV for fibre[1] and on the calculated fibre density among UK infants aged 1½ to 3 years.[94] The suggested fibre intakes at 12 months based on 13-month-old Finnish children[92] are lower than the average NSP intake (8.2 g of NSP per day) for UK children aged 1½ to 3 years.[94]

> Suggested fibre intakes based on Finnish 13-month-old children[92] may be more applicable to infants than extrapolated adult recommendations, because of the greater similarity in age.

TABLE 3.3 Suggested mean fibre intake (grams of non-starch polysaccharides per day) for breastfed infants

Age (months)	Grams-per-day calculation[a]				
	Adult DRV 18g NSP	Adult DRV 12–24g NSP (individual)	Adult DRV 7.2g NSP /1000kcal	NDNS[b] 1½ to 3 years 7.2g NSP/1000kcal	Finnish study[c] 7.6g NSP /1000kcal
6	2.0, 1.9	1.4–2.8, 1.3–2.6	4.5, 4.2	4.5, 4.2	Increase fibre intake
7	2.1, 2.0	1.4–2.8, 1.3–2.6	4.7, 4.2	4.7, 4.2	
8	2.2, 2.1	1.5–3.0, 1.4–2.8	4.7, 4.4	4.7, 4.4	5.1, 4.7
9	2.3, 2.1	1.5–3.0, 1.4–2.8	5.0, 4.5	5.0, 4.5	5.3, 4.8
10	2.4, 2.2	1.6–3.2, 1.5–3.0	5.2, 4.7	5.2, 4.7	5.5, 5.0
11	2.4, 2.2	1.6–3.2, 1.5–3.0	5.3, 4.8	5.3, 4.8	5.6, 5.1
12	2.4, 2.3	1.7–3.4, 1.5–3.0	5.5, 5.0	5.5, 5.0	5.8, 5.3
					7.7, 7.0[d]

Notes: [a]Boy, girl (breastfed); [b]Bates *et al*.[94]; [c]Ruottinen *et al*.[92]; [d]AOAC. DRV, Dietary Reference Value using energy level for which recommendation set[1]; NDNS, The UK National Diet and Nutrition Survey; NSP, non-starch polysaccharides.

> Fibre suggestions based on the adult DRV range for an individual appear to be inappropriate, since these suggestions are lower than previously recorded for UK infants and are lower than fibre intakes which appear to have positive health effects among Finnish children.[92]

The fact that the fibre intakes, based on the UK adult DRV of 18 g of NSP per day are lower than previously recorded UK infant fibre intakes[7,14] implies that these calculated infant fibre intakes are achievable or may be too low. Conversely, it could be argued that fibre intakes in UK infants aged 6–12 months are too high, since they exceed UK adult recommendations (extrapolated for infant body weight). Iron intake during this late infancy period is often compromised, yet a higher fibre intake at 13 months is associated with a higher iron intake.[92] It is possible that the type of fibre consumed, high phytate cereal versus fruit and vegetables,[101] may have a negative effect on iron status in UK infants, as may poor variability in the diet or a relatively low intake of haem iron.[7]

It could be argued that only fibre intake at 12 months can be meaningfully based on fibre intake among 13-month-old Finnish children,[92] since fibre intake in terms of energy density appears to reach a maximum level at 12 months[91] or 2 years,[92] rather than at an earlier age. Indeed, it seems likely that any fibre intake suggestions for infants at the start of complementary feeding would be inappropriate since an infant's diet is so different to that of young children, and more so to that of adults, due to an infant's high milk intake, in terms of total energy intake.

If milk intake is substantially lower at 13 months than at 6–12 months, then fibre intake suggestions should be reduced accordingly – that is, the energy content of the infant diet used in fibre calculations should be for the solid component of the diet only, not of milk. While information on milk intake in the Finnish study of 13-month-old children[92] is not available, intake of dairy products, including milk, was higher[105] than among 6- to 12-month-old infants in a UK study,[7] and thus differences in milk intake may not be large. Further, intake of dairy products, including milk, and of calcium, were not significantly different among Finnish 13-month-old children with low, average or high fibre intakes, suggesting that milk intake was not reduced on a high fibre diet.[92]

> If milk intake is substantially lower at 13 months than at 6–12 months, then fibre intake suggestions should be reduced accordingly – that is, the energy content of the infant diet used in fibre calculations should be for the solid component of the diet only, not of milk.

The early stages of complementary feeding are characterised by the intake of fruit, vegetables and cereals, with the later addition of meat, fish and eggs.[7,14,106] This suggests that fibre intake may increase quite rapidly in the early stages of complementary feeding, and then increase gradually as a more varied diet is consumed. As mentioned earlier, this pattern of fibre intake was seen in a study of German infants,[91] where fibre intake doubled between 6 and 9 months and changed very little to 12 months. Further research is needed to determine appropriate fibre recommendations for infants.

> While there are many difficulties in estimating appropriate fibre intakes for infants based on current research, the suggested fibre range for:
> - 6- to 12-month-old infants is 4.5–5.5 g of NSP per day for boys and 4.2–5.0 g of NSP for girls based on the UK adult DRV for fibre (calculated fibre density) and the fibre intake among UK children aged 1½ to 3 years
> - 8- to 12-month-old infants is 5.1–5.8 g of NSP per day for boys and 4.4–5.5 g of NSP per day for girls based on a Finnish study of 13-month-old infants.
>
> Further research is needed to determine appropriate fibre recommendations for infants.

THE RECOMMENDATIONS FOR NON-MILK EXTRINSIC SUGARS AND STARCH

Carbohydrates consist of sugars, starch and NSP. Dietary sugars are classified as either intrinsic (naturally occurring in the cell structure of a food, as in whole fruits and vegetables) or extrinsic (not located in the cell structure, found free in the food or added to it, such as sugars in fruit juices, table sugar and honey). Non-milk extrinsic sugars (NMES) are extrinsic sugars that are not found in milk or milk products. For groups of children, it is recommended that the average intake of NMES should be limited to about 10% of total dietary energy intake.[1]

COMA[4] concluded that this general population recommendation, aimed at reducing levels of dental caries, is applicable for preschool children, including infants.

> COMA[4] concluded that the recommendation for average intake of NMES (limit to about 10% of total dietary energy intake) is applicable to infants.

Among UK infants, NMES have been found to provide 9% of energy intake at 6–9 months and 12% of energy intake at 6–12 months,[7] the main sources of NMES sugars being infant fruit juices and drinks, and squash.[7]

Ruottinen et al.[92] found that 13-month-old Finnish infants with a high fibre intake had a significantly lower intake of sucrose (one of the NMES) than infants on a lower fibre intake; infants with a low sucrose intake were found to consume less fruit, fruit juice, soft drinks, sweets, pastries, desserts and sugared dairy products than infants with a high sucrose intake, and also more vegetables and cereals.[105]

> Finnish infants with a high fibre intake were found to have a lower intake of sucrose (one of the NMES) than infants on a lower fibre intake.[92]

Following the introduction of solids it is recommended that the proportion of energy derived from starch should increase as the proportion derived from fat decreases, provided that energy intake is adequate.[4] The COMA panel on DRVs[1] recognised that the DRV for starch for the general population of about 37% of energy from starch might only apply from 2 years of age.

> The proportion of energy derived from starch should increase as the proportion derived from fat decreases, provided that energy intake is adequate.[4]

Among UK 6- to 12-month-old infants, the average daily intake of starch was 18% of total energy.[7] Cooked cereal products and vegetables are good sources of starch for infants.

The European Food Safety Authority Panel on Dietetic Products, Nutrition and Allergies[26] proposed a Reference Intake range for carbohydrates of 45%–60% of energy intake for children from 1 year of age, based on their protective health effects on body weight and blood lipids and perceived achievable intakes.

THE RECOMMENDATION FOR PROTEIN

The RNI for protein for infants is 12.7 g per day at 4–6 months, 13.7 g per day at 7–9 months and 14.9 g per day at 10–12 months.[1] COMA[4] also recommended that an adequate intake of protein with a balance of essential amino acids should be ensured during complementary feeding.

Infants are unlikely to be protein deficient following the introduction of solids if they regularly consume meat, fish, eggs, pulses or recommended quantities of milk.[1] However, if energy intake is low, and high amounts of milk or juice are given, or a milk-free diet is given with little meat, eggs or pulses, protein intake may not be sufficient to meet requirements.

> Infants are unlikely to be protein deficient following the introduction of solids if they regularly consume meat, fish, eggs, pulses or recommended quantities of milk.[1]

THE RECOMMENDATION FOR IRON

Iron is needed for the development of brain tissue, forming part of the myelin sheath around nerves. It is also involved in the production of white blood cells, which are a major component of the immune system, and forms part of haemoglobin in red blood cells, which is responsible for carrying oxygen around the body.

For 4- to 6-month-old infants, the Reference Nutrient Intake (RNI, the intake required to meet the needs of those with the highest requirements) for iron is 4.3 mg per day, the Estimated Average Requirement (EAR, the intake required to meet the needs of half the people in a group) is 3.3 mg per day and the Lower Reference Nutrient Intake (LRNI, the intake level sufficient to meet the needs only of those with the lowest requirements) is 2.3 mg per day.[1] For 7- to

12-month-old infants, the RNI is 7.8 mg per day, the EAR 6.0 mg per day, and the LRNI 4.2 mg per day.[1]

Infants introduced to solids before 6 months may require up to 3.7 mg of iron per day from solids if iron stores are low, while infants aged 7–12 months may require up to 7.3 mg per day of iron from solids if infants are consuming the guideline minimum milk intake of 600 and 500 mL of breast or formula per day providing 0.6 mg of iron a day and 0.5 mg of iron a day, respectively.[4] In terms of required iron density of the diet, infants have much higher requirements than adults;[1,107] for example, compared with an average adult male (8.7 mg iron required per 2500 kcal, or 3.5 mg iron per 1000 kcal), a 9-month-old breastfed boy of average weight requires 11.2 mg of iron per 1000 kcal (7.8 mg per 694.2 kcal).

> In terms of required iron density of the diet, infants have much higher requirements than adults. For 4- to 6-month-old infants, the RNI for iron is 4.3 mg per day, the EAR is 3.3 mg per day, and the LRNI is 2.3 mg per day. For 7- to 12-month-old infants, the RNI is 7.8 mg per day, the EAR 6.0 mg per day, and the LRNI 4.2 mg per day.[1]

WHO[108] criteria for iron deficiency (ID) and iron deficiency anaemia (IDA) for infants are a serum ferritin concentration of <12 µg/L for ID, plus a haemoglobin iron concentration <110 g/L for IDA. ESPGHAN[33] has criticised these cut-off values for being too high, since they do not correspond to concentrations of haemoglobin below which functional consequences of anaemia occur. Values from studies in Sweden and Honduras[109] (haemoglobin iron concentration <105 g/L at 4–6 months, <100 g/L at 9 months) and in the United Kingdom[110] (haemoglobin iron concentration <100 g/L at 12 months, serum ferritin <16 µ/L at 12 months) may be more useful measures since they correspond to the lowest levels among representative population samples.

Comparison of levels of ID and IDA with iron intakes suggests that the RNI and the LRNI for iron for infants may be inflated.[111] Current data on infant iron intake in the United Kingdom is lacking, a situation which will be rectified by a new infant survey commissioned by the Food Standards Agency.[40]

> The RNI and the LRNI for iron for infants may be inflated, as shown by comparison of levels of ID and IDA with iron intakes.

Effect of iron deficiency and iron deficiency anaemia on infant development

Randomised controlled trials of iron supplementation suggest that IDA is a cause of poor motor development in the first 3 years of life, the long-term effects being unknown.[107] In addition, children from lower socio-economic groups may be more vulnerable to the long-term effects of IDA on cognitive measures than children from higher socio-economic groups.[112]

Insufficient evidence prevented an assessment by SACN[107] of the effects of IDA and ID on cognitive and language development, while a previous review found inconclusive evidence for a causal relationship between IDA or ID and deficits in cognitive and behavioural function.[113]

In terms of treatment of IDA, a Cochrane systematic review,[114] including only two randomised controlled trials, found that there was plausible but inconclusive evidence that psychomotor development improved if IDA treatment lasted for more than 30 days.

There may be times when the developing brain is particularly sensitive to iron deprivation, which cannot be improved by iron treatment.[115] It is feasible that ID in infants might exist in the brain in the absence of IDA,[112,116] the American Pediatric Association[117] stating that ID in the absence of IDA may irreversibly adversely affect long-term neurodevelopment and behaviour in infants.

While further research is needed, SACN[107] concluded that the effect of iron deficiency on preschool children's cognitive, motor and behavioural development remains controversial.

> While IDA appears to be a cause of poor motor development in the first 3 years of life and ID may exist in the brain in the absence of IDA, the effect of ID and IDA on preschool children's motor, cognitive and behavioural development remains controversial.

Serum ferritin at birth and later risk of iron deficiency

Serum ferritin at birth (cord serum ferritin) was shown to correlate well with serum ferritin at 6 and 12 months among Norwegian infants,[118] inferring that low levels at birth relate to low levels at 6 and 12 months. Low iron stores at birth, which were found to be more prevalent in boys than girls, placed these infants at greater risk of ID at 6 (2% of infants) and 12 months (12% of infants) than infants with higher iron stores at birth.[118] Low cord serum ferritin has also been shown by others[18,119,120] to be associated with low serum ferritin in later infancy, indicating that increased iron absorption cannot completely rectify this situation. An infant who is growing rapidly will require more iron than an infant growing at a slower rate, and is therefore at a greater risk of ID.[18,121]

> Infants born with low iron stores appear to have a greater risk of ID at 6 and 12 months than infants whose iron stores are replete at birth.

Maternal iron deficiency anaemia and later infant risk of iron deficiency anaemia

Several studies in developing countries have found that maternal anaemia is significantly related to infant anaemia, but these studies measured haemoglobin iron only, and thus IDA could not be assessed.[122-124] Maternal IDA at delivery has been shown to lead to over six times the risk of infant IDA at 12 months compared with infants born to non-anaemic women, with risk being independent of birthweight and feeding practice.[122] Higher infant IDA at 12 months among infants born to mothers with IDA than infants born to mothers without IDA has also been shown by others.[125] Further investigation is required to determine whether this reflects low-iron diets in the mother and infant.

> Infants born to mothers with IDA have been shown to have a greater risk of IDA at 12 months than infants born to mothers with no IDA.

Iron status after 6 months of age: iron deficiency anaemia

The prevalence of IDA in infants at 8–12 months of age depends on the population group and the criteria used to define IDA, as described in the following three sections.

Iron deficiency anaemia at 8 months

- 7% prevalence of IDA among infants from the Avon area of England (haemoglobin iron ≤95 g/L, corresponding to impaired motor development at 18 months), 23% using the WHO classification, the authors stating that this high level of IDA was due to the inappropriateness of WHO measures for their capillary haemoglobin sampling method.[126]

Iron deficiency anaemia at 9 months

- No IDA among a small, mixed socio-economic sample of Danish infants (haemoglobin iron levels <105 g/L, serum ferritin <12 µg/L), 66% of whom were exclusively breastfed at 2 months and 40% at 4 months[18]
- 7% IDA among Canadian infants (haemoglobin iron concentration ≤101 g/L or ≤110 g/L with additional markers, serum ferritin <10 µg/L), 18% of infants consuming cow's milk or low iron formula at 9 months, IDA levels significantly associated with duration of breastfeeding, with 15% IDA among infants breastfed for 8 months.[127]

Iron deficiency anaemia at 12 months

- 2.3% IDA (WHO measures) among infants from 11 European centres, IDA being significantly more frequent in low socio-economic groups (5.1%)[128]
- 2.3% IDA (WHO measures) among Icelandic infants, breastfeeding duration and demographics not stated[121]
- 2.6% IDA (WHO measures) among Irish infants predominantly formula fed up to 9 months, while at 12 months only 6% were breastfed and cow's milk was common (infants with IDA were given cow's milk at an early age, had low haemoglobin iron intake and had severely anaemic mothers)[129]
- 4% IDA among infants from the Avon area of England (haemoglobin iron concentration <100 g/L, 18% by WHO definitions), with more breastfed than formula-fed infants having IDA, cow's milk as the main drink being associated with increased IDA.[93] More than 25% of breastfed infants and those receiving cow's milk and 41% of infants having more than six breastfeeds a day had iron intakes below the LRNI, indicating that iron intake was unlikely to meet the needs of these infants[93]
- 7% IDA (WHO measures) among Norwegian breastfed and formula-fed infants.[130]

> Limited findings indicate that in developed countries such as Canada, Norway, Denmark, Iceland, the United Kingdom and Ireland, rates of IDA appear to be between 0% and 7% at 8–12 months, with rates being higher among infants from lower socio-economic groups than among their higher income counterparts (one study only).

Iron status after 6 months of age: iron deficiency

As with IDA, the prevalence of ID in infants at 9–12 months of age depends on the population group and the criteria used to define ID, as shown in the following two sections.

Iron deficiency at 9 months

- 0% ID among Danish infants, 40% exclusively breastfed to 4 months[18]
- 24% ID (serum ferritin <10 µg/L) among Canadian infants, 18% of infants consuming cow's milk or low-iron formula at 9 months and 95% of infants having iron-fortified cereal by 6 months.[127]

Iron deficiency at 12 months

- 0% ID among American infants, those from lower socio-economic groups fully breastfed for 6 months or more having a 19% higher risk of ID than their higher-income counterparts fully breastfed for between 4 and 6 months[131]
- 4.2% ID (serum ferritin <10 µg/L) among UK infants, serum ferritin being significantly related to meat intake at 12 months, while mean iron intake did not meet the RNI[111]
- 5.8% ID (serum ferritin ≤12 µg/L) among Icelandic infants, 38% being exclusively breastfed to 5 months and 20% breastfed at 12 months[132]
- 7.2% ID (serum ferritin <10 µg/L) among infants from 11 European countries, 5.6% for six countries where the sample size was 36 or more[128]
- 10.3% ID (serum ferritin ≤12 µg/L) among Swedish infants[133]
- 20% ID among Icelandic infants with high breastfeeding levels (not stated), the total duration of breastfeeding being significantly shorter in those with ID, while significantly more boys than girls had ID (27% versus 12%).[121]

In developed countries such as the United States, Denmark, Iceland, Sweden and the United Kingdom, rates of ID appear to be between 0% and 24% at 9–12 months, with one study finding that rates of ID were higher among infants from lower socio-economic groups fully breastfed for 6 months than among their higher income counterparts fully breastfed for between 4 and 6 months.

Complementary feeding and iron

In the UK survey of 6- to 12-month-old infants,[7] over 70% of 10- to 12-month-old infants had iron intakes below the RNI, with 21% below the LRNI, indicating a high risk of iron deficiency; the potentially inflated RNI and LRNI levels for iron[111] make it difficult to relate these iron intakes to levels of ID and IDA.

Meat and fish

Meat and fish consumption have been shown to be positively associated with iron status in infants[18,121,132,134,135] and in toddlers,[136] a lack of association in other studies potentially being due to a lack of variability in intake or to a low intake. For example, Male *et al.*,[128] where only 2%–5% of iron intake among 6- to 12-month-old infants was from meat. The UK survey of 6- to 12-month-old infants[7] found that among 6- to 9-month-old and 10- to 12-month-old infants, meat contributed only 3%–7% to total iron intake, respectively. The 2005 UK infant feeding survey,[137] where 98% of infants had been started on solids before 6 months, found that only 64% and 40% of the higher and lower socio-economic groups, respectively, had consumed meat at least three times a week at 8–10 months.

Infants who were exclusively breastfed for 4–6 months were more likely to develop marginal iron status (low haemoglobin) at 10 months if they were given commercial complementary foods with a low versus a high meat content (8% and 12% meat by weight, respectively), while the iron status of infants not exclusively breastfed was adequate.[138]

> Meat and fish consumption have been shown to be positively associated with iron status in infants. Meat intake may be low among UK infants.

Non-milk extrinsic sugars

The 2005 UK infant feeding survey[137] found that compared with higher socio-economic group infants, lower socio-economic group infants were more frequent consumers of sweets, chocolates and biscuits (14% versus 33%) and of crisps (10% versus 21%); these 'empty calories' may have displaced more nutrient dense foods and hence could have contributed to a low iron intake. Similarly, the UK survey of 6- to 12-month-old infants[7] found that NMES provided 12% of energy intake in 9- to 12-month-old infants, mainly from sweetened drinks (biscuits, chocolate and sweets also being eaten by these infants), a higher intake than recommended (about 10% of energy intake),[4] which again could displace more nutrient-dense foods.

> A low iron intake among UK infants may be partly due to low haemoglobin iron intake and displacement of nutrients with sweet foods.

Commercial infant foods

The UK survey of 6- to 12-month-old infants[7] found that infants who did not consume commercial infant foods had a mean iron intake well below the RNI, while approximately 40% of these infants had iron intakes below the LRNI, indicating intakes insufficient to meet needs. Hopkins *et al.*[93] (using 1993 data) found that over 60% of iron intake among 8-month-old UK infants was from commercial infant foods (which were consumed by over 90% of infants), fortified breakfast cereals, vegetables, meat and fish also contributing to iron intake.

> Commercial infant foods appear to be an important source of iron in an infant's diet.

Milk intake

UK infants aged 8 and 12 months were more likely to have satisfactory iron intakes from solids if they had fewer than six breast milk feeds a day (41% of high breast milk–fed infants having iron intakes below the LRNI) or if formula or cow's milk intake was <600 mL a day.[93] Similarly, iron status among Icelandic infants was found to be positively associated with formula intake, while breast-feeding duration was negatively associated with iron status compared with infants given formula.[121,132] Cow's milk intake has been shown in many studies to be negatively related to iron intake and iron status.[93,121,129]

> Fewer than six breast milk feeds a day or <600 mL a day of formula milk or cow's milk appears to lead to more satisfactory iron intakes among infants aged 8 and 12 months.

Fibre intake

NSP levels among UK infants aged 8 and 12 months were not associated with haemoglobin or ferritin levels for breastfed or formula-fed infants,[93] while at 18 months, NSP intake was positively associated with ferritin levels.[139] Similarly, a high fibre intake in the UK National Diet and Nutrition Survey of 1½ to 4½ year-olds was not related to low iron status.[140] Finnish children with a high fibre intake were found to have a higher intake of iron than children with lower fibre intakes,[92] while others have also shown a positive association between NSP intake and iron intake.[141]

> NSP levels have not been found to affect iron levels in infants, while fibre intake in young children has been found to be positively related to iron intake.

Bread intake has been found to have a significant negative effect on ferritin levels among Danish infants[18] and female Icelandic infants[132] and porridge a significant positive effect among Icelandic infants.[132] In addition, intake of iron-fortified infant cereals has been found to be positively related with iron status among American infants.[142] In the United Kingdom, it is doubtful whether infant cereals have such a positive effect on iron status, since infant cereals are not fortified as highly as in the United States, while organic infant cereals (which are growing in popularity) contain no added iron due to organic regulations.[143]

Enhancers of non–haem iron absorption

Non-haem alternatives to meat, such as hard-boiled eggs, beans and lentils, do not contain as much iron as meat, although vitamin C, meat, fish and poultry can enhance the absorption of non-haem iron. For example, meat, in the form of a freeze-dried powder added to infant cereal, was found to increase non-haem iron absorption by 85%, compared with a 39% increase in absorption from added vitamin C, the small particles of meat potentially increasing absorption compared with larger pieces of meat.[144] It is likely that sucking the juices from meat, as in early self-feeding, will not increase non-haem absorption from a meal.[145]

> The absorption of non-haem iron can be enhanced by vitamin C, meat, fish and poultry.

THE RECOMMENDATION FOR ZINC

Zinc is involved in the metabolism of all macronutrients, forming part of over 200 enzymes. It is involved in the immune system, oxygen and carbon dioxide transfer, liver function, storage and release of insulin, the sense of smell and the sense of taste. Along with iron, zinc is essential for normal growth and neurological development.[146]

> For 4- to 12-month-old infants, the EAR for zinc is 3.8 mg per day and the LRNI is 3.0 mg per day. The RNI for zinc is 4.0 mg per day at 4–6 months and 5.0 mg per day at 7–12 months.[1]

In terms of required zinc density of the diet, infants have approximately double the requirements of adults;[1] for example, compared with an average adult male who requires 3.6 mg of zinc per 1000 kcal (9.0 mg of zinc required per 2500 kcal), a 9-month-old breastfed boy of average weight requires 7.2 mg of zinc per 1000 kcal (5.0 mg per 694.2 kcal).

> In terms of required zinc density of the diet, infants have approximately double the requirements of adults.

The zinc content of breast milk appears to decrease during complementary feeding, regardless of maternal zinc status (while the iron content appears to increase), and thus complementary foods become an important source of zinc.[147] Typical early complementary foods such as fruit, vegetables and infant cereals are low in zinc.[148] Pureed beef as a first complementary food has been found to lead to significantly higher zinc intake in 5- to 7-month-old infants than among infants not given beef[149]; it has been suggested that meat would help meet both iron and zinc requirements for breastfed infants after 6 months.[148] Other good sources of zinc include fortified infant foods such as baby porridge, and hard-boiled egg (*see* Tables 4.10 and 4.11).

> The zinc content of breast milk appears to decrease during complementary feeding, regardless of maternal zinc status. Typical early complementary foods such as fruit, vegetables and infant cereals are low in zinc. Good sources of zinc include meat, hard-boiled egg and fortified infant foods such as porridge.

The UK survey of infants aged 6–12 months[7] found that the average zinc intake was 4.5 mg per day, below the RNI; among 9- to 12-month-old infants, the average zinc intake was 4.8 mg per day, while 6% of infants had daily zinc intakes of 3 mg per day, below the LRNI. Meat provided only 10% of zinc intake,[7] indicating that parents may need to be encouraged to give infants larger or more frequent servings of meat,[4] to include zinc-fortified foods and to give a variety of other foods containing zinc.

> For infants to obtain sufficient zinc intake, parents may need to give infants larger or more frequent servings of meat,[4] to include zinc-fortified foods and to give a variety of other foods containing zinc.

THE RECOMMENDATION FOR VITAMIN A

Vitamin A controls cell growth and development, particularly in the skin, respiratory and gastrointestinal tracts; it increases resistance to infection, enhancing the activity of white blood cells, and is important for vision.[146]

> The RNI for vitamin A for infants from 6 to 12 months is 350 μg Retinol Equivalent (RE) per day, the EAR is 250 μg RE per day and the LRNI is 150 μg RE per day.[1]

While mean vitamin A intakes were double the RNI in a UK study of infants aged 6 to 12 months,[7] the mean of the lowest 2.5% of vitamin A intakes was below the RNI. Vitamin A supplements are recommended for infants consuming <500 mL of formula milk a day and for all breastfed infants from 6 months consuming breast milk as their main drink.[4] A supplement of 200 μg of vitamin A (RE) is marketed for infants.[150] As discussed in Chapter 4, some infants may have very high intakes, dependent upon the complementary foods consumed and the use of supplements.

> A daily vitamin A supplement is recommended for infants consuming <500 mL of formula milk a day and for all breastfed infants from 6 months consuming breast milk as their main drink.[4]

The vitamin A content of breast milk is affected by maternal vitamin A status, infant and maternal vitamin A status being positively related.[151] The vitamin A content of breast milk from well-nourished mothers in Europe has been shown to range from 40 to 70 μg per 100 mL[151] and to be 57.2 μg per 100 mL in developed countries.[152]

> The vitamin A content of breast milk is affected by maternal vitamin A status.

THE RECOMMENDATION FOR VITAMIN D

The main function of vitamin D is the regulation of calcium levels in the body; it increases both the absorption of calcium from food and calcium deposition into the skeleton, and is essential for normal bone growth during childhood and tooth enamel formation.[146] Vitamin D is also involved in white blood cell activity, vitamin D deficiency in children being linked with an increased risk of infections and auto-immune diseases.[153]

Vitamin D exists in two forms: (1) vitamin D3 or cholecalciferol, which is produced in the skin from 7-dehydrocholesterol by the action of sunlight, and (2) vitamin D2 (ergocalciferol), which is produced by some plants such as fungi and is less bioavailable than vitamin D3. The main factors affecting an infant's vitamin D status are maternal vitamin D status during pregnancy and the infant's exposure to ultraviolet radiation; ultraviolet exposure is often low.[4]

> The RNI for vitamin D is 8.5 µg per day for infants between 4 and 6 months and 7 µg per day for infants aged 7–12 months.[4]

Formula milk plays a major role in meeting the RNI for vitamin D for infants, the vitamin D content of formula milks currently available in the UK ranging from 1.1 to 1.5 µg per 100 mL.[154] Other foods which could also help to meet the RNI for vitamin D include commercial infant foods fortified with vitamin D, such as infant cereals, other fortified foods such as margarine (which is mandatorily fortified), breakfast cereals and orange juice, plus foods such as fatty fish, eggs and meat (*see* Chapter 4, Vitamin D, p. 136).

> Formula milk plays a major role in meeting the RNI for vitamin D, while other sources include fortified infant foods such as infant cereals, plus other fortified foods such as margarine, breakfast cereals and orange juice.

Breast milk is low in vitamin D (a 'trace' per 100 g).[155] In Danish mothers with apparently normal intakes of vitamin D, the concentration of vitamin D in breast milk (samples taken in winter months) ranged from 0.04 to 0.13 µg per 100 mL,[156] Denmark being at a similar latitude to the United Kingdom. Supplementation of lactating mothers with 10 µg of vitamin D per day for 3 months has been found to increase the vitamin D content of breast milk, but to levels insufficient to meet the infant's requirements (range: 0.08 to 0.17 µg per 100 mL).[157,158] Similarly, supplementation of lactating mothers with 50 µg of vitamin D per day for 3 months has been found to have an insufficient effect on the breastfed infant's vitamin D status.[159]

> Breast milk is low in vitamin D. Supplementation of lactating mothers with 10 µg of vitamin D per day does not meet an infant's vitamin D requirements.

However, maternal supplementation of vitamin D at non-toxic levels of 100 µg per day[159] and 160 µg per day[157] has shown significant effects on infant vitamin D status. For example, maternal supplementation of 160 µg per day for 6 months led to vitamin D concentrations in breast milk of 4.7 µg per 100 mL, and to vitamin D status in infants being equivalent to an infant receiving a daily supplement of 7.5 µg per day.[157] That is, breast milk does appear to be able to meet an infant's vitamin D requirements, providing that there is adequate maternal vitamin D supplementation (in terms of both quantity and duration of vitamin D supplementation). However, such maternal supplementation levels are much higher than currently recommended, and higher than tolerable upper intake levels,[160,161] although clinical trials suggest that current upper safe limits for vitamin D are well below vitamin D toxicity levels.[162]

> Breast milk does appear to be able to meet an infant's vitamin D requirements, providing that there is adequate maternal vitamin D supplementation; however, such maternal supplementation levels are much higher than currently recommended.

The UK survey of 6- to 12-month-old infants found that the mean dietary intake of vitamin D was 3.5 µg per day,[7] well below the RNI of 7 µg per day.[4] Vitamin D supplements are recommended for infants to help meet the RNI as follows.

> From 6 months all breastfed infants and all infants who are not drinking 500 mL or more a day of infant formula are recommended to take a vitamin D supplement of 7 µg a day.[160] A supplement of 7 µg a day is recommended for breastfed infants from 1 month of age if the mother is not taking a supplement (10 µg a day) or did not do so when pregnant.

The recommendation for breastfed infants to be supplemented from 1 month of age only if the mother is not taking a supplement[160] appears inadequate in view of the evidence on the ineffectiveness of a 10 µg a day maternal vitamin D supplement on breast milk vitamin D levels.[158,159]

The recommended vitamin D supplement level for infants is lower than in several countries, as described in Chapter 1 (*see* Vitamin D, p. 8), a supplement of 10 µg a day being recommended for all American and Canadian infants from zero to 12 months,[163,164] for all Norwegian infants from 6 months of age,[30] and for all infants receiving <500 mL of formula a day.[165] SACN[166] stated that there was insufficient evidence to change the DRV for vitamin D at that time; however, SACN[167] agreed to review the DRV for vitamin D because of new evidence, and the review is in progress.

Most cases of vitamin D deficiency in the UK are among South Asian and Afro-Caribbean infants.[168,169] However, levels of vitamin D deficiency appear to be increasing in countries where there is adequate sunlight, and it has been highlighted that deficiency may be partly due to breastfeeding without vitamin D supplementation, and covering the skin against sunlight.[170]

A SACN update on vitamin D[166] highlighted concerns that health professionals were overlooking recommendations for vitamin D supplementation in infants and that uptake of vitamin drops was very low, even among those entitled to free supplements. More recently, a small survey in London[171] found that less than half of health visitors surveyed routinely advised vitamin D supplementation for infants (only a quarter of midwives advising supplementation among pregnant women), although 67% of health visitors did target high-risk groups. Similarly low levels of advice on vitamin D have been found in an NHS trust,[172] where only half of the health visiting teams were aware of the recommendations for vitamin D supplementation.

> A SACN update on vitamin D[166] highlighted concerns that recommendations for vitamin D supplementation in infants were being overlooked by health professionals and that uptake of vitamin drops was very low. It appears that not all health visiting teams are aware of the recommendations for vitamin D supplementation.

Health visitors may be wary of publicising the need for vitamin D supplementation among breastfeeding women and their infants, in case this detrimentally affects breastfeeding continuation rates. Infant feeding booklets produced by national agencies (*see* Chapter 2) may give confusing advice to parents on vitamin D – for example, not specifically stating that supplements are recommended for breastfed infants.[173] In addition, some NHS trusts produce their own infant feeding leaflets for parents which do not include information on vitamin D, and do not provide the free Department of Health, NHS and Unicef[174] infant feeding booklet, which includes advice on vitamin D, as described in Chapter 2. Investigation of these issues should be undertaken.

While pregnant and breastfeeding women on income support and their infants are entitled to free vitamin D supplements, under the 'Healthy Start' scheme,[175] vitamin D status does not vary by socio-economic group,[176] and it is important that midwives, health visitors and general practitioners are aware of the importance of vitamin D supplementation and pass this information on to clients.

THE RECOMMENDATION FOR CALCIUM

Calcium is needed to form strong bones and teeth, but it is also important in blood clotting, muscle contraction (skeletal and heart muscle) and nerve transmission.[146]

> For infants up to 12 months of age, the RNI for calcium is 525 mg per day, the EAR is 400 mg (based on 40% absorption from infant formula), while the LRNI is 240 mg per day.[1]

The absorption of calcium from breast milk is about 66%[1] and was thought to be about 40% from infant formula,[1] although absorption rates may be similar to breast milk.[177] The rate of calcium retention in infancy is about 160 mg per day, indicative of requirements; based on the absorption rate from breast milk, 240 mg per day of calcium is adequate to meet the needs of infants.[1] If the absorption rate of calcium from infant formula is similar to that from breast milk, then this suggests that the RNI for calcium may be too high; based on 66% absorption, and an EAR of 240 mg per day, the RNI would be 312 mg per day and the LRNI 168 mg per day (EAR + 30% and EAR − 30%, respectively).

> Based on the absorption rate from breast milk, 240 mg per day of calcium will meet the needs of infants.[1] If the absorption rate of calcium from infant formula is similar to that from breast milk, then the RNI for calcium may be too high.

Compared with breast milk and infant formula, calcium absorption from whole cow's milk is lower, the calcium content being 34 mg per 100 g,[155] 50 mg per 100 g[178] (minimum; guidance upper limit, 140 mg per 100 g[178]) and 118 mg[155] per 100 g, respectively.

Milk and dairy products are rich sources of bioavailable calcium,[155] although they are also high in protein, sodium and phosphorus, which can increase the loss of body calcium, while vitamin D promotes calcium absorption. Other good sources of calcium (*see* Chapter 4, Calcium, p. 138) include oily fish, such as sardines or salmon, and fortified breakfast cereals (calcium availability being lower from high-phytate cereals), while most vegetables contain only a little calcium, high levels of oxalate in spinach resulting in very little available calcium.[146,179]

> Milk and dairy products are very good sources of calcium, while oily fish and fortified breakfast cereals are also good sources.

The UK survey of 6- to 12-month-old infants[7] found that 65% of calcium in the diet came from milk and milk products, with calcium intakes being almost 50% above the RNI. The American Academy of Pediatrics[179] commented that there appeared to be no advantage to increasing the intake of calcium usually obtained at 6–12 months from milk and solids.

A high sucrose intake from 13 months has been shown to lead to lower than recommended intakes of calcium at 9 years of age,[105] while consumption of NMES (e.g. from sweetened drinks, sugars and sweetened grains) has also been shown to be associated with a decreased calcium density of the diet among 5- to 17-year-old Irish and American children and adolescents.[180,181]

While calcium and vitamin D have been implicated in the development of obesity, there is insufficient evidence regarding its role,[182] ESPGHAN[183] stating that no recommendations could be made on the role of calcium or dairy products in the development of obesity, owing to a lack of evidence.

THE RECOMMENDATION FOR IODINE

Iodine is required for the production of the thyroid hormone thyroxine, selenium being required for the conversion of thyroxine to the more active component of the thyroid hormone, triiodotyrosine.[146] The thyroid hormones are important regulators of cell activity and growth, particularly the skeletal and nervous systems, iodine deficiency during infancy resulting in hypothyroidism, growth retardation and psychomotor damage.

The UK RNI and LRNI for iodine are 60 and 40 μg per day, respectively, at 4–12 months,[1] while the WHO RNI is 90 μg per day for infants.[184] The iodine requirements for infants are higher than for adults, per kilogram body weight. WHO[184] states that in iodine deficient countries or areas (that is, where the median urinary iodine level among schoolchildren and pregnant women is less <100 µg/L) where there is limited iodised salt distribution (<90% of households using iodised salt), iodine supplements should be given to infants and to pregnant and lactating women. For infants aged 7–12 months in iodine deficient countries, WHO[184] recommends an annual iodine supplement of 200 mg or a daily supplement so that total iodine intake meets the RNI of 90 µg per day, and for pregnant and lactating women, an annual iodine supplement of 400 mg or a daily supplement so that total iodine intake meets the RNI of 250 µg per day.

This recommendation appears to apply to the United Kingdom, where median urinary iodine levels among 14- to 15-year-old schoolgirls were 80.1 µg/L,[185] WHO[184] defining mild iodine deficiency at population median urinary iodine excretion levels of 50–99 µg/L.

> For infants aged 7–12 months in iodine deficient countries, WHO[184] recommends an annual iodine supplement of 200 mg or a daily supplement. This recommendation appears to apply to the United Kingdom.

Iodine intakes are below the UK RNI for 11- to 18-year-old girls but above the UK RNI for young children.[94] Cow's milk intake has decreased in the United Kingdom, low cow's milk intake being an indicator of lower urinary iodine levels.[186] In addition, the availability of iodised salt is limited in the United Kingdom,[187] making up <5% of all salt consumed.[188]

The iodine content of breast milk may also indicate that the United Kingdom appears to be a mildly iodine-deficient country, since the iodine content is 7 µg per 100 mL,[189] while levels of 10–15 µg per 100 mL would be expected if the United Kingdom was iodine sufficient.[190]

> The iodine content of breast milk is 7 µg per 100 mL, while 10–15 µg per 100 mL would be expected if the United Kingdom was iodine sufficient.[190]

Iodine and selenium deficiencies are common in mountainous regions and flood areas where there is leaching of these minerals from the soil; inland areas of Wales and western England may be considered as low-iodine soil areas.[191] The use of non-local foods in low-iodine soil areas may help improve infants' iodine status, while the use of iodised salt would be inappropriate since added salt is not recommended for infants.[4]

While mild iodine deficiency was previously felt to have no adverse health effects,[192] it appears to impair cognition in children,[193] European studies indicating that mild iodine deficiency among children may lead to neurological disorders,[194-196] although confounding factors in these studies may have affected child development.[190]

The current iodine status of UK infants is unclear, because of a lack of data. Previous intake data from the UK survey of 6- to 12-month-old infants[7] indicates that iodine intakes were three and a half times the RNI at 6–9 months and over four and a half times the RNI at 9–12 months, while iodine status from urinary iodine samples was not measured. While milk provided over half the average intake of iodine, cow's milk intake was high, making up over a third of the total milk intake at 6–9 months and over three-quarters of the total milk intake at 9–12 months.[7] More recently, the 2005 Infant Feeding Survey[137] found that only 6% of infants aged 6 months or over had cow's milk as their main drink (23% having some cow's milk, mixed with food), while at 8–10 months, 83% of infants had infant formula as their only source of milk.

> The iodine status of UK infants is unclear.

This apparent substantial reduction in intake of cow's milk among UK infants would be expected to have an equally substantial impact on iodine intake, if infant formula, like breast milk, is considerably lower in iodine than whole cow's milk. Legislation stipulates a minimum iodine content of 10 µg per 100 kcal,[197] similar to the iodine content of breast milk at 7 µg per 100 g,[189] and a maximum content of 50 µg per 100 kcal,[197] similar to the iodine content of whole cow's milk at 30 µg per 100 g.[198]

However, the actual iodine content of infant formula in the United Kingdom is unclear, because of a lack of data, the iodine content of infant formula in other countries being much lower than the iodine content of cow's milk. For example, the average iodine content of infant formula on sale in the United States has been reported as 23.5 µg in 5 oz, approximately 16.6 µg in 100 g,[199] while the iodine content in follow-on formula in Poland has been found to range from 10.7 to 25.6 µg per 100 kcal.[200] However, the iodine content in some infant milks has been found to exceed the European Commission guideline upper limit.[201]

The impact of a reduced intake of cow's milk on UK infants' iodine intake may have been partly alleviated by a doubling of the iodine content of cow's milk from 1990 to 2007.[198,202] In addition, the regulations on the content of infant formula and follow-on formula[197] may have had a positive impact on the adequacy of iodine intake among formula-fed infants, since these regulations stipulate substantially higher iodine levels than the previous 3.3 μg of iodine per 100 g of infant formula.[74]

Mean urinary iodine concentrations among Swiss infants have been found to be 91 μg/L at 6 months and 103 μg/L at 12 months,[203] even though median urinary iodine concentrations among schoolchildren and pregnant women and use of iodised salt were above WHO indicators of iodine sufficiency.[184] The median iodine content of breast milk (4.9 μg per 100 g) was lower than in the United Kingdom, while urinary iodine concentrations were lower in breastfed infants than in formula-fed infants (73 μg /L versus 109 μg/L).[203]

It has been argued that iodine should be routinely added to commercial complementary foods for infants, to improve iodine status[204]; the iodine content of popular commercial cereal complementary foods in Switzerland has been found to range from 18 to 46 μg per portion.[203] Alexy et al.[205] produced a simulated diet to estimate the iodine intake of an 8-month-old German infant receiving three meals a day, from either home-made or commercial complementary foods, half of the commercial complementary foods being fortified with iodine, in addition to breast milk or iodine-fortified formula milk. The iodine intake of a breastfed infant receiving home-made complementary foods was found to be 45 μg per day, <50% of the RNI, while the iodine intake for an infant receiving infant formula and commercial complementary foods was 39% or 100% above the RNI, dependent upon the chosen complementary foods.[205] In the United States, 90% of the iodine intake for infants over 6 months has been shown to come from dairy produce, infant formula and infant foods.[206]

> It has been argued that iodine should be routinely added to commercial complementary foods for infants to improve iodine status.[204]

The iodine content of complementary foods in the United Kingdom is unclear, as manufacturers do not provide this information. While infants should consume 500 mL or more of breast milk or infant formula a day,[4] with 500 or 600 mL of breast milk, iodine intake will only meet the UK RNI with additional iodine from one portion of meat alternatives (fresh fish or hard-boiled egg), as described in Chapter 4.

REFERENCES

1. Department of Health. *Dietary Reference Values for energy and nutrients for the UK. Report of the Committee on Medical Aspects of Food Policy*. Report on Health and Social Subjects, 41. London: HMSO; 1991.

2. Scientific Advisory Committee on Nutrition. *Dietary Reference Values for Energy 2011*. London: The Stationery Office; 2012. Available at: www.sacn.gov.uk/pdfs/sacn_dietary_reference_values_for_energy.pdf (accessed 10 June 2012).

3. Royal College of Paediatrics and Child Health (RCPCH). *UK-WHO Growth Charts: early years*. London: RCPCH; 2011. Available at: www.rcpch.ac.uk/growthcharts (accessed 28 July 2011).

4. Department of Health. *Weaning and the Weaning Diet. Report of the Working Group on the Weaning Diet of the Committee on Medical Aspects of Food Policy*. Report on Health and Social Subjects, 45. London: The Stationery Office; 1994.

5. Satter E. Feeding dynamics: helping children to eat well. *J Pediatr Health Care*. 1995; 9(4): 178–84.

6. Rapley G, Murkett T. *Baby-Led Weaning: helping your baby love good food*. London: Vermilion; 2009.

7. Mills A, Tyler HA. *Food and Nutrient Intakes of British Infants Aged 6–12 Months*. London: HMSO; 1992.

8. Department of Health. *Infant Feeding Recommendation*. London: Department of Health; 2003. Available at: www.dh.gov.uk/assetRoot/04/09/69/99/04096999.pdf (accessed 17 March 2011).

9. Rapley G. Baby-led weaning: transitioning to solid foods at the baby's own pace. *Community Pract*. 2011; **84**(6): 20–3.

10. Paul AA, Whitehead RG, Black AE. Energy intakes and growth from two months to three years in initially breast-fed children. *J Hum Nutr Diet*. 1990; **3**(2): 79–92.

11. Skinner JD, Carruth BR, Houck KS, *et al*. Longitudinal study of nutrient and food intakes of infants aged 2 to 24 months. *J Am Diet Assoc*. 1997; **97**(5): 496–504.

12. Noble S, Emmett P. Differences in weaning practice, food and nutrient intake between breast- and formula-fed 4-month-old infants in England. *J Hum Nutr Diet*. 2006; **19**(4): 303–13.

13. Koletzko B, Tsang R, Zlotkin SH, *et al*. *Nutrition During Infancy: principles and practice*. Cincinnati, OH: Digital Educational Publishing; 1997. pp. 123–53.

14. Noble S, Emmett P; for ALSPAC Study Team; Avon Longitudinal Study of Pregnancy and Childhood. Food and nutrient intake in a cohort of 8-month-old infants in the south-west of England in 1993. *Eur J Clin Nutr*. 2001; **55**(8): 698–707.

15. Gondolf UK, Tetens I, Michaelsen KF, *et al*. Dietary habits of partly breast-fed and completely weaned infants at 9 months of age. *Public Health Nutr*. 2012; **15**(4): 578–86.

16. Conn JA, Davies MT, Walker RB, *et al*. Food and nutrient intakes of 9-month-old infants in Adelaide, Australia. *Public Health Nutr*. 2009; **12**(12): 2448–56.

17. Ernst JA, Brady MS, Rickard KA. Food and nutrient intake of 6- to 12-month-old infants fed formula or cow milk: a summary of four national surveys. *J Pediatr*. 1990; **117**(2 Pt. 2): S86–100.

18. Michaelsen KF. Nutrition and growth during infancy: the Copenhagen Cohort Study. *Acta Paediatr Suppl*. 1997; **420**: 1–36.

19. Robinson S, Marriott L, Poole J, *et al*. Dietary patterns in infancy: the importance of maternal and family influences on feeding practice. *Br J Nutr*. 2007; **98**(5): 1029–37.

20. Hart CN, Raynor HA, Jelalian E, *et al*. The association of maternal food intake and infants' and toddlers' food intake. *Child Care Health Dev*. 2010; **36**(3): 396–403.

21. Prentice AM, Paul AA. Fat and energy needs of children in developing countries. *Am J Clin Nutr.* 2000; **72**(5 Suppl.): S1253–65.

22. Michaelsen KF, Dewey KG, Perez-Exposito AB, *et al.* Food sources and intake of n-6 and n-3 fatty acids in low-income countries with emphasis on infants, young children (6–24 months), and pregnant and lactating women. *Matern Child Nutr.* 2011; **7**(Suppl. 2): S124–40.

23. Nordic Committee on Foods. *Nordic Nutrition Recommendations.* 2nd ed. Copenhagen: Nordic Council of Ministers; 1989.

24. Food and Agriculture Organization (FAO); World Health Organization. *Fats and Oils in Human Nutrition: report of a joint expert consultation.* FAO Food and Nutrition Paper, 57, Chapter 7, pp.49–55. Rome: FAO; 1993. Available at: www.fao.org/docrep/V4700E/V4700E00.htm (accessed 18 July 2011).

25. American Academy of Paediatrics. Committee on Nutrition. Statement of cholesterol. *Pediatrics.* 1992; **90**: 469–72.

26. European Food Safety Authority Panel on Dietetic Products, Nutrition, and Allergies. Scientific opinion on dietary reference values for fats, including saturated fatty acids, polyunsaturated fatty acids, monounsaturated fatty acids, trans fatty acids, and cholesterol. *EFSA Journal.* 2010; **8**(3): 1461–568.

27. Health Council of the Netherlands. *Dietary Reference Intakes: energy, proteins, fats and digestible carbohydrates.* Publication no. 2001/19. The Hague: Health Council of the Netherlands; 2001. Available at: www.gr.nl/sites/default/files/01@19ER. (accessed 23 June 2010).

28. Institute of Medicine. *Dietary Reference Intakes for Energy, Carbohydrate, Fibre, Fat, Fatty Acids, Cholesterol, Protein, and Amino Acids.* Washington, DC: National Academies Press; 2005. Summary Tables, pp. 1324–25. Available at: www.nap.edu/openbook.php?record_id=10490&page=1324 (accessed 12 March 2010).

29. Hermoso M, Tabacchi G, Iglesi-Altaba I, *et al.* The nutritional requirements of infants. Towards EU alignment of reference values: the EURRECA network. *Matern Child Nutr.* 2010; **6**(Suppl. 2): S55–83.

30. Nordic Council of Ministers. *Nordic Nutrition Recommendations 2004: integrating nutrition and physical activity.* 4th ed. Copenhagen: Nordic Council of Ministers; 2004. Available at: www.norden.org/fi/julkaisut/julkaisut/2004-013/excerpt (accessed 24 July 2010).

31. Joint Food and Agriculture Organization; World Health Organization; United Nations University Expert Consultation on Human Energy Requirements. *Human Energy Requirements: report of a Joint FAO/WHO/UNU Expert Consultation.* FAO Food and Nutrition Technical Report Series, no.1. Rome: FAO; 2004. Available at: www.fao.org/docrep/007/y5686e/y5686e00.htm (accessed 3 October 2011).

32. World Health Organization. *Guiding Principles for Feeding Non-Breastfed Children 6–24 Months of Age.* Geneva, Switzerland: WHO; 2005. Available at: www.who.int/maternal_child_adolescent/documents/9241593431/en.index.html (accessed 12 June 2011).

33. Agostoni C, Decsi T, Fewtrell M, *et al.*; for ESPGHAN Committee on Nutrition. Complementary feeding: a commentary by the ESPGHAN Committee on Nutrition. *J Pediatr Gastroenterol Nutr.* 2008; **46**(1): 99–110.

34. Australian Government National Health and Medical Research Council. *Infant Feeding Guidelines for Health Workers. Draft for public consultation.* Canberra, Australia:

National Health and Medical Research Council; 2011. Available at: www.nhmrc.gov.
au/guidelines/publications/n20 (accessed 3 April 2012).

35. Health Canada. *Nutrition for Healthy Term Infants Statement of the Joint Working
Group: Canadian Paediatric Society, Dietitians of Canada and Health Canada.* Ottawa,
ON: Health Canada; 2005. Available at: www.hc-sc.gc.ca/fn-an/nutrition/infant-
nourisson/inf-nutrition-nour-eng.php (accessed 10 August 2012).

36. US Department of Agriculture; US Departments of Health and Human Services.
Dietary Guidelines for Americans 2010. 7th edition. Washington, DC: US Government
and Printing Office; 2010. Available at: www.cnpp.usda.gov/publications/dietary
guidelines/2010/policydoc/policydoc.pdf (accessed 22 May 2011).

37. Becker W, Lyhne N, Pedersen AN, *et al.* Nordic Nutrition Recommendations 2004:
integrating nutrition and physical activity. *Scand J Food Nutr.* 2004; **48**(4): 178–87.

38. Health Council of the Netherlands. *Guidelines for a Healthy Diet 2006.* Publication
no. 2006/1. The Hague: Health Council of the Netherlands; 2006.

39. Prentice A, Branca F, Decsi T, *et al.* Energy and nutrient dietary reference values for
children in Europe: methodological approaches and current nutritional recommendations. *Br J Nutr.* 2004; **92**(Suppl. 2): S83–146.

40. National Infant Diet and Health Study. Available at: www.mrc-hnr.cam.ac.uk/NIDHS
(accessed 17 September 2011).

41. Uauy R, Dangour AD. Fat and fatty acid requirements and recommendations for
infants of 0–2 years and children of 2–19 years. *Ann Nutr Metab.* 2009; **55**(1–3):
76–96.

42. Michaelsen KF, Jorgensen MH. Dietary fat content and energy density during infancy
and childhood; the effect on energy intake and growth. *Eur J Clin Nutr.* 1995; **49**(7):
467–83.

43. Niinikoski H, Lagstrom H, Jokinen E, *et al.* Impact of repeated dietary counselling
between infancy and 14 years of age on dietary intakes and serum lipids and lipoproteins: the STRIP study. *Circulation.* 2007; **116**(9): 1032–40.

44. Rask-Nissila L, Jokinen E, Terho P, *et al.* Neurological development of 5-year-old
children receiving a low-saturated fat, low-cholesterol diet since infancy. *J Am Med
Assoc.* 2000; **1284**(8): 1035–36.

45. Fuchs GJ, Farris RP, DeWier M, *et al.* Effect of dietary fat on cardiovascular risk factors in infancy. *Pediatrics.* 1994; **93**(5): 756–63.

46. Mize CE, Uauy R, Kramer R, *et al.* Lipoprotein-cholesterol responses in healthy
infants fed defined diets from ages 1 to 12 months: comparison of diets predominant in oleic acid versus linoleic acid, with parallel observations in infants fed a
human milk-based diet. *J Lipid Res.* 1995; **36**(6): 1178–87.

47. Friedman G, Goldberg SJ. An evaluation of the safety of a low-saturated fat, low-
cholesterol diet beginning in infancy. *Pediatrics.* 1976; **58**(5): 655–57.

48. Makrides M, Gibson RA, Udell T, *et al.*; for International LCPUFA Investigators.
Supplementation of infant formula with long-chain polyunsaturated fatty acids does
not influence the growth of term infants. *Am J Clin Nutr.* 2005; **81**(5): 1094–101.

49. Scientific Advisory Committee on Nutrition; Committee on Toxicity. *Advice on Fish
Consumption: benefits & risks.* London: The Stationery Office; 2004. Available at: www.
sacn.gov.uk/pdfs/fics_sacn_advice_fish.pdf (accessed 12 June 2011).

50. Makrides M, Smithers LG, Gibson RA. Role of long-chain polyunsaturated fatty acids

in neurodevelopment and growth. *Nestle Nutr Workshop Ser Pediatr Program*. 2010; 65: 123–36.

51. Makrides M, Collins CT, Gibson RA. Impact of fatty acid status on growth and neuro-behavioral development in humans. *Matern Child Nutr*. 2011; 7(Suppl. 2): 80–8.

52. Hakanen M, Lagstrom H, Kaitosaari T, *et al*. Development of overweight in an athero-sclerosis prevention trial starting in early childhood: the STRIP study. *Int J Obes (Lond)*. 2006; 30(4): 618–26.

53. Mace K, Shahkhalili Y, Aprikian O, *et al*. Dietary fat and fat types as early determi-nants of childhood obesity: a reappraisal. *Int J Obes (Lond)*. 2006; 30(Suppl. 4): S50–57.

54. ESPGHAN Committee on Nutrition, Agostoni C, Braegger C, *et al*. Role of dietary factors and food habits in the development of childhood obesity: a commentary by the ESPGHAN Committee on Nutrition. *J Pediatr Gastroenterol Nutr*. 2011; 52(6): 662–69.

55. Hu FB, Manson JE, Willett WC. Types of dietary fat and risk of coronary heart dis-ease: a critical review. *J Am Coll Nutr*. 2001; 20(1): 5–19.

56. Uauy R, Castillo C. Lipid requirements of infants: implications for nutrient com-position of fortified complementary foods. *J Nutr*. 2003; 133(9): S2692–972.

57. Ohlund I, Hörnell A, Lind T, *et al*. Dietary fat in infancy should be more focused on quality than on quality. *Eur J Clin Nutr*. 2008; 62(9): 1058–65.

58. Klag MJ, Ford DE, Mead LA, *et al*. Serum cholesterol in young men and subsequent cardiovascular disease. *N Engl J Med*. 1993; 328(5): 313–18.

59. Law MR, Wald NJ, Thompson SG. By how much and how quickly does reduction in serum cholesterol concentration lower risk of ischaemic heart disease? *BMJ*. 1994; 308(6925): 367–72.

60. Niinikoski H, Pahkala K, Ala-Korpela M, *et al*. Effect of repeated dietary counsel-ling on serum lipoproteins from infancy to adulthood. *Pediatrics*. 2012; 129(3): e704–13.

61. World Health Organization (WHO); Food and Agriculture Organization. *Interim Summary of Conclusions and Dietary Recommendations on Total Fat and Fatty Acids. From the Joint FAO/WHO expert consultation on fats and fatty acids in human nutrition, 10-14 November, 2008*. Geneva, Switzerland: WHO; 2008. Available at: http://who.int/nutrition/topics/FFA_summary_rec_conclusion.pdf (accessed 10 July 2010).

62. Siri-Tarino PW, Sun Q, Hu FB, *et al*. Saturated fat, carbohydrate and cardiovascular disease. *Am J Clin Nutr*. 2010; 91(3): 502–9.

63. Calder PC, Dangour AD, Diekman C, *et al*. Essential fats for future health. Proceedings of the 9th Unilever nutrition symposium, 26–27 May 2010. *Eur J Clin Nutr*. 2010; 64(Suppl. 4): S1–13.

64. Gibson RA, Muhlhausler B, Makrides M. Conversion of linoleic acid and alpha-linolenic acid to long-chain polyunsaturated fatty acids (LCPUFAs), with a focus on pregnancy, lactation and the first 2 years of life. *Matern Child Nutr*. 2011; 7(Suppl. 2): S17–26.

65. Makrides M, Neumann MA, Jeffrey B, *et al*. A randomized trial of different ratios of linoleic to alpha-linolenic acid in the diet of term infants: effects on visual function and growth. *Am J Clin Nutr*. 2000; 71(1): 120–9.

66. Pot GK, Prynne CJ, Roberts C, *et al*. National Diet and Nutrition Survey: fat and fatty

acid intake from the first year of the rolling programme and comparison with previous surveys. *Br J Nutr.* 2012; **107**(3): 405–15. Epub 2011 Jul 18.

67. Briend A, Dewey KG, Reinhart GA. Fatty acid status in early life in low-income countries – overview of the situation, policy and research priorities. *Matern Child Nutr.* 2011; **7**(Suppl. 2): S141–8.

68. Wan ZX, Wang XL, Xu L, *et al.* Lipid content and fatty acids composition of mature human milk in rural North China. *Br J Nutr.* 2010; **103**(6): 913–16.

69. Brenna JT, Varamini B, Jensen RG, *et al.* Docosahexaenoic and arachidonic acid concentrations in human breast milk worldwide. *Am J Clin Nutr.* 2007; **85**(6): 1457–64.

70. Schwartz J, Dube K, Alexy U, *et al.* PUFA and LC-PUFA intake during the first year of life: can dietary practice achieve a guideline diet? *Eur J Clin Nutr.* 2010; **64**(2): 124–30.

71. Bier DM, Brosnan JT, Flatt JP, *et al.* Report of the IDECG Working Group on lower and upper limits of carbohydrate and fat intake. *Eur J Clin Nutr.* 1999; **53**(Suppl. 1): S177–8.

72. Dewey KG, Brown, KH. Update on technical issues concerning complementary feeding of young children in developing countries and implications for intervention programs. *Food Nutr Bull.* 2003; **24**(1): 5–28.

73. Uauy R, Juanita R, Camila C, *et al.* Prevention and control of obesity in preschool children: importance of normative standards. *J Pediatr Gastroenterol Nutr.* 2006; **43**(Suppl. 3): S26–37.

74. Codex Alimentarius Commission. Commission of the European Communities. Directive on infant formulae and follow-on formulae. 91/321/EEC. *Official Journal of the European Community.* 1991; L175: 35–49. Available at: http://eur-lex.europa.eu/LexUriServ/LexUriServ.do?uri=OJ:L:1991:175:0035:0049:EN:PDF (accessed 23 March 2011).

75. Aggett PJ, Haschke F, Heine W, *et al.* Committee report: childhood diet and prevention of coronary heart disease. ESPGAN Committee on Nutrition. European Society of Paediatric Gastroenterology and Nutrition. *J Pediatr Gastroenterol Nutr.* 1994; **19**(3): 261–9.

76. Food and Agriculture Organization (FAO). *Fats and Fatty Acids in Human Nutrition: report on an expert consultation. FAO Food Nutrition Paper 91.* Rome: FAO; 2010. Available at: http://foris.fao.org/preview/25553-0ece4cb94ac52f9a25af77ca5cfba7a8c.pdf (accessed 17 April 2011).

77. Scientific Committee for Food. *Reports of the Scientific Committee for Food. Nutrient and energy intakes for the European Community.* 31st Series. Luxembourg: Commission of the European Communities; 1992. Available at: http://ec.europa.eu/food/fs/sc/scf/out89.pdf (accessed 19 June 2011).

78. Smit LA, Mozaffarian D, Willett W. Review of fat and fatty acid requirements and criteria for developing dietary guidelines. *Ann Nutr Metab.* 2009; **55**(1–3): 44–55.

79. Burdette HL, Whitaker RC, Hall WC, *et al.* Breastfeeding, introduction of complementary foods, and adiposity at 5 y of age. *Am J Clin Nutr.* 2006; **83**(3): 550–58.

80. Michels KB, Willett WC, Graubard BI, *et al.* A longitudinal study of infant feeding and obesity throughout life course. *Int J Obes (Lond).* 2007; **31**(7): 1078–85.

81. Owen CG, Martin RM, Whincup PH, *et al.* The effect of breastfeeding on mean body mass index throughout life: a quantitative review of published and unpublished observational evidence. *Am J Clin Nutr.* 2005; **82**(6): 1298–307.

82. Scientific Advisory Committee on Nutrition. *The Influence of Maternal, Fetal and Child Nutrition on the Development of Chronic Disease in Later Life*. London: The Stationery Office; 2011. Available at: www.sacn.gov.uk/pdfs/sacn_early_nutrition_final_report_20_6_11.pdf (accessed 10 March 2012).

83. Kramer MS, Matush L, Vanilovich I, et al. Effects of prolonged and exclusive breastfeeding on child height, weight, adiposity, and blood pressure at age 6.5 y: evidence from a large randomized trial. *Am J Clin Nutr*. 2007; **86**(6): 1717–21.

84. Toschke AM, Martin RM, von Kries R, et al. Infant feeding method and obesity: body mass index and dual-energy X-ray absorptiometry measurements at 9–10 y of age from the Avon Longitudinal Study of Parents and Children (ALSPAC). *Am J Clin Nutr*. 2007; **85**(6): 1578–85.

85. Baird J, Fisher D, Lucas P, et al. Being big or growing fast: systematic review of size and growth in infancy and later obesity. *BMJ*. 2005; **331**(7522): 929–36.

86. Monasta L, Batty GD, Cattaneo A, et al. Early-life determinants of overweight and obesity: a review of systematic reviews. *Obes Rev*. 2010; **11**(10): 695–708.

87. Moorcroft KE, Marshall JL, McCormick FM. Association between timing of introducing solid foods and obesity in infancy and childhood: a systematic review. *Matern Child Nutr*. 2011; **7**(1): 3–26.

88. Codex Alimentarius Commission. Joint FAO/WHO Food Standards Programme, Secretariat of the Codex Alimentarius Commission. *Guidelines on nutrition labelling CAC /GL 2-1985*. Rome: Food and Agriculture Organization; 2010. Available at: www.codex alimentarius.org/input/download/report/742/al33_22e. (accessed 16 March 2011).

89. Gibney M. *EURODIET: a framework for food-based dietary guidelines in the European Union*. Brussels: Health & Consumer Protection; 2000. Available at: http://nutrition. med.uoc.gr/eurodiet/conference/first.html (accessed 18 November 2011).

90. Lunn J, Buttriss JL. Carbohydrates and dietary fibre. *Nutr Bull*. 2007; **32**: 21–64.

91. Alexy U, Kersting M, Sichert-Hellert W. Evaluation of dietary fibre intake from infancy to adolescence against various references: results of the DONALD Study. *Eur J Clin Nutr*. 2006; **60**(7): 909–14.

92. Ruottinen S, Lagström HK, Niinikoski H, et al. Dietary fiber does not displace energy but is associated with decreased serum cholesterol concentrations in healthy children. *Am J Clin Nutr*. 2010; **91**(3): 651–61.

93. Hopkins D, Emmett P, Steer C, et al. Infant feeding in the second 6 months of life related to iron status: an observational study. *Arch Dis Child*. 2007; **92**(10): 850–4.

94. Bates B, Bates C, Prentice A, et al., editors. *National Diet and Nutrition Survey, headline results from years 1 and 2 (combined) of the rolling programme (2008/09–2009/10)*. London: Department of Health; 2011. Available at: www.dh.gov.uk/en/ Publicationsandstatistics/Publications/PublicationsStatistics/DH_130728 (accessed 16 March 2012).

95. Alexy U, Kersting M, Sichert-Hellert W, et al. Macronutrient intake of 3- to 36-month-old German infants and children: results of the DONALD Study. *Ann Nutr Metab*. 1999; **43**(1): 14–22.

96. Simell O, Niinikoski H, Ronnemaa T, et al. Special Turku coronary risk factor intervention project for babies (STRIP). *Am J Clin Nutr*. 2000; **72**(5 Suppl.): S1316–31.

97. Agostoni C, Riva E, Giovannini M. Dietary fiber in weaning foods of young children. *Pediatrics*. 1995; **96**(5 Pt. 2): 1002–5.

98. Dwyer J. Overview: dietary approaches for reducing cardiovascular disease risks. *J Nutr*. 1995; **125**(3 Suppl.): S656–65.

99. Williams CL, Dwyer J, Agostonu C, *et al*. A summary of conference recommendations on dietary fiber in childhood. *Pediatrics*. 1995; **96**(1): 1023–8.

100. Institute of Grocery Distribution (IGD). *Report of the IGD/PIC Industry Nutrition Strategy Group Technical Working Group on Guideline Daily Amounts*. Watford, UK: IGD; 2005. Available at: www.igd.com/index.asp?id=1&fid=5&sid=42&tid=62&cid=448 (accessed 19 September 2010).

101. Amirabdollahian F, Ash R. An estimate of phytate intake and molar ratio of phytate to zinc in the diet of the people in the United Kingdom. *Public Health Nutr*. 2010; **13**(9): 1380–88.

102. Scientific Advisory Committee on Nutrition (SACN). *Statement on Dietary Fibre*. London: SACN; 2008. Available at: www.sacn.gov.uk/pdfs/final_sacn_position_statement_for_website_dietary_fibre.pdf (accessed 12 June 2011).

103. Edwards CA, Parrett AM. Dietary fibre in infancy and childhood. *Proc Nutr Soc*. 2003; **62**(1): 17–23.

104. Aggett PJ, Agastoni, C, Axelsson I, *et al*.; for ESPGHAN Committee on Nutrition. Nondigestible carbohydrates in the diets of infants and young children: a commentary by the ESPGHAN Committee on Nutrition. *J Pediatr Gastroenterol Nutr*. 2003; **36**(3): 329–37.

105. Ruottinen S, Niinikoski H, Lagström H, *et al*. High sucrose intake is associated with poor quality of diet and growth between 13 months and 9 years of age: the Special Turku Coronary Risk Factor Intervention project. *Pediatrics*. 2008; **121**(6): e1676–85.

106. Siega-Riz AM, Deming DM, Reidy KC, *et al*. Food consumption patterns of infants and toddlers: where are we now? *J Am Diet Assoc*. 2010; **110**(12 Suppl.): S38–51.

107. Scientific Advisory Committee on Nutrition. *Iron and Health*. London: The Stationery Office; 2010. Available at: www.sacn.gov.uk/pdfs/sacn_iron_and_health_report_web.pdf (accessed 12 June 2011).

108. World Health Organization. *Iron Deficiency Anaemia: assessment, prevention, and control; a guide for programme managers*. Geneva, Switzerland: WHO; 2001. Available at: www.who.int/nutrition/publications/en/ida_assessment_prevention_control.pdf (accessed 9 September 2011).

109. Domellöf M, Dewey KG, Lönnerdal B, *et al*. The diagnostic criteria for iron deficiency in infants should be reevaluated. *J Nutr*. 2002; **132**(12): 3680–86.

110. Sherriff A, Emond A, Hawkins N, *et al*. Haemoglobin and ferritin concentrations in children aged 12 and 18 months. *Arch Dis Child*. 1999; **80**(2): 153–7.

111. Taylor A, Redworth EW, Morgan JB. Influence of diet on iron, copper, and zinc status in children under 24 months of age. *Biol Trace Elem Res*. 2004; **97**(3): 197–214.

112. Lozoff B. Perinatal iron deficiency and the developing brain. *Pediatr Res*. 2000; **48**(2): 137–9.

113. McCann JC, Ames BN. An overview of evidence for a causal relation between iron deficiency during development and deficits in cognitive or behavioral function. *Am J Clin Nutr*. 2007; **85**(4): 931–45.

114. Logan S, Martins S, Gilbert R. Iron therapy for improving psychomotor development and cognitive function in children under the age of three with iron deficiency anaemia. *Cochrane Database Syst Rev*. 2001; **2**: CD001444.

115. Kordas K, Siegel EH, Olney DK, *et al.* Maternal reports of sleep in 6–18 month-old infants from Nepal and Zanzibar: association with iron deficiency anemia and stunting. *Early Hum Dev.* 2008; **84**(6): 389–98.

116. Allen LH. Pregnancy and iron deficiency: unresolved issues. *Nutr Rev.* 1997; **55**(4): 91–101.

117. Baker RD, Greer FR; for Committee on Nutrition American Academy of Pediatrics. Diagnosis and prevention of iron deficiency and iron deficiency anaemia in infants and young children (0–3 years of age). *Pediatrics.* 2010; **126**(5): 1040–50.

118. Hay G, Refsum H, Whitelaw A, *et al.* Predictors of serum ferritin and serum soluble transferrin receptor in newborns and their associations with iron status during the first 2y of life. *Am J Clin Nutr.* 2007; **86**(1): 64–73.

119. Puolakka J, Jänne O, Vihko R. Evaluation by serum ferritin assay of the influence of maternal iron stores on the iron status of newborns and infants. *Acta Obstet Gynecol Scand Suppl.* 1980; **95**: 53–6.

120. Georgieff MK, Wewerka SW, Nelson CA, *et al.* Iron status at 9 months of infants with low iron stores at birth. *J Pediatr.* 2002; **141**(3): 405–9.

121. Thorsdottir I, Gunnarsson BS, Atladottir H, *et al.* Iron status at 12 months of age: effects of body size, growth and diet in a population with high birth weight. *Eur J Clin Nutr.* 2003; **57**(4): 505–13.

122. Colomer J, Colomer C, Gutierrez D, *et al.* Anaemia during pregnancy as a risk factor for infant iron deficiency: report from the Valencia Infant Anaemia Cohort (VIAC) study. *Paediatr Perinat Epidemiol.* 1990; **4**(2): 196–204.

123. De Pee S, Bloem MW, Sari M, *et al.* The high prevalence of low haemoglobin concentration among Indonesian infants aged 3–5 months is related to maternal anaemia. *J Nutr.* 2002; **132**(8): 2215–21.

124. Meinzen-Derr JK, Guerrero ML, Altaye M, *et al.* Risk of infant anaemia is associated with exclusive breast-feeding and maternal anaemia in a Mexican cohort. *J Nutr.* 2006; **136**(2): 452–8.

125. Kilbride J, Baker TG, Parapia LA, *et al.* Anaemia during pregnancy as a risk factor for iron-deficiency anaemia in infancy: a case-control study in Jordan. *Int J Epidemiol.* 1999; **28**(3): 461–8.

126. Sherriff A, Emond A, Bell JC, *et al.* Should infants be screened for anaemia? A prospective study investigating the relation between haemoglobin at 8, 12 and 18 months and development at 18 months. *Arch Dis Child.* 2001; **84**(6): 480–5.

127. Innis SM, Nelson CM, Wadsworth LD, *et al.* Incidence of iron deficiency anemia and depleted iron stores among nine-month-old infants in Vancouver, Canada. *Can J Public Health.* 1997; **88**(2): 80–4.

128. Male C, Persson LA, Freeman V, *et al.* Prevalence of iron deficiency in 12-mo-old infants from 11 European areas and influence of dietary factors on iron status (Euro-Growth study). *Acta Paediatr.* 2001; **90**(5): 492–8.

129. Freeman VE, Mulder J, Van't Hof MA, *et al.* A longitudinal study of iron status in children at 12, 24 and 36 months. *Public Health Nutr.* 1998; **1**(2): 93–100.

130. Hay G, Sandstad B, Whitelaw A, *et al.* Iron status in a group of Norwegian children aged 6–24 months. *Acta Paediatr.* 2004; **93**(5): 592–8.

131. Chantry CJ, Howard CR, Auinger P. Full breastfeeding duration and risk for iron deficiency in U.S. infants. *Breastfeed Med.* 2007; **2**(2): 63–73.

132. Thorisdottir AV, Thorsdottir I, Palsson GI. Nutrition and iron status of 1-year olds following a revision in infant dietary recommendations. *Anemia*. 2011; 2011: 986303. Epub 2011 Jul 18.

133. Bramhagen A, Svahn J, Hallström I, *et al*. Factors influencing iron nutrition among one-year-old healthy children in Sweden. *J Clin Nurs*. 2011; **20**(13): 1887–94.

134. Haschke F, Pietschnig B, Vanura H, *et al*. Iron intake and iron nutritional status of infants fed iron-fortified beikost with meat. *Am J Clin Nutr*. 1988; **47**(1): 108–12.

135. Engelmann MD, Sandström B, Michaelsen KF. Meat intake and iron status in late infancy: an intervention study. *J Pediatr Gastroenterol Nutr*. 1998; **26**(1): 26–33.

136. Thane C, Walmsley C, Bates C, *et al*. Risk factors for poor iron status in British toddlers: further analysis of data from the National Diet and Nutrition Survey of children aged 1.5–4.5 years. *Public Health Nutr*. 2000; **3**(4): 433–40.

137. Department of Health. *Infant Feeding Survey 2005*. London: Department of Health; 2007. Available at: www.ic.nhs.uk/statistics-and-data-collections/health-and-lifestyles-related-surveys/infant-feeding-survey (accessed 17 March 2011).

138. Dube K, Schwartz J, Mueller MJ, *et al*. Complementary food with low (8%) or high (12%) meat content as source of dietary iron: a double-blinded randomised controlled trial. *Eur J Nutr*. 2011; **49**(1): 11–18.

139. Cowin I, Emond A, Emmett P, *et al*. Association between composition of the diet and haemoglobin and ferritin levels in 18-month-old children. *Eur J Clin Nutr*. 2001; **55**(4): 278–86.

140. Gregory JR, Collins DL, Davies PSW, *et al*. *National Diet and Nutrition Survey: children aged 1.5 to 4.5 years. Volume 1: Report of the Diet and Nutrition Survey*. London: HMSO; 1995.

141. Hampl JS, Betts NB, Benes BA. The 'age+5' rule: comparisons of dietary fibre intake among 4- to 10-year-old children. *J Am Diet Assoc*. 1998; **98**(12): 1418–23.

142. Dewey KG. Increasing iron intake of children through complementary foods. *Food Nutr Bull*. 2007; **28**(4): S595–609.

143. The Organic Products Regulations 2009. No. 842, part 5, regulation 28; 2009. Available at: www.legislation.gov.uk/uksi/2009/842/regulation/28 (accessed 12 June 2011).

144. Hallberg L, Hoppe M, Andersson M, *et al*. The role of meat to improve the critical iron balance during weaning. *Pediatrics*. 2003; **111**(4 Pt. 1): 864–70.

145. Martinez C, Fox T, Eagles J, *et al*. Evaluation of iron bioavailability in infant weaning foods fortified with haem concentrate. *J Pediatr Gastroenterol Nutr*. 1998; **27**(4): 419–24.

146. Zimmermann M. *Burgerstein's Handbook of Nutrition: micronutrients in the prevention and therapy of disease*. 9th ed. Stuttgart/New York: Thieme; 2000.

147. Domellöf M, Lönnerdal B, Dewey KG, *et al*. Iron, zinc, and copper concentrations in breast milk are independent of maternal mineral status. *Am J Clin Nutr*. 2004; **79**(1): 111–15.

148. Krebs NF. Dietary zinc and iron sources, physical growth and cognitive development of breastfed infants. *J Nutr*. 2000; **130**(2S Suppl.): S358–60.

149. Westcott JL, Simon NB, Krebs NF. Growth, zinc and iron status, and development of exclusively breastfed infants fed meat vs cereal as a first weaning food. *Faseb J*. 1998; **12**: A847.

150. Leaf AA; for RCPCH Standing Committee on Nutrition. Vitamins for babies and young children. *Arch Dis Child*. 2007; **92**(2): 160–4.

151. Ross S, Harvey PWJ. Contribution of breastfeeding to vitamin A nutrition of infants: a simulation model. *Bull World Health Organ*. 2003; **81**(2): 1–7.

152. Penniston KL, Tanumihardjo SA. The acute and chronic toxic effects of vitamin A1-4. *Am J Clin Nutr*. 2006; **83**(2): 191–201.

153. Dawodu A, Wagner CL. Prevention of vitamin D deficiency in mothers and infants worldwide: a paradigm shift. *Pediatr Int Child Health*. 2012; **32**(1): 3–13.

154. Crawley H, Westland S. *Infant Milks in the UK*. Abbots Langley: The Caroline Walker Trust; 2011. Available at: www.cwt.org.uk/pdfs/infantsmilk_web.pdf (accessed 16 March 2012).

155. Food Standards Agency. *McCance and Widdowson's The Composition of Foods*. 6th summary ed. Cambridge: Royal Society of Chemistry; 2002.

156. Leerbeck E, Søndergaard H. The total content of vitamin D in human milk and cow's milk. *Br J Nutr*. 1980; **44**(1): 7–12.

157. Wagner CL, Hulsey TC, Fanning D, *et al*. High dose vitamin D3 supplementation in a cohort of breastfeeding mothers and their infants: a 6-month follow-up pilot study. *Breastfeed Med*. 2006; **1**(2): 59–70.

158. Taylor SN, Wagner CL, Hollis BW. Vitamin D supplementation during lactation to support infant and mother. *J Am Coll Nutr*. 2008; **27**(6): 690–701.

159. Hollis BW, Wagner CL. Assessment of dietary vitamin D requirements during pregnancy and lactation. *Am J Clin Nutr*. 2004; **79**(5): 717–26.

160. Department of Health. *Nutrition and Bone Health: with particular reference to calcium and vitamin D. Report of the Subgroup on Bone Health, Working Group on the Nutritional Status of the Population, Committee on Medical Aspects of Food and Nutrition Policy*. London: The Stationery Office; 1998.

161. Scientific Committee on Food; Scientific Panel on Dietetic Products, Nutrition and Allergies. *Tolerable Upper Intake Levels for Vitamins and Minerals*. 2006. Available at: www.efsa.europa.eu/en/ndatopics/docs/ndatolerableuil.pdf (accessed 19 June 2011).

162. Hathcock JN, Shoa A, Vieth, *et al*. Risk assessment for vitamin D. *Am J Clin Nutr*. 2007; **85**(1): 6–18.

163. Institute of Medicine. Committee to review dietary reference intakes for vitamin D and calcium. *Dietary Reference Intakes for Calcium and Vitamin D*. Washington, DC: Institute of Medicine; 2011. Available at: www.iom.edu/reports/2010/Dietary-Reference-Intakes-for-Calcium-and-Vitamin-D (accessed 19 June 2011).

164. American Academy of Pediatrics. Breastfeeding and the use of human milk. *Pediatrics*. 2012; **129**: e827–41.

165. Health Council of the Netherlands. *Towards an Adequate Intake of Vitamin D*. Publication no. 2008/15E. The Hague: Health Council of the Netherlands; 2008. Available at: www.gezondheidsraad.nl/en/publications/towards-adequate-intake-vitamin-d-0 (accessed 23 June 2011).

166. Scientific Advisory Committee on Nutrition (SACN). *Update on Vitamin D*. London: SACN; 2007. Available at: www.sacn.gov.uk/pdfs/sacn_position_vitamin_d_2007_05_07.pdf (accessed 12 June 2011).

167. Scientific Advisory Committee on Nutrition (SACN). *Vitamin D Working Group. 2nd*

meeting. Draft minutes. London: SACN; 2011. Available at: www.sacn.gov.uk/pdfs/minutes_vitamin_d_meeting_071211.pdf (accessed 10 March 2012).

168. Shaw NJ, Pal BR. Vitamin D deficiency in UK Asian families: activating a new concern. *Arch Dis Child.* 2002; **86**(3): 147–9.

169. Zipitis CS, Markides GA, Swann IL. Vitamin D deficiency: prevention or treatment? *Arch Dis Child.* 2006; **91**(12): 1011–14.

170. Holick MF, Chen TC. Vitamin D deficiency: a worldwide problem with health consequences. *Am J Clin Nutr.* 2008; **87**(4): S1080–6.

171. Jain V, Raychaudhuri R, Barry W. A survey of healthcare professionals' awareness of vitamin D supplementation in pregnancy, infancy and childhood: midwives, GPs and health visitors have their say. *Arch Dis Child.* 2011; **96**: A16–18.

172. Lockyer V, Parcellato L, Gee I. Vitamin D deficiency and supplementation: are we failing to prevent the preventable? *Community Pract.* 2011; **84**(3): 23–6.

173. National Health Service; Unicef; Department of Health. *Introducing Solid Foods.* London: Department of Health; 2011 Available at: www.dh.gov.uk/prod_consum_dh/groups/dh_digitalassets/documents/digitalasset/dh_125828.pdf (accessed 8 March 2012).

174. Department of Health; National Health Service; Unicef. *Weaning: starting solid food.* London: Department of Health; 2008 Available at: www.dh.gov.uk/prod_consum_dh/groups/dh_digitalassets/documents/digitalasset/dh_084164.pdf (accessed 17 March 2011).

175. www.healthystart.nhs.uk

176. Davies JH, Reed JM, Blake E, *et al.* Epidemiology of vitamin D deficiency in children presenting to a pediatric orthopaedic service in the UK. *J Pediatr Orthop.* 2011; **31**(7): 798–802.

177. Abrams SA. Calcium absorption in infants and small children: methods of determination and recent findings. *Nutrients.* 2010; **2**(4): 474–80. Epub 2010 Apr 6.

178. Codex Alimentarius Commission. *Commission of the European Communities. Standard for infant formula and formulas for special medical purposes intended for infants. Codex Standard 72-1981*; 1981. Available at: www.codexalimentarius.org/input/download/standards/288/CXS_072e.pdf (accessed 13 March 2011).

179. Baker SS, Cochran WJ, Flores CA, *et al.* American Academy of Pediatrics. Committee on Nutrition. Calcium requirements of infants, children and adolescents. *Pediatrics.* 1999; **104**(5 Pt. 1): 1152–7.

180. Joyce T, Gibney MJ. The impact of added sugar consumption on overall dietary quality in Irish children and teenagers. *J Hum Nutr Diet.* 2008; **21**(5): 438–50.

181. Frary CD, Johnson RK, Wang MQ. Children and adolescents' choices of foods and beverages high in added sugar are associated with intakes of key nutrients and food groups. *J Adolesc Health.* 2004; **34**(1): 56–63.

182. Song Q, Sergeev IN. Calcium and vitamin D in obesity. *Nutr Res Rev.* 2012; **25**(1): 130–41.

183. ESPGHAN Committee on Nutrition, Agostoni C, Braegger C, *et al.* Role of dietary factors and food habits in the development of childhood obesity: a commentary by the ESPGHAN Committee on Nutrition. *J Pediatr Gastroenterol Nutr.* 2011; **52**(6): 662–9.

184. World Health Organization (WHO); United Nations Children's Fund; International

Council for the Control of Iodine Deficiency Disorders. *Assessment of Iodine Deficiency Disorders and Monitoring their Elimination*. 3rd ed. Geneva, Switzerland: WHO; 2007. Available at: www.unicef.org/ukraine/2_Guide_for_IDD_managers_eng.pdf (accessed 1 February 2011).

185. Vanderpump MPJ, Lazarus JH, Smyth PP, *et al*. Iodine status of UK schoolgirls: a cross-sectional survey. *Lancet*. 2011; **377**(9782): 2007–12.

186. Soriguer F, Gutierrez-Repiso C, Gonzalez-Romero S, *et al*. Iodine concentration in cow's milk and its relation with urinary iodine concentrations in the population. *Clin Nutr*. 2011; **30**(1): 44–8.

187. Bath S, Button S, Rayman MP. Iodised salt availability in the United Kingdom. *Proc Nutr Soc*. 2011; **70**(OCE4); e117.

188. Lazarus JH, Smyth PPA. Iodine deficiency in the UK and Ireland. *Lancet*. 2008; **372**(9642): 888.

189. DHSS. *The Composition of Mature Human Milk*. Report on Health and Social Subjects: 12. London: HMSO; 1977.

190. Zimmermann MB. Iodine deficiency in pregnancy and the effects of maternal iodine supplementation in the offspring: a review. *Am J Clin Nutr*. 2009; **89**(2): S668–72.

191. Zimmermann MB. Symposium on 'Geographical and geological influences on nutrition: iodine deficiency in industrialised countries'. *Proc Nutr Soc*. 2010; **69**(1): 133–43.

192. Stanbury JB, Ermans AM, Hetzel BS, *et al*. Endemic goitre and cretinism: public health significance and prevention. *WHO Chron*. 1974; **28**(5): 220–8.

193. Vanderpump MPJ. Commentary: iodine deficiency as a new challenge for industrialised countries: a UK perspective. *Int J Epidemiol*. Epub 2012 May 13.

194. Glinoer D, Delange F. The potential repercussions of maternal, fetal, and neonatal hypothyroxinemia on the progeny. *Thyroid*. 2000; **10**(10): 871–87.

195. Vitti P, Delange F, Pinchera A, *et al*. Europe is iodine deficient. *Lancet*. 2003; **361**(9364): 1226.

196. Santiago-Fernandez P, Torres-Barahona R, Muela-Martinez JA, *et al*. Intelligence quotient and iodine intake: a cross-sectional study in children. *J Clin Endocrinol Metab*. 2004; **89**(8): 3851.

197. HM Government. *The Infant Formula and Follow-On Formula (England) Regulations 2007, no. 3521*; 2007. Available at: www.legislation.gov.uk/uksi/2007/3521 (accessed 1 June 2011).

198. Food Standards Agency (FSA). *Retail Survey of Iodine in UK Produced Dairy Foods*. Food Survey Information Sheet No. 02/08. London: FSA; 2008. Available at: www.food.gov.uk/multimedia/pdfs/fsis0208.pdf (accessed 17 April 2011).

199. Pearce EN, Pino S, He X, *et al*. Sources of dietary iodine: bread, cow's milk, and infant formula in the Boston area. *J Clin Endocrinol Metab*. 2004; **89**(7): 3421–4.

200. Osterc A, Stos K, Stibilj V. Investigation of iodine in infant starting, special and follow-on formulae. *Food Control*. 2006; **17**(7): 522–6.

201. MacLean W, Van Dael P, Clemens R, *et al*. Upper levels of nutrients in infant formulas: comparison of analytical data with the revised Codex infant formula standard. *J Food Compos Anal*. 2010; **23**(1): 44–53.

202. Ministry of Agriculture, Fisheries and Food (MAFF). *Total Diet Study*. London: MAFF; 1985.

203. Andersson M, Aeberli I, Wüst N, *et al*. The Swiss iodized salt program provides adequate iodine for school children and pregnant women, but weaning infants not receiving iodine-containing complementary foods as well as their mothers are iodine deficient. *J Clin Endocrinol Metab*. 2010; **95**(12): 5217–24.

204. Dunn JT. Iodine should be routinely added to complementary foods. *J Nutr*. 2003; **133**(9): S3008–10.

205. Alexy U, Drossard C, Kersting M, *et al*. Iodine intake in the youngest: impact of commercial complementary food. *Eur J Clin Nutr*. 2009; **63**(11): 1368–70.

206. Murray CW, Egan SK, Kim H, *et al*. US Food and Drug Administration's Total Diet Study: dietary intake of perchlorate and iodine. *J Expo Sci Enironv Epidemiol*. 2008; **18**(6): 571–80.

CHAPTER 4

Meeting dietary requirements

Key facts

1. Early complementary fruit, vegetable and cereal purees, mashes and finger foods contain less energy than breast milk. Most contain little or no fat.

2. Daily consumption of 200 mL of breast or formula milk will meet the recommendation for omega-3 and omega-6 fatty acids.

3. The consumption of a wide variety of foods should help meet iron requirements; however, without fortified cereals and meat, these requirements will be difficult to attain. The best sources of iron for infants are tinned sardines and meat (beef). Good sources include fortified infant cereals and fortified breakfast cereals.

4. At 6–9 months, for an average weight infant to obtain >35% of energy from fat, he could consume 70–175 kcal or 3–7 tablespoons of solids per day before solids containing fat were needed (with 500 mL of milk per day).

5. Between ½ and 4 tablespoons of solids will provide 0.5 g of non-starch polysaccharides (one fibre serving).

6. Four to nine fibre servings are suggested at 6–9 months, and five to eleven servings at 10–12 months. It is suggested that after 6 months of age, one or two servings a day of wheat cereals are given.

MEETING DIETARY REQUIREMENTS

The dietary requirements outlined in Chapter 3 can be met by the adoption of a varied, balanced diet following the introduction of solids, with the addition of vitamin A and vitamin D supplements where required. Energy needs should be met by ensuring that fat intake is sufficient. In particular:

- iron rich solids should be introduced early on, such as meat and fortified cereals
- zinc rich foods should be introduced, such as meat and meat products, fortified cereals and hard-boiled eggs
- foods containing vitamin D, such as oily fish, eggs, fortified infant cereals and fortified breakfast cereals should also be included
- phytate levels should not be high (to ensure that the absorption of iron and zinc is not reduced)
- breast or formula milk should meet omega-3 and omega-6 polyunsaturated fatty acid requirements, oily fish and rapeseed and sunflower oil providing additional sources
- reduced-fat foods are not needed
- 500–600 mL of breast or formula milk will help ensure that fat intake is sufficient.

ENERGY RECOMMENDATIONS

As stated in Chapter 3, revised Estimated Average Requirements (EARs) for energy are as follows: 96 kcal/kg per day for formula-fed boys and girls at 5–6 months, 72 kcal/kg per day for breastfed boys and girls at 5–6 months, and 72 kcal/kg per day for breastfed and formula-fed boys and girls at 7–12 months.[1] There should be a balanced intake of foods from different food groups (*see* Chapter 5). Based on the revised EARs for energy for infants (SACN, 2012; *see* Table 3.1) and following Committee on the Medical Aspects of Food Policy (COMA)[2] minimum guidelines for breast or formula milk intake of 600 mL at 4–6 months and 500 mL at 7–12 months, the average amount of energy required from solids for a breastfed boy, taking the energy content of 100 mL of breast milk as 69 kcal, would be:

- 206 kcal at 6 months (if introduced to solids before 6 months)
- 340 kcal at 9 months
- 417 kcal at 12 months.

This equates to 67% of daily energy intake from milk at 6 months, 50% at 9 months and 45% of daily energy intake from milk at 12 months. The contribution of milk to total energy intake, based on the lower revised EARs for energy[1] is higher than based on previous EARs for energy[2] by 13%, 11% and 9% at 6, 9 and 12 months, respectively.

> Based on revised EARs for energy[1] and minimum intake of breast or formula milk of 500 mL at 7–12 months, breast and formula milk contribute 50% of energy to the total daily energy intake at 9 months and 45% at 12 months, approximately 10% more than based on previous EARs for energy.[2]

Reducing minimum guidelines for milk intake by 100 mL, to 500 mL at 6 months (for infants introduced to solids before 6 months) and 400 mL at 7–12 months, would lead to a similar contribution being made by milk to total energy intake as previously.[2] It is unclear when infants commencing solids at 6 months 'catch up' in terms of the proportion of energy provided by solids compared with infants commencing solids before 6 months.

The World Health Organization (WHO)[3] recommends that in order to increase energy intake, 10–20 g of fat should make up part of an infant's diet after initiation of complementary feeding if milk intake is low at 300–400 mL per day and no foods from animal sources are present in the diet. WHO[3] also suggests that 5 g of fat are added to the diet even if animal products are present in the diet and milk intake is low (300–400 mL per day).

SUGGESTED FAT INTAKE

To obtain the suggested fat intake of >35% of energy from fat, a suitable balance between intake of breast or formula milk and solids is needed.

Amount of solids before fat required

If we take >35% of energy from fat as the minimum suggested fat intake for infants at 6–12 months of age (*see* Chapter 3), the amount of solids low in fat (such as infant rice and fruit and vegetable purees, mashes or finger foods) that can be offered before higher-fat solids are required is dependent upon the volume of milk consumed. As mentioned earlier, the minimum guideline for breast or formula milk is 600 mL per day at 4–6 months and 500 mL per day at 7–12 months.[2] In addition, breast milk contains 69 kcal and 4.1 g of fat per 100 mL, while the calorific value of 1 g of fat is 9 kcal. Thus, between 4 and

6 months, for a breastfed infant consuming 600 mL of milk a day, to obtain >35% of energy from fat, he could consume up to *210 kcal a day* from solids before needing solids containing fat (4.1 g of fat per 100 mL of milk gives 24.6 g of fat in 600 mL of milk; 600 mL of milk contains 6 × 69 kcal = 414; (24.6 × 9) / (414 + 210) = 35.5% of energy from fat; 214 kcal from solids containing no fat gives 35.4% of energy from fat).

Between 7 and 9 months, for an infant consuming a minimum of 500 mL of milk a day, to obtain >35% of energy from fat, he could consume up to *175 kcal* a day from solids before needing food containing fat (4.1 g of fat per 100 mL of milk gives 20.5 g of fat in 500 mL of milk; 500 mL of milk contains 5 × 69 kcal = 345; (20.5 × 9) / (345 + 175) = 35.5% of energy from fat; 176 kcal from solids containing no fat gives 35.4% of energy from fat).

In the first weeks of solids, a tablespoon of solids is about 15–20 kcal and about 25 kcal in later weeks, 1 tablespoon of solids weighing 20–25 g (calculated using information from the Food Standards Agency (FSA),[4] infant food manufacturers and the author's weighed measurements). The earlier calculations of kilocalories from solids that can be consumed before solids containing fat are needed can be translated into tablespoons of food, where the energy content of 1 tablespoon of solids is approximately 25 kcal (*see* Table 4.1).

Thus, when an infant starts having less milk or more food, or both, the amount of fat in the food will need to increase to give the suggested level of fat intake (>35% of energy from fat).

The relative amounts of breast or formula milk and solids (kilocalories from solids and tablespoons of solids) required to obtain >35% of energy from fat per day are shown in Table 4.1

TABLE 4.1 Intake of breast milk, formula milk and solids before fat is needed from solids*

Milk intake per day	Number of kilocalories from solids before fat required	Number of tablespoons of solids before fat required
600 mL[a]	210	8
500 mL[b]	175	7

Notes: *To obtain >35% of energy from fat; [a]at 4–6 months; [b]at 7–9 months.

> Foods containing fat, such as yoghurt, meat and cheese, should be included in the infant diet once a maximum of 8 tablespoons of solids are consumed with 600 mL of breast or formula milk at 4–6 months, and 7 tablespoons of solids with 500 mL of breast or formula milk at 7–9 months.

As outlined in Chapter 3 (Role of milk in energy provision following the introduction of solids, p. 42), the volume of milk required is unclear, 500–600 mL being suggested intakes only.[2] As shown earlier (Energy recommendations, p. 102), 500 mL of milk at 4–6 months and 400 mL of milk at 7–9 months give similar contributions of milk to total energy intake as suggested by COMA,[2] while 200 mL of milk will meet suggested omega-3 and omega-6 polyunsaturated fatty acid requirements (*see* Omega-3 and omega-6 polyunsaturated fatty acids, p. 116).

WHO[3] recommends that solids containing the same amount of fat as milk or more per 100 g are used; solids with approximately the same fat content as milk (4.1 g of fat per 100 g of milk) will give >35% of energy from fat (4 g of fat per 100 g of food will give 36% of energy from fat; 4.1 g will give 36.9% of energy from fat). That is, as long as a balance of foods from different food groups are eaten, an infant's fat intake should be adequate (*see* Chapter 5).

> As long as a balance of foods from different food groups are eaten, an infant's fat intake should be adequate.

Fat content of foods

In addition to milk, yoghurt, cheese, meat, fish, nuts and oils (such as rapeseed oil) can provide fat as part of a balanced infant diet (*see* Chapter 5). Table 4.2 gives the fat and energy content of many foods suitable for infants. Note that milk would be added to dry breakfast cereals such as Weetabix or Wheaty Biscuits, porridge and Ready Brek; it is suggested that between 50 and 80 mL of milk will be added per serving, the lower range value and median value found for 1- to 3-year-old children, where the median portion size of Weetabix was one biscuit[5] equivalent to two suggested servings for infants, which may be consumed in infancy. A portion will be used as 50 mL of milk, providing 2.0–3.1 g of fat. Some dry infant cereals, such as Creamy Oat Porridge, contain milk powder and only water is added, while others, such as baby rice, do not contain milk powder and milk is added (*see* Table 4.2). For mixed commercial (ready-made) or home-made meals, such as beef stew and spaghetti bolognaise, a serving size of 3½ tablespoons is assumed, or 70 g, which equates to the median daily consumption of such meals among 6- to 12-month-old UK infants[6]; however, nutritional information for a tablespoon portion is given.

TABLE 4.2 Fat and energy content per food portion (1 tablespoon, 20 g, unless stated otherwise)*

Food	Grams of fat per portion	Grams of saturated fat per portion	Kilocalories per portion
Vegetables and fruit (excluding avocado)	0	0	Various (5–19)
Pasta	0.1	0	17.2
Lentils (½ tablespoon, 10 g)	0.1	0	10.5
Baked beans, butter beans (½ tablespoon, 10 g)	0.1	0	7.5
Vegetable casserole	0.1	0	10.4
Organic apple, pork and root vegetable casserole[a]	0.1	0	9.6
Pasta, chicken and broccoli[b]	0.2	0.1	10.8
Boiled rice (white and brown)	0.2	0	27.9
White fish (steamed plaice)	0.2	0	18.4
White bread (½ slice)	0.2	0.1	21.9
Weetabix (½ biscuit)	0.3	0	33.5
Wheaty Biscuits[c] (½ biscuit)	0.3	0	32.1
Brown, wholemeal bread (½ slice)	0.3	0.1	21.0
Turkey (breast, grilled)	0.3	0.1	31.0
Parsnips, Chicken and Leeks[d]	0.3	0.1	11.0
Chickpeas (½ tablespoon, 10 g)	0.3	0	11.5
Baby rice (3 g made with 22 g formula milk per 10 g dry weight)[d]	0.3/0.1	0.4/0	18.7/38.4
Hearty Lamb Hotpot[e]	0.4	0.2	12.8
Home-made spaghetti bolognaise[f]	0.6	0.5	21.2
Plain yoghurt	0.6	0.3	15.8
Infant rice pudding[g]	0.6	0	45.0
Chicken (light meat)	0.7	0.4	30.6
Porridge (½ tablespoon, 10 g dry weight)	0.8	0.2	35.6
Lean pork	0.8	0.3	24.6
Beef stew[f]	0.9	0.3	21.4
Turkey strips, stir-fried	0.9	N	32.8
Lean beef	0.9	0.3	30.6
Custard	0.9	0.6	23.6
Rice pudding	0.9	0.5	26.0

Food	Grams of fat per portion	Grams of saturated fat per portion	Kilocalories per portion
Ready Brek (½ tablespoon, 10 g dry weight)	0.9	0.2	37.3
Creamy Oat Porridge[g] (½ tablespoon, 10 g dry weight) (add water)	1.1	0.5	42.2
Roast chicken (light and dark meat)	1.5	0.6	35.4
Lean lamb	1.6	0.7	30.6
Pilchards in tomato sauce	1.6	0.3	28.8
Tinned tuna (in oil, drained)	1.8	0.3	37.8
Sardines in tomato sauce	1.9	0.6	34.4
Whole milk on cereal (50 mL)	2.0	1.3	33.0
Greek-style yoghurt	2.0	1.4	26.6
Macaroni cheese	2.0	1.0	32.4
Ice cream	2.0	1.2	35.4
Hard-boiled egg (½ small, 22 g)	2.2	0.7	29.4
Salmon (steamed)	2.4	0.4	38.8
Hummus	2.6	N	37.4
Cheese sauce	2.9	1.4	39.6
Cheddar cheese (grated, 1 tablespoon, 10 g)	3.5	2.2	41.6
Avocado	3.9	0.8	38.0
Butter (½ teaspoon, 5 g)	4.1	2.6	37.3
Margarine, not polyunsaturated, polyunsaturated (½ teaspoon, 5 g)	4.1	1.4, 0.9	37.3
Flaxseed (½ tablespoon, 10 g)	4.6	0.4	51.0
Vegetable oil, rapeseed oil, sunflower oil, olive oil (½ teaspoon, 5 g)	5.0	0.6, 0.3, 0.6, 0.7	45.0
Peanut butter (½ tablespoon, 10 g)	5.2	1.3	60.6
Ground walnuts (½ tablespoon, 10 g)	5.2	0.6	52.5
Ground almonds (½ tablespoon, 10 g)	5.4	0.4	56.5
Pork (fatty)	10.2	4.1	103.0
Beef (fatty)	10.5	5.0	106.6
Lamb (fatty)	11.3	5.3	113.6

Notes: *Values calculated from Food Standards Agency[4] and food manufacturers' information; [a,b,d,e]Organix[7]: [a]from 7 months, [b]from 10 months, [d]from 4 months, [e]from 12 months; [c]Cow & Gate,[8] from 6 months; [f]more than 40% meat sauce; [g]Heinz,[9] 4+ months; N not available.

Providing foods that contain <0.8 g of fat per 20 g portion together with foods containing more than this will help ensure an appropriate level of fat intake (*see* Table 4.2). Each 100 kcal of food does not have to contain the right amount of fat; one meal may be lower in fat and another higher. Providing the correct amount of fat on a daily basis is probably easier to remember than on a meal basis or over several days.

> Providing foods which contain <0.8 g of fat per 20 g portion together with foods containing more than this will help ensure an appropriate level of fat intake.

Table 4.3 gives the fat content per 100 g of food, which together with the information given in Table 4.2 on the fat content per portion should enable comparisons of the fat content of different foods.

TABLE 4.3 Fat content per 100 g of food

Grams of fat per 100 g	Food
<1 g	Fruit (not avocado), vegetables, pasta, baked beans, butter beans, lentils, some ready meals, baby rice (dry)
1–2 g	Boiled rice, baby rice (made with formula), white fish, turkey (grilled), bread and some ready meals
2.8–3.9 g	Weetabix, Wheaty Biscuits, infant rice pudding, chickpeas, home-made spaghetti bolognaise,[a] yoghurt, chicken (light meat)
4.0–9 g	Lean pork, hard-boiled egg, turkey (stir-fried), beef stew, lean beef, hummus, milk on cereal, custard, rice pudding, porridge, roast chicken (white and dark), pilchards in tomato sauce, peanut butter, Ready Brek, lean lamb, tinned tuna in oil
9.5–15 g	Sardines in tomato sauce, Greek-style yoghurt, macaroni cheese, ice cream, Creamy Oat Porridge, steamed salmon, cheese sauce
16–20 g	Avocado
21–35 g	Cheddar cheese
45–60 g	Flaxseed, ground walnuts, ground almonds, pork, beef, lamb (lean and fat)
>80 g	Butter, margarine, rapeseed oil, sunflower oil, olive oil

Note: [a]More than 40% meat sauce.

Providing foods containing <4.0 g of fat per 100 g together with foods containing more than this, in the correct proportions (*see* Chapter 5), will enable attainment of the suggested daily intake of fat (*see* Table 4.3).

Suggested daily intake of fat for infants

Suggested average daily requirements for fat for infants can be calculated using the revised EARs for energy.[1] These suggested average daily values will be slightly higher for formula-fed infants and for infants receiving both breast and formula milk, due to their higher body weight and thus higher total energy intake (*see* Tables 3.1 and 3.2).

Taking the suggested value of >35% of energy from fat and the potential upper limit of 45% of energy from fat (*see* Chapter 3), the average grams of fat per day requirements for infants can be calculated by multiplying the percentage of energy from fat value and dividing by the energy content of 1 g of fat (9.0 kcal) to give the estimated grams of fat per day requirement. For example, for a 9-month-old breastfed boy, the estimated grams of fat per day requirement at >35% of energy from fat would be calculated as follows:

Estimated grams of fat per day at the suggested level of >35% of energy from fat:

$$> (0.35 \times 694.2) / 9.0$$
$$> 27.0$$

The calculations of average grams of fat per day requirements for breastfed boys and girls from 6 to 12 months are shown in the Appendix. Ranges of average grams of fat per day requirements for boys and girls are shown in Table 4.4. These are based on average energy requirements, taking the suggested fat intake of >35% of energy from fat as the lower end of the range and the reasonable upper limit of 45% of energy from fat (*see* Chapter 3, A conservative suggestion for fat intake in the UK, p. 50).

TABLE 4.4 Range of average grams-of-fat-per-day requirements for breastfed boys and girls[a]

Age (months)	Range for boys (g/day)	Range for girls (g/day)
6*	>24.3 to 31.2	>22.4 to 28.8
7	>25.2 to 32.4	>22.8 to 29.3
8	>26.1 to 33.5	>24.0 to 30.8
9	>27.0 to 34.7	>24.6 to 31.6
10	>27.9 to 35.9	>25.5 to 32.7
11	>28.5 to 36.7	>26.1 to 33.5
12	>29.4 to 37.8	>27.0 to 34.7

Notes: *Introduced to solids before 6 months; [a]based on the suggested fat intake of >35% of energy from fat and the reasonable upper limit of 45% of energy from fat.

Table 4.4 shows that for boys, the suggested grams of fat values increase by approximately 1 g per month; for girls, the suggested grams of fat values increase by approximately 0.5 g between 6 and 7 months, and from 8 months the suggested grams of fat values alternately increase by 0.6 g and 0.9 g per month. For ease of use, these values could be simplified as follows.

> At 6 months, boys require >24 g of fat and girls require >22 g of fat. *Requirements increase by approximately 1 g of fat per month.*

Now, since 100 mL of breast milk contains 4.1 g of fat[4]:
- 400 mL contains 16.4 g of fat
- 500 mL of breast milk contains 20.5 g of fat
- 600 mL of breast milk contains 24.6 g of fat.

Similarly, 1000 mL of breast milk contains 40.1 g of fat. A 2011 study of breast-feeding support groups in Scotland found that 33 infants exclusively breastfed at 25 weeks of age[10] consumed on average 999 g of breast milk per day, accompanied by normal infant growth. Assuming a reduction in breast milk intake of 100 mL per month, boys consuming almost 1000 mL of milk at 6 months may not require fat from solids until around 9 months of age. The suggested minimum intake of breast or formula milk was 500 mL at 7 months when the recommended introduction of solids was 4–6 months[2]; that is, a maximum of 3 months following the introduction of solids, equating to 500 mL of milk at 9 months of age if solids were introduced at 6 months.

At 9 months, consuming the guideline minimum of 500 mL of milk,[2] a boy would require 6 g of fat or more from solids per day, while a girl would require 3.5 g of fat or more a day; consumption of 600 mL of breast milk at 9 months would mean that a boy would need 2 g of fat or more from solids per day, while a girl would need no fat from solids. By 12 months of age, a boy receiving 500 mL of milk would require 8.5 g of fat or more from solids per day, while a girl would require 6 g of fat or more. These results could be simplified for ease of use as follows.

> At 7 months, consuming the guideline minimum of 500 mL of breast milk per day[2] on average:
> - A boy would require 4 g of fat or more from solids per day.
> - A girl would require 2 g of fat or more from solids per day, to meet the suggested >35% of energy from fat per day.

- These grams of fat per day requirements from solids would increase by approximately 1 g of fat per month.
- Infants introduced to solids at 6 months may not require fat from solids until later, for example at 8 months (assuming 600 mL of milk at 8 months).

Since we may expect fat intake to decrease gradually from 7 to 12 months (as milk intake gradually decreases), and for ease of use, we could further simplify the fat requirements from solids as follows.

Fat requirements from solids at 7–12 months:
- 4 g of fat for girls with 600 mL of breast milk
- 6 g of fat for boys with 600 mL of breast milk
- 8 g of fat for girls with 500 mL of breast milk
- 10 g of fat for boys with 500 mL of breast milk.

In addition:
- Fat requirements from solids at 9 months would be 6 g or more per day for boys and 4 g or more for girls.
- There may be no fat requirements from solids until about 8 months for infants introduced to solids at 6 months, assuming an intake of 600 mL of milk at 8 months.

Number of tablespoons of food to meet daily fat requirements

To translate the information in the previous section on grams of fat requirements from solids into intake of foods, information on grams of fat per tablespoon (20 g) of food can be used (*see* Table 4.2 and Table 4.3).

Table 4.2 shows that other than rice pudding, custard and breakfast cereals (such as Weetabix, Wheaty Biscuits, porridge, Creamy Oat Porridge and Ready Brek), chickpeas, hummus and avocado, all other foods providing >0.4 g of fat per tablespoon are either dairy foods (including macaroni cheese), meat and alternatives, or fats (butter, margarine and oils).

When considering food groups and fat intake, rice pudding, custard and breakfast cereals with milk could be included under dairy foods, since most of the fat comes from milk. Butter could also be placed with dairy foods, while margarine and oils could be grouped with dairy foods, since they could be considered as alternatives to butter, or they could be viewed separately. For ease, margarine and oils will be placed with dairy foods, which will be called 'dairy foods and alternatives', while chickpeas, hummus and avocado will be placed with 'meat and alternatives'. Addition of these foods to 'meat and alternatives' might seem strange, as they may seem better fitted to 'fruits and vegetables'; however, their fat and iron content is comparable with other meat alternative foods.

Again for ease, those foods containing 0.4 g of fat or less per tablespoon (other fruit and vegetables, pasta, lentils, home-made vegetable casserole, some commercial meat and vegetable and pasta dishes, rice, white fish and bread) will provide additional fat to that obtained from these two food groups. While these foods may be eaten several times a day in total, it is estimated that their contribution to daily fat intake will be less than approximately 3 g of fat, or approximately an additional 10% of total fat intake. If, for example, five cereals are consumed per day, the maximum fat intake from cereals would be 2.4 g of fat per day, assuming two portions of breakfast cereals such as Ready Brek (1.8 g of fat) and three portions of rice or bread (0.6 g of fat). While it would be more accurate to include these foods, this simplified approximation appears adequate.

'Meat and alternatives' and 'dairy foods and alternatives' can be organised into five categories based on their fat content per portion, using the following portion sizes: ½ teaspoon or 5 g of butter, margarine and oils; ½ tablespoon or 10 g of peanut butter and ground walnuts and almonds; 1 tablespoon or 10 g of grated cheese and dry breakfast cereals; plus 1 tablespoon or 20 g for other foods, as shown in Table 4.5. While more groups could have been used, five groups were selected for ease of use.

TABLE 4.5 Fat content per portion of 'meat and alternatives' and 'dairy products and alternatives'*

Grams of fat per portion	Meat and alternatives	Dairy products and alternatives
1	Home-made spaghetti bolognaise and beef stew, chicken, turkey (stir-fried), lean beef, lamb and pork	Yoghurt, rice pudding and custard; porridge, Creamy Oat Porridge and Ready Brek (10 g dry weight)
2	Pilchards and sardines in tomato sauce, tinned tuna in oil, salmon	Greek-style yoghurt, ice cream, whole milk (on cereal, 50 mL), macaroni cheese
3	Hard-boiled egg (half small, 22 g), hummus, avocado	Cheese sauce, grated cheese (1 tablespoon, 10 g)
5	Flaxseed, ground walnuts and almonds, peanut butter (½ tablespoon, 10 g)	Butter, margarine and oils (½ teaspoon, 5 g)
10 (meat)	Pork, beef, lamb (lean and fat)	

Note: *One tablespoon or 20 g unless stated otherwise.

It is clear from Table 4.5 and the suggested fat intakes from solids at 7–12 months that daily consumption of four portions of meat or alternatives per day plus one to two dairy products or alternatives, or five portions of meat or alternatives per day and one or two dairy products or alternatives (*see* Chapter 5), could easily lead to a fat intake 7 g above the potential upper fat limit if foods with 3, 5 or 10 g of fat per portion were used frequently. For example, consumption of four portions of meat or alternatives, as two portions of lean meat, half a hard-boiled egg and one portion of nuts, could equate to 9.4 g of fat, while one portion of dairy products or alternatives, as a portion of oil, could equate to 5 g of fat. Thus four portions of meat or alternatives and one portion of dairy products or alternatives could equate to 14.4 g of fat in a day from solids, well above the suggested lower limit of fat intake of 10 g of fat for a boy with 500 mL of milk, but within the reasonable upper limit of 45% of energy from fat.

The average amount of fat per day required from solids to meet the suggested total fat requirements with 500 mL of breast milk (4 g per day for a boy and 2 g per day for a girl at 7 months, increasing by 1 g per month, as outlined in 'Suggested daily intake of fat for infants', p. 109) could be obtained in various ways, as shown in the menu in Table 4.6.

As shown in Table 4.6, the suggested average daily fat intake at 7 months with 500 mL of breast or formula milk a day (4 g of fat or more for a boy and 2 g or more for a girl) and at 8 months with 600 mL of breast or formula milk a day can easily be obtained by the inclusion of one portion from 'meat and alternatives' and one portion from 'dairy products and alternatives' per day. To obtain <5 g of fat from solids per day, only the shown portion sizes of the lower-fat value dairy products and alternatives (such as cheese sauce, custard, ice cream, yoghurt, porridge and Ready Brek with milk), and lower-value meat and alternatives (such as lean meat, including chicken, turkey, and lean cuts of lamb, beef and pork, chickpeas, oily fish, half a hard-boiled egg, avocado and hummus) can be included (*see* Table 4.5). Alternatively, smaller portion sizes than shown in Table 4.5 could be used for nuts, seeds, butter, margarine and oils. Foods that contain <0.4 g of fat per tablespoon can also be used, such as pasta, rice, bread, baked beans, lentils, white fish and some commercial mixed dishes.

Where the suggested average daily fat intake from solids is between 8 and 10 g of fat, more than one portion per day of lower-fat value meat, dairy and alternatives can be consumed per day, or larger portion sizes. Alternatively, one portion of higher-fat value meat, dairy and alternatives can be consumed per day, such as ground nuts, butter, margarine, oil or cheese, in addition to

TABLE 4.6 Daily menus for infants aged 7–12 months providing 2–10 g of fat*

Fat from solids (g)	Breakfast	Dinner	Tea	Supper or snack
2	Creamy Oat Porridge **1** & banana	Chicken **1**, rice & carrots		
3	Yoghurt **1** & pear	Beef stew **1** & bread	Lamb **1**, butternut squash & rice	
4	Ready Brek **1** & whole milk **2** & banana	White fish & baby rice & orange	Beef **1** & sweet potatoes	
5	Porridge **1** & banana	2 Spaghetti bolognaise **2**, pear	Tuna **2**, toast, broccoli & carrot pieces	
6	Toast & butter **5**, apple	Turkey **1** & potatoes, melon	Lentil, spinach and tomato curry & rice	
7	Weetabix & whole milk **2** & blueberries	2 Beef **2**, potatoes, peas & gravy, Raspberries	Sardines **2**, sweet potato & parsnip mash, yoghurt **1**	Rice cakes
8	Ready Brek **1** & whole milk **2** & apricots	Pasta & tomato sauce	Sweet potato cakes fried in rapeseed oil **5**	
9	Cheese **3** on toast, orange	Plaice, pasta & butternut squash sauce	Hard-boiled egg (small) **6** & toast, orange	
10	2 Creamy Oat Porridge **2** & orange	2 Beef stew **2** & broccoli, infant rice pudding **1**	Salmon **2**, rice & avocado **3**, apricots	

Note: *Values in bold are the grams of fat from a food, where a serving is 1 tablespoon (20 g) of foods unless stated otherwise.

lower-fat value meat, dairy and alternatives, plus additional foods which contain <0.4 g of fat per tablespoon.

When <10 g of fat is suggested, non-lean lamb, beef or pork would provide too much fat if eaten frequently, as would two or more daily servings of nuts.

> One portion of higher-fat value meat and alternatives (such as nuts) and of dairy products and alternatives (such as cheese) per day can meet suggested total fat requirements. However, two to five portions of meat or alternatives (including up to one high-fat version, such as nuts or oil) and one to three dairy products (including up to one portion of cheese; three dairy products if one portion of milk and two portions of yoghurt only) provide a more realistic means of meeting total suggested fat requirements on a daily basis at 7–12 months.

Saturated fat

While there are no saturated fat recommendations for infants in the UK, recommendations for adults state that saturated fats should provide a population average of 10% of total dietary energy.[11] As mentioned in Chapter 3, it has been suggested[12] that saturated fats should not exceed 10% of total energy intake for children after 2 years of age, and that this level can also be considered for infants after 6 months of age who are at high risk of cardiovascular disease (presumably most Western infants). Use of reduced-fat milk and dairy products and limiting solid fats are highlighted as methods for reducing saturated fat intake.[12,13]

However, this level of saturated fat intake is not feasible for infants consuming 600 or 500 mL of breast or formula milk a day. For example, 500 mL of breast milk (which contains 1.8 g of saturated fat per 100 g) equates to 9 g of saturated fat, while ≤10% of energy from saturated fat equates to ≤7.6 g of saturated fat a day for a 9-month-old breastfed boy and ≤8.5 g of saturated fat a day for a 12-month-old breastfed boy, based on revised EARs for energy[1] of 685 kcal a day and 762 kcal a day for a 9-month-old and a 12-month-old breastfed boy, respectively.

A daily intake of 400 mL of breast milk (the amount providing an equivalent proportion of calories from milk as the COMA[2] suggestion of 500 mL of milk at 7–12 months), but virtually no fat from solids, would meet the ≤10% of energy from saturated fat suggestion; 200 mL of breast milk (the amount meeting suggested omega-3 and omega-6 polyunsaturated fatty acid requirements) would enable 4–5 g of fat to be obtained from solids at 9 and 12 months respectively, or three meat and alternatives and one dairy product and alternatives at 9 months and four meat and alternatives and two dairy products and alternatives (or five meat and alternatives and one dairy product and alternatives) at 12 months. However, such a low intake of milk may compromise calcium intake if food sources of calcium are insufficient to meet requirements (*see* Chapter 3).

The saturated fat content from foods (*see* Table 4.2) can be limited by having lean meat rather than fatty meats, and limiting the amount of dairy products and alternatives, such as butter and cheese. The highest saturated fat values per serving of dairy products and alternatives (with butter and oils as alternatives) from Table 4.2 are 2.6 g for butter and 2.2 g for cheese; similarly, the highest saturated fat values per serving of meat and alternatives are 5.3 g for lamb (fatty; lean lamb contains 0.7 g of saturated fat), 5.0 g for fatty beef and 4.1 g for fatty pork (as opposed to 0.3 g of saturated fat for lean beef and pork).

Thus, for example, consumption of three servings of fatty meat (such as lamb, 5.3 g of saturated fat per portion) a day could lead to a maximum of 20.9% of an infant's total daily food energy coming from saturated fat, compared with only 1.3% if lean meat were used!

Omega-3 and omega-6 polyunsaturated fatty acids

While there are no UK recommendations for omega-3 and omega-6 polyunsaturated fatty acids for infants, to meet the adult COMA[11] recommendations of 0.2% of total daily energy intake from omega-3 linolenic acid and 1% of total daily energy intake from omega-6 linoleic acid, adjusted for energy intake using the revised EARs for energy[1] of 72 kcal/kg per day for breastfed and formula-fed boys and girls from 7 to 12 months (*see* Table 3.1), an infant from 7 to 12 months of age would need:

$0.002 \times 72 = 0.14$ kcal/kg body weight of omega-3 linolenic acid, and
$0.01 \times 72 = 0.72$ kcal/kg body weight from omega-6 linoleic acid.

These values also correspond to the energy adjusted requirements for a 6-month-old breastfed infant for whom the revised EAR for energy is also 72 kcal/kg,[1] while a 6-month-old formula-fed infant, for whom the revised EAR for energy is 96 kcal/kg[1] would require 0.2 kcal/kg body weight a day of omega-3 linolenic acid and 1.0 kcal/kg body weight a day of omega-6 linoleic acid.

> While there are no UK recommendations for omega-3 and omega-6 polyunsaturated fatty acids for infants, to meet the adult recommendations of 0.2% of total daily energy intake from omega-3 linolenic acid and 1% of total daily energy intake from omega-6 linoleic acid, a 7- to 12-month-old infant would need:
> - 0.1 kcal/kg body weight a day of linolenic acid (omega-3) and
> - 0.7 kcal/kg body weight a day of linoleic acid (omega-6).

Based on average weights for infants[14] as shown in Table 3.2, the average daily grams of omega-3 and omega-6 polyunsaturated fat requirements for a 7-month-old boy would be:

[0.1 kcal linolenic acid per kilogram × 8.3 kg (weight)]/9 (kilocalories/grams fat) = 0.1 g
[0.7 kcal linoleic acid per kilogram × 8.3 kg (weight)]/9 (kilocalories/grams fat) = 0.6 g

Similarly, the average daily grams of omega-3 and omega-6 polyunsaturated fat requirements for 6- to 12-month-old boys and girls would be as follows.

- Omega-3:
  - 0.1 g for boys and girls at 7–12 months and 6-month-old breastfed infants
  - 0.2 g for 6-month-old formula-fed infants.
- Omega-6:
  - 0.6 g for 6-month-old breastfed girls, 7-month-old boys and 7- to 9-month-old girls
  - 0.7 g for 8- to 11-month-old boys and 10- to 12-month-old girls
  - 0.8 g for 12-month-old boys and 6-month-old formula-fed boys.

> Based on UK adult recommendations of 0.2% of total daily energy intake from omega-3 linolenic acid and 1% of total daily energy intake from omega-6 linoleic acid, average weight infants at 6–12 months would require:
> - 0.1–0.2 g of omega-3 per day, and
> - 0.6–0.8 g of omega-6 per day.

To enable the recommended intake of essential fatty acids to be met (*see* Chapter 3, Recommended intake of omega-3 and omega-6 fatty acids, p. 51, and Recommended and suggested saturated fat intake, p. 53), it has been suggested that the proportion of omega-6 to omega-3 fatty acids in commercial complementary foods could be lowered, by using an appropriate vegetable oil[15] such as rapeseed oil.[16] Similarly, manipulation of the proportion of omega-6 to omega-3 fatty acids could also feasibly be made in home-made complementary foods.

As shown in Table 4.6, 200 mL of breast milk will meet omega-3 and omega-6 suggestions for infants.

Taking the suggested levels[13] for omega-3 (at least 0.5% of daily energy intake) and omega-6 fatty acids (at least 3%–4.5% of daily energy intake):

- 200 mL of breast milk would meet omega-3 requirements for 6- to 12-month-old infants
- 650 mL of breast milk would meet omega-6 requirements for 6- to 9-month-old girls and 7-month-old boys
- 725 mL of breast milk would meet omega-6 requirements for 8- to 11-month-old boys and 10- to 12-month-old girls
- 800 mL of breast milk would meet omega-6 requirements for 12-month-old boys (at 3% of daily energy intake).

While the average volume of breast milk consumed by UK infants exclusively breastfed for 6 months is unclear, average intakes among a small Scottish sample were found to be as high as 999 mL per day.[17] This information, together with the suggestion by COMA[2] of a minimum intake of 500 mL of milk at 7 months of age (i.e. 3 months after the minimum age for the introduction of solids), suggests that breast milk intake could meet omega-6 requirements for 6- to 9-month-old girls and 7-month-old boys.

At 500 mL of breast milk a day, additional omega-6 requirements could be met from solids such as a serving of oil (rapeseed, blended vegetable oil or olive oil, sunflower oil giving >4.5% of daily energy from omega-6[4]), margarine, eggs, tinned sardines or tuna in oil, or hummus, as shown in Table 4.7.

Table 4.7 also shows that while rapeseed oil has half the polyunsaturated fat content of corn and sunflower oils (rapeseed oil is higher in monounsaturated fat than these oils), it is higher in omega-3 polyunsaturated fat. All three oils are suitable for infants.

> A 200 mL amount of breast milk will meet UK adult recommendations for omega-3 polyunsaturated fatty acids (0.2% of omega-3 polyunsaturated fatty acids per day) and suggested recommendations for infants for omega-3 polyunsaturated fatty acids (at least 0.5% of daily energy from omega-3 fatty acids). A 500 mL amount of breast milk (the minimum guideline amount at 7–12 months) plus a portion of dairy alternatives or meat alternatives (oil, margarine, eggs, hummus, or tinned sardines or tuna in oil) would meet suggested recommendations for infants for omega-6 polyunsaturated fatty acids (at least 3%–4.5% of daily energy from omega-6 polyunsaturated fatty acids).

Long-chain omega-3 polyunsaturated fatty acids

The Scientific Advisory Committee on Nutrition (SACN) and the Committee on Toxicity (COT)[21] recommendation of 0.45 g of long-chain omega-3 polyunsaturated fatty acids (containing 20–22 carbons) a day for adults equates to 0.2% of daily energy intake from long-chain omega-3 polyunsaturated fatty acids for an adult [0.45 g = 4.05 kcal (0.45 g × 9 kcal/g); 4.05 kcal/2595 or 4.05 kcal/2071 kcal (daily energy requirements for males and females, respectively; SACN, 2012) = 0.2% energy from omega-3 polyunsaturated fatty acids]. In terms of fish intake, the recommendation from SACN and COT[21] is to consume at least two portions of fish a week, one of which should be oily, the average portion size for an adult being 140 g.[22] A guideline range of oily fish

TABLE 4.7 Food sources of omega-3 and omega-6 fatty acids

Food	Omega-3		Omega-6	
	Per 100 g	Per portion	Per 100 g	Per portion
Dairy foods and alternatives: (5 g (½ teaspoon) of oil, butter and margarine, 10 g (1 tablespoon) of cheese, 100 mL of breast and formula milk, 50 mL of whole cow's milk)				
Walnut oil	11.5	0.6	58.4	2.9
Rapeseed oil	9.6	0.5	19.7	1.0
Blended vegetable oil	6.5	0.3	23.3	1.2
Soya margarine	3.8	0.2	30.8	1.5
Soft margarine (not polyunsaturated)	2.7	0.1	9.8	0.5
Butter	0.7	0	1.4	0.1
Sunflower oil	0.1	0	63.2	3.2
Corn oil	0.9	0	50.4	2.5
Olive oil	0.7	0	7.5	0.4
Cheddar cheese	0.3	0.0	1.0	0.0
Breast milk, whole milk, formula milk[b]	0.1, 0, 0.1		0.4, 0.1, 0.1[c]	
Meat and alternatives: (10 g (½ tablespoon) of nuts and seeds, 22 g (half) of hard-boiled egg)				
Walnuts	7.5	0.8	39.3	3.9
Flaxseed	24.1	2.4	7.1	0.7
Taramasalata	5.0	1.0	10.8	2.2
Pilchards in tomato sauce	3.0	0.6	0.3	0.1
Sardines in tomato sauce	2.7	0.5	0.3	0.1
Tinned sardines in oil	2.3	0.5	2.6	0.5
Tinned salmon in brine	1.9	0.4	0.3	0.1
Tinned tuna in oil	1.2	0.2	3.3	0.7
Hummus	0.5	0.1	4.6	0.9
Hard-boiled egg	0.1	0	0.8	0.3
Beef, lamb, pork	0.1, 0.2, 0.1	0	0.4, 0.5, 1.0	0.1, 0.1, 0.2
Avocado	0.1	0	1.6	0.3

Notes: *Ministry of Agriculture, Fisheries and Food[18]; [a]grams per 100 g and per portion (20 g, 1 tablespoon, unless stated otherwise); [b]maximum recommendations for omega-3 and omega-6 in formula milk are 1% and 2% of total fat, respectively[19]; [c]omega-6 levels vary by brand, e.g. Hipp Organic First Infant Milk[20] contains 0.6 g of omega-6 per 100 mL; non-oily fish is low in omega-3 and omega-6 (e.g. plaice, 0.3 and 0 g per 100 g, respectively), as is tinned tuna in brine (0.2 and 0 g per 100 g, respectively).

consumption was set, since it was noted that more than two portions of fish a week would benefit some people; the guideline range for girls and women of reproductive age was one to two portions of oily fish per week, while for boys, men, and women past reproductive age, the guideline range was one to four portions of oily fish per week.[21]

If we use this adult recommendation of 0.45 g of long-chain omega-3 poly-unsaturated fatty acids a day for infants, using revised EARs for energy,[1] as shown in Table 3.1, we get a range of 0.5%–0.7% of energy from long-chain omega-3 polyunsaturated fatty acids per day for breastfed infants aged 6–12 months (0.5% energy from long-chain omega-3 polyunsaturated fatty acids per day for 11- to 12-month-old boys, 0.6% energy for 7- to 10-month-old boys and 9- to 12-month-old girls, and 0.7% energy from long-chain omega-3 polyunsaturated fatty acids per day for 6-month-old boys and 6- to 8-month-old girls).

> Based on energy-adjusted adult recommendations for long-chain omega-3 polyunsaturated fatty acids, recommendations for 6- to 12-month-old breastfed infants would be 0.5%–0.7% of energy from long-chain omega-3 polyunsaturated fatty acids per day.

Since the energy intake of a 12-month-old breastfed boy is 0.3 times that of an adult, and the recommended intake of fish for an adult is at least 280 g a week (equivalent to at least two portions of fish, one of which should be oily),[21] then perhaps the energy-adjusted adult recommendation for a 12-month-old infant of 84 g (0.3 × 280 g) or four 20 g portions (or two 40 g portions) of fish a week, one of which should be oily, may be appropriate. Similarly, an appropriate intake of fish for a 6-month-old infant (where energy intake is 0.2 times that of an adult) may be 69 g or three 20 g portions (or two 30 g portions) of fish a week (one of which should be oily).

> Based on the recommended intake of fish for an adult, the suggested intake of fish for 6- to 12-month-old infants would be three 20 g portions at 6 months and four 20 g portions at 12 months, or two portions a week with a portion size of 30 g at 6 months and 40 g at 12 months, one portion of which should be oily.

FIBRE INTAKE

As described in Chapter 3, the suggested range for fibre intake for infants at 6–12 months based on UK adult dietary reference values is 4.5–5.5 g of non-starch polysaccharides (NSP) per day for boys and 4.2–5.0 g per day for girls; based on fibre intakes among Finnish infants at 13 months of age,[23] the suggested range for fibre intake for infants at 8–12 months is 5.1–5.8 g of NSP per day for boys and 4.7–5.3 g NSP per day for girls.

As can be seen from Tables 4.8 and 4.9, these suggested fibre intakes can be achieved by intake of low-fibre (<3 g of fibre per 100 g of food) to medium-fibre foods (≥3 g but <6 g of fibre per 100 g of food) together with high-fibre foods (6 g or more of fibre per 100 g of food)[24]; it was not clarified whether this definition[24] of low/medium/high fibre foods was based on NSP or AOAC, and the definition is used here as NSP.

TABLE 4.8 Non-starch polysaccharides (NSP) and AOAC values for different foods (grams per 100 g)[*]

Food[a]	NSP per 100 g	AOAC per 100 g
Fruit (low to medium fibre)		
fruit (apple, apricot, pear) (low fibre)	1.6, 1.7, 2.2	2.3, 2.3, 2.9
strawberries, banana, raspberries (low fibre)	1.1, 1.1, 2.5	1.5, 1.5, 3.3
avocado[b] (medium fibre)	3.4	4.5
Vegetables (low to medium fibre)		
potatoes (old) (low fibre)	1.2	1.5
vegetables (broccoli, carrot) (low fibre)	2.3, 2.5	3.1, 3.3
parsnip (medium fibre)	4.7	6.3
Cereals (low to high fibre)		
rice (white/brown) (low fibre)	0.1/0.8	0.1/1.1
breakfast cereal (Rice Krispies, porridge) (low fibre)	0.7, 0.9	0.9, 1.1
pasta (spaghetti white/wholemeal) (low/medium fibre)	1.2/3.5	1.6/4.7
bread (white/brown/wholemeal) (low/medium fibre)	1.9/3.5/5.0	2/4.7/6.7
breakfast cereal (Weetabix, Shredded Wheat, Wheaty Biscuits) (high fibre)	9.7, 9.8, 11	12.9, 13, 13.2
Ground nuts and seeds (medium to high fibre)		
walnuts (medium fibre)	3.5	4.7
peanut butter (medium fibre)	5.4	7.2
sunflower seeds, almonds (high fibre)	6, 7.4	8, 9.8

Notes: *Food Standards Agency[4]; [a]low/medium/high fibre (<3 g, 3 g but <6 g, 6 g or more)[24]; [b]included under fruit for ease, included as a meat alternative (*see* Chapter 5).

Table 4.9 gives the fibre content per portion of food, AOAC values also being given where NSP values were derived from manufacturer's information, which is given as AOAC. As shown in Table 4.9, the range of NSP per portion of food is 0–1.3 g.

> The NSP content per portion of food is 0–1.3 g.

TABLE 4.9 Fibre content of foods for infants

Food	Fibre content (grams NSP per 100 g)	Fibre content per portion (20 g (1 tablespoon))*
Fruit	**0.7–3.4**	**0.1–0.7**
Grapes, banana, strawberry, tangerine, orange, apricot, apple, kiwi, pear, raspberry	0.7, 1.1, 1.1, 1.3, 1.7, 1.7, 1.8, 1.9, 2.2, 2.5	0.1, 0.2, 0.2, 0.3, 0.3, 0.3, 0.4, 0.4, 0.4, 0.5
Vegetables	**1.0–5.1**	**0.2–1.0**
Tomato, potato, sweetcorn, green beans, broccoli, sweet potatoes, carrot	1.0, 1.1, 1.4, 2.2, 2.3, 2.3, 2.5	0.2, 0.2, 0.3, 0.4, 0.5, 0.5, 0.5
Parsnip	4.7	0.9
Cereals	**0.1–9.8**	**0–1.0**
Rice		
white rice, brown rice	0.1, 0.8	0, 0.2
baby rice[a]	3.9 (5.2 AOAC)	0.2 (0.3 AOAC) per 6 g and 10 g mixed, 0.4 per 10 g dry
Bread		
white, granary, brown	1.9, 3.3, 3.5	0.4, 0.7, 0.7 (½ slice)
wholemeal	5.0	1.0 (½ slice)
white pitta, brown pitta	2.4, 5.2	0.5, 1.0 (½ small)
Pasta		
egg noodles, macaroni	0.6, 0.9	0.1, 0.2
spaghetti	1.2	0.2
baby pasta[b]	1.8 (2.4 AOAC)	0.3 (0.4 AOAC) per 15 g, 0.2 per 10 g
wholemeal spaghetti	3.5	0.7
Rice cakes[c]	1.6 (2.1 AOAC)	0.2 per 2 large (10 g)
Apple rice cakes[a]	1.9 (2.5 AOAC)	0.2 per 6 small (12 g)
Weetabix	9.7	0.9 for ½ biscuit
Wheaty Biscuits[e]	11	1.0 for ½ biscuit

Food	Fibre content (grams NSP per 100 g)	Fibre content per portion (20 g (1 tablespoon))*
Breakfast cereals (dry weight, 1 tablespoon, 10 g)		
Rice Krispies, Cornflakes,	0.7, 0.9	0.1, 0.1
Baby porridge[d]	1.1 (1.5 AOAC)	0.1 (0.2 AOAC)
Creamy Oat Porridge[b]	2.9 (3.8 AOAC)	0.3 (0.4 AOAC)
Porridge	6.8 (9 AOAC)	0.7 (0.9 AOAC)
Ready Brek	8.0	0.8
Milk, dairy products and alternatives	**0**	**0**
Milk, yoghurt (plain), cheese	0	0
Rice pudding, custard	0.1, 0	0, 0
Butter, vegetable margarine/oils	0	0
Meat and alternatives	**0–7.4**	**0–0.7**
Fish, poultry, meat, eggs	0	0
Baked beans (½ tablespoon, 10 g)	3.7	0.4
Lentils, chickpeas, butter beans, soya beans, red kidney beans (½ tablespoon, 10 g)	3.8, 4.3, 4.6, 6.1, 6.7	0.4, 0.4, 0.5, 0.6, 0.7
Peanut butter (½ tablespoon, 10 g)	5.4	0.5
Nuts (ground) (½ tablespoon, 10 g)		
walnuts, sunflower seeds, almonds	3.5, 6.0, 7.4	0.4, 0.6, 0.7
Avocado	3.4	0.7
Peas (½ tablespoon, 10 g)	5.1	0.5
Savoury dishes	**0.5–2.5**	**0.1–0.5**
Home-made savoury food		
macaroni cheese	0.5	0.1
beef stew	0.7	0.1
spaghetti bolognese	0.9	0.2
vegetable casserole	2.1	0.4
Ready-made savoury food		
Pasta, Chicken and Broccoli	0.7 (0.9 AOAC)	0.1 (0.2 AOAC)
Organic Apple, Pork and Root Vegetable Casserole[a]	0.9 (1.2 AOAC)	0.2 (0.2 AOAC)
Hearty Lamb Hotpot[a]	1.8 (2.4 AOAC)	0.4 (0.5 AOAC)
Parsnips, Chicken and Leeks[a]	2.5 (3.3 AOAC)	0.5 (0.7 AOAC)

Notes: *Unless stated otherwise. [a]Organix[7]: baby rice 100 g dry weight, 6 g with 45 mL milk; Apple Rice Cakes; Parsnips, Chicken and Leeks (4–6 months); Apple, Pork and Root vegetable casserole (from 7 months); Pasta, Chicken and Broccoli (from 10 months); Hearty Lamb Hotpot (from 12 months). [b]Heinz[9] Pasta Stars (from 7 months), 15 g average serving; Heinz[9] Creamy Oat Porridge; [c]Kallo Foods[25] – Food Standards Agency[4] – states no reliable information; [d]Hipp Organic[26]; [d]Cow & Gate[8] Wheaty Biscuits.

Number of portions to provide 0.5 g of fibre

The number of portions of different foods required to provide 0.5 g of fibre are given in Table 4.10, where a portion is typically one tablespoon or 20 g of food. Foods which contain zero or 0.1 g of fibre per tablespoon such as white rice, Rice Krispies, milk, dairy products and alternatives, poultry, meat, fish, egg noodles, macaroni cheese, beef stew, and some commercial dishes are not included in Table 4.10 or in further calculations of fibre intake, and can be viewed as 'additional fibre foods', providing a small amount of fibre in addition to the total calculated fibre intake.

Table 4.11 is a summary version of Table 4.10, showing that the highest fibre sources (where only ½ tablespoon, half a portion or one portion of food provides 0.5 g of fibre) are whole-wheat cereals – breakfast cereals (Weetabix and Wheaty biscuits (quarter of a biscuit), Ready Brek), wholemeal bread and brown pitta bread, wholemeal spaghetti; parsnips, and meat alternatives – lentils, peas, beans, peanut butter and nuts.

> The highest fibre sources are whole-wheat cereals, wholemeal bread and brown pitta bread, wholemeal spaghetti, parsnips and meat alternatives (lentils, peas, beans, peanut butter and nuts).

As outlined in Chapter 3, the suggested range of NSP intake for breast-fed infants is 4.7–5.3 g per day for girls and 5.1–5.8 g per day for boys at 8–12 months, based on the fibre density among Finnish 13-month-old children.[23] Translated into number of servings of food containing 0.5 g of fibre, this equates to 9–11 servings of food containing 0.5 g of fibre for girls and 10–12 servings for boys.

> The suggested fibre intake for breastfed infants from 8 to 12 months of age, increasing gradually, equates to:
> - 9–11 servings of food containing 0.5 g of fibre for girls
> - 10–12 servings of food containing 0.5 g of fibre for boys.

Providing both fruit and vegetables and cereals per day, these fibre servings are further described in terms of daily menus in Table 4.12. Examples of daily menus are also included which provide fewer than nine fibre servings, which may be appropriate for infants aged younger than 8 months.

TABLE 4.10 Number of portions of food required to give 0.5 g of fibre

Food	Number of portions*
Fruit[a]	
Banana, strawberry, tangerine, orange, apricot	2
Apple, kiwi, pear, raspberry	1
Vegetables	
Tomato, potato, sweetcorn	2
Broccoli, carrot, sweet potatoes, green beans	1
Parsnip	½
Cereals	
Brown rice, baby rice[b]	2
White bread, white pitta, granary, brown	2 (1 slice, 1 small pitta)
Wholemeal bread, brown pitta	1 (½ slice, ½ small pitta)
Pasta	
macaroni, spaghetti, baby pasta[c]	2
wholemeal spaghetti	½
Rice cakes,[d] apple rice cakes[b]	4 large, 12 small
Creamy Oat Porridge[c]	2 (20 g dry)
Porridge	1 (10 g dry)
Ready Brek	½ (5 g dry)
Weetabix, Wheaty Biscuits[e]	½ (¼ dry biscuit)
Meat and alternatives	
Avocado	1
Baked beans, lentils, peas, chickpeas, butter beans, soya beans, red kidney beans	1 (½ tablespoon, 10 g)
Peanut butter	1 (½ tablespoon, 10 g)
Ground nuts and seeds	1 (½ tablespoon, 10 g)
Savoury mixed dishes	
Home-made savoury food	
spaghetti bolognaise	2
vegetable casserole (and parsnip dish)	1
Ready-made savoury food	
Organic Apple, Pork and Root Vegetable Casserole[b]	2
Hearty Lamb Hotpot,[b] Parsnips, Chicken and Leeks[b]	1

Notes: *Where one portion is 20 g or 1 tablespoon unless stated otherwise; [a]banana (1 small), apple/pear (½ small). [b]Organix[7]: baby rice, Apple Rice Cakes, Parsnips, Chicken and Leeks, Apple, Pork and Root vegetable casserole, Pasta, Chicken and Broccoli, Hearty Lamb Hotpot. [c]Heinz[9]: Pasta Stars, Creamy Oat Porridge; [d]Kallo Foods[25] – Food Standards Agency[4] – states no reliable information; [e]Cow & Gate[8] Wheaty Biscuits.

TABLE 4.11 Summary table showing number of portions of food required to give 0.5 g of non-starch polysaccharides

Food	Number of portions*	Amount
Weetabix, Wheaty Biscuits[a]	½	¼ biscuit
Parsnip, peas, wholemeal spaghetti		½ tablespoon, 10 g
Ready Brek		½ tablespoon, 5 g dry
Baked beans, beans, lentils, peanut butter, nuts and seeds	1	½ tablespoon, 10 g
Wholemeal bread, brown pitta bread		½ slice
Apple and pear (½ small), kiwi, raspberry, avocado, broccoli, carrots, sweet potatoes, green beans, mixed vegetable or parsnip dishes (home-made or ready-made)		1 tablespoon, 20 g
Porridge		½ tablespoon, 10 g dry
Banana and tangerine (1 small), orange (½), strawberries, apricots, tomato, potato, sweetcorn, macaroni, spaghetti, baby pasta,[b] brown rice, baby rice,[c] spaghetti bolognaise, meat and vegetable dishes	2	2 tablespoons, 40 g
White, granary or brown bread, white pitta bread		1 slice
Creamy Oat Porridge[b]		2 tablespoons, 20 g dry
Rice cakes (small[c] and large[d])		12 small, 4 large

Notes: *Where one portion is 20 g or 1 tablespoon unless stated otherwise; [a]Cow & Gate[8] Wheaty Biscuits; [b]Heinz[9]: Pasta Stars, Creamy Oat Porridge; [c]Organix[7]: baby rice, Apple Rice Cakes; [d]Kallo Foods.[25]

TABLE 4.12 Daily menus providing the suggested number of servings of fibre for infants (nine to twelve servings)*,[a]

Fibre servings (g fibre)	Breakfast	Dinner	Tea	Supper or snack
1 (0.5 g)	1 tablespoon Creamy Oat Porridge **½** (& *milk*) & ½ small banana **½**			
2 (1 g)	2 tablespoons baby rice **1** (& *milk*)	1 tablespoon sweet potato **1** (& *beef*)		
3 (1.5 g)	½ tablespoon Ready Brek **1** (& *milk*) & ½ pear **1**	1 tablespoon home-made vegetable casserole **1** (& *turkey*)		

Fibre servings (g fibre)	Breakfast	Dinner	Tea	Supper or snack
4 (2 g)	½ Weetabix **2** (& *milk*)	1 tablespoon carrots **1** & 2 tablespoon baby pasta **1** (& *lamb*)		
5 (2.5 g)	½ brown toast **½** (& *1 small hard-boiled egg*) & 1 tablespoon strawberries **½**	2 tablespoons commercial chicken and vegetables **1** & 1 tablespoon baby pasta **½**	1 tablespoon avocado **1** & 1 tablespoon parsnips **1** & 6 small rice cakes **½**	(*Greek-style yoghurt*)
6 (3 g)	½ brown pitta **1** (& *grated cheese*) & ½ small apple **1**	2 tablespoons home-made beef & vegetables **1**	2 tablespoons baby rice **1** & 1 tablespoon broccoli **1** (& *salmon*)	1 small banana **1**
7 (3.5 g)	1 tablespoon porridge **1** (& *milk*) & 1 tablespoon kiwi **1**	1 white toast **1** & ½ tablespoon peanut butter **1** & 1 small banana **1**	1 tablespoon brown rice **½** & 1 tablespoon carrots **1** (& *beef*)	6 small rice cakes **½**
8 (4 g)	½ Weetabix **2** (& *milk*) & 1 tablespoon raspberries **1**	2 tablespoon baby pasta **1** (& *grated cheese*) & 1 tablespoon avocado **1**	2 tablespoon mashed potatoes **1** & ½ tablespoon baked beans **1** (& *mackerel*)	½ pear **1**
9 (4.5 g)	1 tablespoon Ready Brek (dry) **2** (& *milk*) & 1 tangerine **1**	3 tablespoons parsnip & lamb casserole **3** & ½ apple **1** (& *natural yoghurt*)	1 tablespoon brown rice **½** & ½ tablespoon ground nuts **1** (& *turkey*)	½ small banana **½**
10 (5 g)	1 Wheaty Biscuit **4** (& *milk*) & 1 kiwi **1**	2 tablespoons baby pasta **2** & 2 tablespoons tomato sauce **1** (& *beef & rapeseed oil*)	1 tablespoon sweet potato **1** (& *salmon*) & 1 tablespoon carrots **1**	
11 (5.5 g)	1 wholemeal toast **2**, ½ tablespoon peanut butter **1** & ½ orange **1**	3 tablespoon home-made vegetable curry **3** & 1 tablespoon brown rice **½** (& *natural yoghurt*)	2 tablespoons mixed pork & parsnips **2** & 1 tablespoon potatoes **½**	½ apple **1**
12 (6 g)	1 Weetabix (& *milk*) **4** & 1 small tangerine **1**	1 brown toast **1** & 1 tablespoon baked beans **2** & ½ pear **1**	2 tablespoons baby pasta **1** & broccoli **1** (& *chicken & natural yoghurt*)	½ small banana **1**

Notes: *Food Standards Agency[4]; one serving of fibre equates to 0.5 g of non-starch polysaccharides; bold italics show the number of fibre servings; [a]with a minimum of 600 mL of milk a day at 6 months and 500 mL of milk a day at 7–12 months; foods in brackets do not add to fibre intake, but ensure suggested intake of dairy and meat.

It is clear from the menu in Table 4.12 that the suggested number of fibre servings (9–12) can be achieved more easily when three meals a day are eaten, with two or more fibre servings from cereals (one or more wholegrain cereals) plus two or more fibre servings from fruit and vegetables, with or without beans, ground nuts or peanut butter. In terms of food groups, lentils, beans (not green) and nuts are seen as 'meat alternatives'.[2]

> The suggested fibre intake can be achieved with three to five portions of cereals (three portions if two wholegrain breakfast cereals are consumed, four portions otherwise, always one or more wholegrain cereal), three to five portions of fruit and vegetables and one portion of meat alternatives (nuts, beans, peas or avocado). This suggested fibre intake could be further simplified to four portions of fruit and vegetables and four portions of cereals a day (always one wholemeal), with or without one portion of meat alternatives a day.

The guideline number of servings of 'starchy foods', 'vegetables and fruit' and 'meat and meat alternatives' outlined by COMA[2] are as follows: a total of five to six servings a day at 6–9 months (two to three servings, two servings and one serving respectively), and a total of seven to ten servings or more a day at 9–12 months (three to four servings of starchy foods, three to four servings of vegetables and fruit, and a minimum of one serving of meat or two of meat alternatives). That is, the suggested number of fibre servings from 8 months based on 13-month-old Finnish children[23] correspond to COMA food group frequency guidelines at 9–12 months, although the serving size is not specified by COMA.[2] In comparison, the fibre suggestions based on UK adult fibre recommendations (see Table 3.3) are slightly low compared with COMA[2] food group frequency guidelines at 9–12 months.

> The suggested number of fibre servings from 8 months, based on fibre intake among 13-month-old Finnish children,[23] correspond to COMA food group frequency guidelines at 9–12 months.[2]

NON-MILK EXTRINSIC SUGARS

As described in Chapter 3, the COMA[2] recommendation for non-milk extrinsic sugars (NMES) for groups of children is that the average intake should be limited to about 10% of total dietary energy intake. The main sources of NMES in a representative study of the diets of UK infants aged 9–12 months being fruit juices and sweet drinks.[6] NMES were found to provide 12% of infants' daily energy intake.[6] Advice for parents on NMES from COMA[2] is to encourage water as a drink other than milk (while diluted fruit juice can be provided at a meal time in a beaker), to use unsweetened versions of foods such as yoghurts and breakfast cereals, and only to add sugar to tart fruit, if needed.

IRON

As outlined in Chapter 3, the RNI for iron is 4.3 mg per day at 4–6 months and 7.8 mg per day at 7–12 months.[11] Table 4.13 lists foods with 0.1 mg or more of iron per portion, from meat sources (haem iron) such as beef and tinned sardines, and non-meat sources (non-haem iron), such as apricots, avocado and fortified breakfast cereals. The absorption of non-haem iron from a meal can be increased by including foods containing vitamin C in the meal, such as fruit and vegetables, and by excluding high-fibre foods such as wholewheat breakfast cereals or wholewheat bread from the meal. Provision of a wide variety of foods should help enable iron requirements to be met.

From Table 4.13, it is clear that obtaining the required iron without formula milk, fortified cereals, wholemeal bread, sardines and beef is difficult. Taking average values for meat and alternatives and cereals as 0.5 mg of iron per portion and of fruit and vegetables as 0.1 mg, at 7–12 months, with 500 mL of follow-on formula milk, three portions each of meat and alternatives, cereals and fruit and vegetables meets iron requirements. With 500 mL of breast milk, even ensuring that the highest iron containing foods are consumed from each food group (including three portions of beef and two portions of sardines, two portions of wholegrain breakfast cereals and two portions of wholemeal bread, apricots, peas and broccoli), it is difficult to meet iron requirements with five portions of meat and alternatives, cereals and fruit and vegetables. However, iron availability in foods and the infant's ability to absorb a greater percentage of iron from food when iron status is low play important roles in infant iron status.

> Obtaining the required iron without formula milk, fortified cereals, wholemeal bread, sardines and beef appears to be difficult.

TABLE 4.13 Amount of iron in a portion of food (1 tablespoon, 20 g, unless stated otherwise)*

Food	Amount of iron (mg) per portion
Fruit and vegetables	
Apricots (fresh)	0.7
Spinach (not well absorbed)	0.3
Broccoli	0.2
Sweet potato, parsnips, carrots, sweetcorn, tinned tomatoes	0.1
Banana, strawberries, kiwi	0.1
Cereals	
Ready Brek (1 tablespoon, 10 g dry weight)	1.2
Weetabix (½), Wheaty Biscuits (½)	0.7
Wholemeal bread, brown pitta (½ slice, 18 g), Creamy Oat Porridge[a] (1 tablespoon, 10 g dry weight)	0.5
Brown bread, white pitta (½ slice, 18 g), Banana porridge[a]	0.4
White bread (½ slice, 18 g)	0.3
Porridge, baby porridge, macaroni, other pasta, boiled potato	0.1
Meat and alternatives	
Cashews, sunflower seeds (½ tablespoon, 10 g)	0.6
Tinned sardines or pilchards in tomato sauce or oil (after 6 months), beef	0.5
Hummus, lentils (½ tablespoon, 10 g)	0.4
Tinned tuna in oil (after 6 months), lamb, commercial meat-based dishes (71 g**), hard-boiled egg (½, 22 g)	0.3
Almonds, walnuts, peas (½ tablespoon, 10 g)	0.3
Tinned mackerel, turkey, sausages, beef stew, bolognaise sauce, peanut butter	0.2
Chicken, steamed salmon, taramasalata, pork, avocado	0.1
Baked beans (½ tablespoon, 10 g)	0.1
Milk, dairy and alternatives	
Formula milk (per 100 mL), First milk	0.5 to 0.8***
Follow-on milk (suitable from 6 months)	1.0 to 1.3***
Breast milk (0.08 mg per 100 mL)	0.1

Notes: *Food Standards Agency[4]; **71 g median portion from UK 6–12 month survey,[6] 0.4 g/100 g average intake from Hipp database for meat-based infant dishes (personal communication (e-mail) to author from Hipp, 2011 – non-analysed data, with varying nutrient content of ingredients); ***Crawley and Westland[20]; [a]Hipp.[26]

ZINC

As outlined in Chapter 3, the RNI for zinc is 4.0 mg per day at 4–6 months and 5.0 mg per day at 7–12 months.[11] Table 4.14 lists foods with 0.1 mg or more of zinc per portion.

TABLE 4.14 Amount of zinc in a portion of food (1 tablespoon, 20 g, unless stated otherwise)[*]

Food	Amount of zinc (mg) per portion
Fruit and vegetables	
Sweet potatoes, broccoli, parsnips, sweetcorn, spinach	0.1
Apricots	0.1
Cereals	
Brown pitta (½)	0.4
Wheaty Biscuits (½), Ready Brek (1 tablespoon, 10 g), brown bread (½ slice, 18 g), wholemeal bread (½ slice, 18 g)	0.3
Porridge, baby porridge, Weetabix (½), white bread (½ slice), white pitta bread (½)	0.2
Brown rice, white rice, macaroni, other pasta, boiled potatoes	0.1
Meat and alternatives	
Beef	0.8
Lamb	0.7
Cashews, sunflower seeds (½ tablespoon, 10 g)	0.6
Beef stew, bolognaise sauce, sardines in tomato sauce	0.5
Pork, chicken, turkey, tinned sardines in oil	0.4
Hummus, lentils (½ tablespoon, 10 g), sausages, pilchards in tomato sauce	0.3
Almonds, walnuts (½ tablespoon, 10 g)	0.3
Tuna in oil, hard-boiled egg (½, 22 g)	0.2
Boiled peas (½ tablespoon, 10 g)	0.2
Cod, plaice, tinned mackerel, steamed salmon, taramasalata, avocado	0.1
Baked beans (½ tablespoon, 10 g)	0.1
Milk, dairy products and alternatives	
Cheddar cheese (½ tablespoon, 10 g)	0.4
Formula milk (100 mL), First milk,	0.5–0.9,
follow-on milk suitable from 6 months[**]	0.5–0.7
Breast milk (100 mL)	0.3
Whole cow's milk (50 mL)	0.2
Plain yoghurt, Greek-style yoghurt, ice cream, custard, rice pudding	0.1

Notes: *Food Standards Agency[4]; **Crawley and Westland.[20]

As shown in Table 4.14, over half of the RNI for zinc can be met by 500 mL of infant formula. Estimating the zinc content of cereals as 0.2 g per portion, of fruit and vegetables as 0.1 g, of meat and alternatives as 0.4 g and of dairy products as 0.4 g per portion, then with 500 mL of breast milk the following number of portions will meet zinc requirements: five portions of cereals and of fruit and vegetables, four portions of meat and alternatives and one portion of dairy products will meet zinc requirements, or four portions each of cereals, fruit and vegetables and meat and alternatives plus two portions of dairy products.

> Over half of the RNI for zinc can be met by 500 mL of infant formula. With 500 mL of breast milk, the following number of portions will meet zinc requirements: five portions of cereals and of fruit and vegetables, four portions of meat and alternatives and one portion of dairy products, or four portions each of cereals, fruit and vegetables and meat and alternatives plus two portions of dairy products.

COMMON EARLY PUREES, MASHES AND BABY RICE: ENERGY, FAT, IRON, ZINC AND FIBRE

If common early complementary foods, such as fruit and vegetables, are served pureed or mashed with added milk or water, then their nutritional composition per portion changes compared with serving pieces of the food, or mashed with no added water or milk, as described in earlier tables. Table 4.15 shows the energy, fat, iron, zinc and fibre content of fruit and vegetable purees. Any food above 0.7 kcal/g (the amount of energy per gram of milk) is defined by the WHO[3] as suitable for complementary feeding.

> Any food above 0.7 kcal/g (the amount of energy per gram of milk) is defined by the WHO[3] as suitable for complementary feeding.

As shown in Table 4.15, baby rice in the United Kingdom contains very little iron. Manufacturers' information can be confusing, since only the amount of iron in 100 g of dried rice is shown on food labels. Many brands of baby rice in the United Kingdom for infants under 6 months are no longer fortified with iron, while the iron content of baby rice varies; for example, Hipp Organic[26] baby rice contains 0.7 mg of iron in 10 g of baby rice powder, and approximately 0.1 mg of iron per 2 g, while Heinz[9] baby rice is fortified with iron, containing 7 mg of iron per 100 g of rice powder, and about 0.7 mg of iron per 20 g. By comparison, baby rice in the United States is fortified to a much higher level than in the United Kingdom, 'Earth's Best'[27] baby rice, for example, containing 45% of the RNI for iron in one 14g portion.

UK fortified baby rice contains only a little iron per portion, organic baby rice containing negligible iron per portion.

Baby rice is an adequate source of energy as a first complementary food, even though it contains slightly fewer kilocalories than milk when it is made quite runny (16 kcal per 20 g of runny baby rice compared with 21 kcal per 20 g of milk). The fat content of baby rice is similar to that of milk, since milk is mixed with the powdered rice. When a thicker baby rice is made – for example, for infants introduced to solids at 6 months – the energy value of baby rice increases (to 25 kcal per 20 g), while the fat content decreases (to 0.5 g of fat per 20 g), since the ratio of milk to powdered rice decreases.

TABLE 4.15 Energy, fat, iron, zinc and fibre content of common early purees (2 tablespoons, 20 g per portion)

Puree*	Energy [kcal (kcal/g)]	Fat per portion	Iron per portion	Zinc per portion	Fibre per portion
Avocado	45.1 (2.3)	1.6	0.4	0	0.4
Sweet potato	39.3 (2.0)	0.1	0.1	0	1.0
Potato	38.1 (1.9)	0.1	0.1	0.1	0.5
Parsnip	25.7 (1.3)	0.1	0.1	0	1.5
First rice	16.3 (0.8)	0.6	0.1	0.1	0
Butternut squash	14.5 (0.7)	0.1	0.1	0	0.6
Banana	11.7 (0.6)	0.3	0	0.1	0.4
Carrot	11.1 (0.6)	0.3	0.1	0	1.4
Apple	6.5 (0.3)	0.1	0.1	0	0.4

Note: *Most of the vegetable purees and banana puree are made with milk; apple puree is made with water and hence the fat and energy content of apple puree will be lower.

Increasing the energy, fat and iron content of purees and mashes

The energy and fat content of vegetable and fruit purees or mashes could be improved by adding yoghurt or cheese sauce, while the addition of meat would also increase the iron content. The addition of butter or vegetable oils, such as rapeseed or sunflower oil, will increase the energy and fat content of purees and mashes. However, while the addition of a little fat will improve the texture, too much fat, especially solid fat, will make it difficult to eat and to digest.

VITAMIN A

As outlined in Chapter 3, the RNI for vitamin A is 350 µg per day at 6–12 months.[11,28] Vitamin A is obtained as retinol from animal products, or can be made from carotenoids from plant foods. Milk and dairy products appear to be the main sources of vitamin A in the infant diet, providing 57% of daily retinol intake in UK infants aged 6–12 months.[6]

TABLE 4.16 Amount of vitamin A in a portion of food (1 tablespoon, 20 g, unless stated otherwise)

Food	*Amount of vitamin A or retinol equivalent** (µg) per portion
Liver (calf; chicken)	5040; 2100
Carrots, boiled (old; young)	446; 256
Spinach	128
Cabbage (curly kale)	112
Formula and follow-on formula milk (100 mL)[a]	minimum 42, maximum 126 65[b]
Cantaloupe-type melon	58.8
Breast milk (100 mL)	58
Butter (½ teaspoon, 5 g)	47.9
Boiled egg (½ small, 22 g)	41.8
Cheddar cheese (1 tablespoon, 10 g)	36.4
Polyunsaturated margarine (½ teaspoon, 5 g)	33.8
Pumpkin, boiled	32
Mango	23.2
Cereal-based infant foods (1 tablespoon, 10 g dry weight)[c]	minimum 23, maximum 69
Boiled peas (½ tablespoon, 10 g)	19
Ice cream, avocado	18.2
Green beans/runner beans	17.4
Whole cow's milk (50 mL)	16.5
Grilled mackerel	9
Custard and milk puddings	7.6
Yoghurt, whole plain	5.6
Roast chicken	4.8

Notes: *Food Standards Agency[4]; **retinol equivalent for fruit and vegetables, retinol only for other foods; [a]based on 60–180 µg per 100 kcal[32]; [b]Hipp Organic Follow-on milk (personal communication (e-mail) to author from Hipp – non-analysed data, with varying nutrient content of ingredients); [c]based on Codex Alimentarius[33] values for processed cereal-based foods (60–180 µg per 100 kcal), using energy values for infant cereals shown in Table 4.2.

While liver is the best source of vitamin A (*see* Table 4.16), current advice on liver consumption by infants is not to consume liver before 6 months[29] and not to have more than one portion per week at 6–12 months due to the high vitamin A content.[30] Fifteen per cent of total retinol intake among 6- to 12-month-old UK infants came from offal, such as liver[6]; offal is now infrequently eaten[31] and hence would not be expected to contribute significantly to vitamin A intake.

Taking the vitamin A content of formula milk as 65 µg per 100 mL (Hipp Organic Follow-on milk[20]), the RNI for vitamin A is achieved with 600 mL of breast or formula milk a day; with 500 mL of breast or formula milk a day, an additional 60 and 25 µg of vitamin A (retinol equivalent) per day is required, respectively.

> The RNI for vitamin A is achieved with 600 mL of breast or formula milk a day; with 500 mL of breast or formula milk a day, an additional 60 and 25 µg of vitamin A per day is required, respectively.

One portion of liver per month would more than meet additional monthly requirements of vitamin A, while two daily portions of dairy products and alternatives (as cow's milk, breast or formula milk, cheese, butter or polyunsaturated margarine) will also provide this additional vitamin A. One portion of these dairy products and alternatives with half a hard-boiled egg, or one whole hard-boiled egg will also provide the required additional vitamin A; this would realistically cover vitamin A intake on only 3–4 days.

One or two portions of carrots a week (old or young, respectively), one portion of spinach or curly kale cabbage a day or two or more portions of a limited number of other vegetables and fruit a day (cantaloupe-type melon, pumpkin, mango and green beans) or meat alternatives (peas and avocado) would generally also provide the required additional vitamin A, dependent upon the absorption rate.

Regulations for commercial cereal-based infant foods[34] stipulate that the vitamin A content should be 60–180 µg of retinol equivalent per 100 kcal. Based on the energy content of infant cereals (*see* Table 4.2), this corresponds to 23–69 µg of vitamin A per 10 g portion of dry cereal. Thus, two portions (20 g) of breakfast cereal (one Wheaty Biscuit), or one portion of infant rice or infant pasta per day would meet additional vitamin A requirements. The Ministry of Agriculture, Fisheries and Food (MAFF) study of 6- to 12-month-old infants[6] found that 10% of retinol intake and 20% of carotene intake came from commercial infant foods.

The MAFF survey of 6- to 12-month-old infants[6] found that while the mean daily intake of vitamin A as retinol equivalent was more than double the RNI, the mean of the lowest 2.5% of intakes was below the RNI while the mean of the highest 2.5% of intakes was over five times the RNI.

> With 500 mL a day of breast or formula milk, vitamin A requirements may be met by consumption of liver once a month, carrots once or twice a week, one to two daily portions of infant cereals or dairy products, or two or more daily portions of specific fruit and vegetables or meat alternatives.

As described in Chapter 3 (The recommendation for vitamin A, p. 78), the vitamin A content of breast milk is dependent upon maternal vitamin A intake and status,[34] while a daily vitamin A supplement is recommended for infants consuming <500 mL of formula milk a day and for all breastfed infants from 6 months consuming breast milk as their main drink.[2] Food composition data[4] suggest that vitamin A supplements may be required occasionally for some infants consuming 500 mL of breast milk or infant formula a day, dependent upon the complementary foods consumed, while a daily supplement with <500 mL of breast or formula milk a day may provide excess vitamin A, again dependent upon the complementary foods consumed.

The MAFF study of 6- to 12-month-old infants[6] found that approximately 40% of infants received a vitamin A supplement, providing approximately 20% of their total vitamin A intake, average intake being over two and a half times the RNI. In 2012, COT[35] stated that further examination is needed of the potential risks from high levels of vitamin A intake during complementary feeding.

> Further examination is needed of the potential risks from high levels of vitamin A intake during complementary feeding.[35]

VITAMIN D

As outlined in Chapter 3, the RNI for vitamin D is 8.5 µg per day at 4–6 months and 7.0 µg per day at 7–12 months.[11] The main dietary sources of vitamin D are fish, oil, margarine, and formula milk, as shown in Table 4.15. As highlighted by a 2011 Caroline Walker Trust report,[20] 500 mL of infant formula will supply

79%–100% of the RNI for vitamin D from 6 months, dependent upon the infant formula (*see* Table 4.17).

TABLE 4.17 Amount of vitamin D in a portion of food (1 tablespoon, 20 g, unless stated otherwise)*

Food	Amount of vitamin D (µg) per portion
Tinned pilchards in brine	2.8
Sunflower oil (½ teaspoon, 5 g)	2.5
Grilled mackerel	1.8
Steamed salmon	1.7
Tinned sardines in tomato sauce	1.6
Formula milk (follow-on milk, suitable from 6 months) (100 mL)*	1.2–1.5
Rapeseed oil (½ teaspoon, 5 g)	1.1
Formula milk (first milk) (100 mL)*	1.1–1.2
Creamy Oat Porridge (1 tablespoon, 10 g), baby rice[a]	1.1
Wheaty Biscuits (½ biscuit, 9 g)[b]	1.0
Tinned sardines in oil, mackerel	1.0
Corn oil (½ teaspoon, 5 g)	0.9
Tinned sardines in brine, grilled beefburger	0.9
Tuna in brine	0.7
Tuna in oil	0.6
Hard-boiled egg (½ small, 22 g)	0.5
Ready Brek (1 tablespoon, 10 g)	0.4
Polyunsaturated margarine (½ teaspoon, 5 g)	0.4
Beef, pork, lamb, beef stew, turkey, macaroni cheese, ice cream	0.1

Notes: *Crawley and Westland[20]; [a]Heinz[9]; [b]Cow & Gate.[8]

Taking the median vitamin D content of specific meat alternatives (sunflower oil, rapeseed oil, corn oil, oily fish and hard-boiled egg) as 1.0 µg per portion and of fortified infant cereals (Wheaty Biscuits, Creamy Oat Porridge or baby rice) as 1.1 µg per portion, daily consumption of one meat alternative and two fortified infant cereals a day would provide half the RNI for vitamin D. Intake of these foods every day may be monotonous, while three to four 20 g portions of white fish per week are also required (as suggested to meet long-chain omega-3 polyunsaturated fatty acid requirements), in addition to other meat and alternatives to meet other nutritional requirements. It is clear that even consuming these foods high in vitamin D, breastfed infants would be unable to achieve vitamin D intakes close to the RNI, and the recommended vitamin D supplement[2] would be required.

> The main dietary sources of vitamin D are fish, oil, margarine, and formula milk. Daily consumption of one portion of specific meat alternatives and two of fortified infant cereals would provide half the RNI for vitamin D; however, this may be difficult to achieve every day. Even consuming these foods high in vitamin D, breastfed infants would be unable to achieve vitamin D intakes close to the RNI.

CALCIUM

As outlined in Chapter 3, the RNI for calcium is 525 mg per day, with a LRNI of 240 mg per day.[11] The main source of calcium for infants is milk, providing over half the average intake in a UK study of 6- to 12-month-old infants, owing to consumption of infant formula and cow's milk.[6] Dairy products, oily fish, breakfast cereals and bread are good sources of calcium, while fruit and vegetables also contain small amounts, as shown in Table 4.18.

> Good sources of calcium include milk, dairy products, oily fish, breakfast cereals and bread.

Consumption of 500 mL of breast milk, the minimum guideline amount from 7 months,[2] will provide 170 mg of calcium, although it is likely that infants introduced to solids at 6 months will consume a greater quantity of breast milk at 7 and 8 months.[10] Consumption of 600, 700 and 800 mL of breast milk will provide 204, 238 and 272 mg of calcium, respectively.

From Table 4.17, median calcium intakes by food group are approximately 59 mg from dairy products (whole plain yoghurt, cheese or whole milk); 37 mg from cereals (fortified breakfast cereals and bread); 8 mg from fruit and vegetables (oranges, apricots, carrots and broccoli), plus 11 mg from meat and alternatives (fish, hard-boiled egg, peas, beans and tofu).

As described in Chapter 3, while the RNI for calcium is 525 mg a day, a daily calcium intake of 240 mg a day has been deemed adequate to meet the needs of breastfed infants (equivalent to the EAR for calcium for breastfed infants, based on the higher absorption rate of calcium from breast milk than infant formula[2]); the RNI for calcium for breastfed infants would then be 312 mg per day.[2]

TABLE 4.18 Dietary sources of calcium

Food	Calcium content (mg) per 100 g[*]	Calcium content (mg) per portion[**]
Milk, dairy products and alternatives		
cheddar cheese (1 tablespoon, 10 g)	739	73.9
whole milk plain yoghurt	200	40
whole cow's milk (50 mL)	118	59
formula milk (100 mL)	50 (minimum)[a]	50 (minimum)[a]
first milk (100 mL)	42–60[b]	42–60[b]
follow-on milk (100 mL)	50–90[b]	50–90[b]
breast milk (100 mL)	34	34
Meat and meat alternatives		
tofu (fried)	1480	296
sardines in brine/oil/tomato sauce	540, 500, 430	108, 100, 86
tinned pilchards in tomato sauce	250	50
baked beans (1 tablespoon, 10 g)	53	5.3
peas (½ tablespoon, 10 g)	42	4.2
hard-boiled egg (½ small, 22 g)	29	12.8
salmon (steamed)	23	4.6
Fruit and vegetables		
apricots, oranges	73, 47	14.6, 9.4
broccoli, carrots	40, 24	8, 4.8
Cereals		
Ready Brek (1 tablespoon, 10 g dry weight)	1200	120
Creamy Oat Porridge[c] (1 tablespoon, 10 g dry weight)	470	47
bread: brown, white, wholemeal (½ slice)	186, 177, 106	37.2, 35.4, 21.2

Notes: *Food Standards Agency[4]; **1 tablespoon, 20 g unless stated otherwise; [a]Codex Alimentarius[33]; [b]Crawley and Westland[20]; [c]Heinz.[9]

With 600 mL of breast milk, containing 204 mg of calcium, a calcium intake above 312 mg a day can be realistically achieved with:

- one portion each of the specified foods from cereals, fruit and vegetables, meat and alternatives and dairy products
- two portions of dairy products on some but not all days (as consuming two portions every day may become too monotonous)
- three portions of cereals on some days.

With 500 mL of breast milk providing 170 mg of calcium, a calcium intake above 312 mg a day can be realistically achieved with:

- two portions of cereals, one portion of dairy products, plus one fruit and vegetables or one meat and alternatives
- two portions of dairy products on some but not all days
- four portions of cereals on some days.

With infant follow-on formula, taking the average calcium content as 70 mg per 100 mL,[20] 600 mL of follow-on formula a day will provide 420 mg of calcium, while 500 mL will provide 350 mg of calcium a day, i.e. greater than the RNI for calcium based on 66% absorption of calcium.[36] A calcium intake above 525 mg a day can be realistically achieved with:

- 600 mL of follow-on formula and two portions of dairy products
- 600 mL of follow-on formula and one portion of the specified foods from each food group
- 500 mL of follow-on formula, two portions of dairy products and two portions of cereals on some days
- 500 mL of follow-on formula, two portions of dairy products and one portion from the other food groups on some days
- 500 mL of follow-on formula, three portions of cereals plus one portion of fruit and vegetables or meat and alternatives on some days.

> With 500 mL of breast milk or infant formula a day, the RNI for calcium is harder to achieve than with 600 mL of breast milk or infant formula a day.

The RNI for calcium of 525 mg per day could be achieved by breastfed infants with 700 or 800 mL of breast milk, plus two portions of dairy products and four portions of cereals on some days.

> With 500 mL of breast milk, a calcium intake above 312 mg a day can be realistically achieved with:
> - two portions of cereals, one portion of dairy products, plus one fruit and vegetables or one meat and alternatives
> - two portions of dairy products on some but not all days, or
> - four portions of cereals on some days.

IODINE

As outlined in Chapter 3, the UK RNI for iodine for infants aged 4–12 months is 60 µg per day,[11] while the WHO[37] RNI is 90 µg per day. Milk, dairy products and fish are good dietary sources of iodine for infants, as shown in Table 4.19.

> Milk, dairy products and fish are good dietary sources of iodine for infants.

As shown in Table 4.19, a portion of meat alternatives as fish or hard-boiled egg will give a median intake of 12.6 µg of iodine per portion, while one portion of dairy products as whole milk yoghurt or whole milk will give 13.8 µg of iodine per portion.

Thus, to meet the UK RNI for iodine with 35 µg of iodine from 500 mL of breast milk a day, an infant would need to consume:

- two portions of meat alternatives (fish or hard-boiled egg) a day (unachievable every day, since this would be monotonous and far removed from an infant's usual dietary intake), plus one portion of dairy products (whole milk yoghurt or whole milk), or
- one portion of meat alternatives (fish or hard-boiled egg) a day (more achievable, since three 20 g portions of fish per week at 6 months and four 20 g portions per week at 12 months are suggested to meet long-chain omega-3 polyunsaturated fatty acid intake, although hard-boiled egg three times every week would be too repetitive), plus two portions of dairy products (whole milk yoghurt or whole milk) per day (which would be achievable on some but not all days).

Similarly, to meet the UK RNI for iodine with 42 µg of iodine from 600 mL of breast milk a day, an infant would need to consume:

- two portions of meat alternatives (fish or hard-boiled egg a day), two portions of dairy products (whole milk yoghurt or whole milk a day), or one portion of meat alternatives and one portion of dairy products a day.

> With 600 mL of breast milk, the RNI for iodine appears to be achievable if specific foods are consumed, while 500 mL of breast milk would result in iodine intake not meeting the RNI on some days, due to the required food group combinations being too limited. This implies that iodine-fortified foods or an iodine supplement would be required for infants consuming 500 mL of breast milk a day, or that the iodine content of breast milk needs to be increased (by maternal iodine supplementation or use of iodine-fortified foods).

TABLE 4.19 Dietary sources of iodine

Food	Iodine content (µg) per 100 g*	Iodine content (µg) per portion**
Milk, dairy products and alternatives		
Whole cow's milk	30[a]	15 (50 mL)
Whole milk plain yoghurt	63	12.6
Cheddar cheese	30	3 (1 tablespoon, 10 g)
Butter	38	1.9 (½ teaspoon, 5 g)
Formula milk (per 100 kcal)[b]	10 (minimum) 50 (maximum)	10 (minimum) 50 (maximum)
Breast milk	7[c]	7 (100 mL)
Meat and meat alternatives		
Haddock (steamed)	260	52
Mackerel (grilled)	170	34
Cod (baked)	130	26
Tinned pilchards in tomato sauce	64	12.8
Hard-boiled egg	53	11.7 (½ small, 22 g)
Salmon (grilled)	44	8.8
Tinned sardines in brine/oil	23	4.6
Brazil nuts, cashews, walnuts, almonds	20, 11, 9, 2	2, 1.1, 0.9, 0.2 (½ tablespoon, 10 g)
Tinned tuna in oil/brine	14/13	2.8/2.6
Lean beef, lamb, pork	10, 6, 5	2, 1.2, 1
Chicken, turkey	8	1.6
Peas	2	0.2 (½ tablespoon, 10 g)
Fruit and vegetables		
Strawberries, bananas	9, 8	1.8, 1.6
Carrots, sweet potatoes	2	0.4
Cereals		
Pasta (plain, fresh)	36	7.2
Breakfast cereals	Significant amounts but no reliable data	
Bread: brown, white, wholemeal	6	1.2 (20 g, ½ slice)
Boiled potatoes	3	0.6

Notes: *Food Standards Agency[4]; **1 tablespoon, 20 g unless stated otherwise; [a]Food Standards Agency[38]; [b]thus approximately equal to breast milk per 100 mL; [c]Department of Health.[2]

REFERENCES

1. Scientific Advisory Committee on Nutrition. *Dietary Reference Values for Energy 2011*. London: The Stationery Office; 2012. Available at: www.sacn.gov.uk/pdfs/sacn_dietary _reference_values_for_energy.pdf (accessed 10 June 2012).

2. Department of Health. *Weaning and the Weaning Diet. Report of the Working Group on the Weaning Diet of the Committee on Medical Aspects of Food Policy*. Report on Health and Social Subjects, 45. Department of Health, London: The Stationery Office; 1994.

3. World Health Organization. *Guiding Principles for Feeding Non-Breastfed Children 6–24 Months of Age*. Geneva, Switzerland: WHO; 2005. Available at: www.who.int/maternal _child_adolescent/documents/9241593431/en/index.html (accessed 12 June 2011).

4. Food Standards Agency. *McCance and Widdowson's The Composition of Foods*. 6th summary ed. Cambridge: Royal Society of Chemistry; 2002.

5. Wrieden WL, Longbottom PJ, Adamson AJ, *et al.* Estimation of typical food portion sizes for children of different ages in Great Britain. *Br J Nutr*. 2008; **99**(6): 1344–53.

6. Mills A, Tyler HA. *Food and Nutrient Intakes of British Infants Aged 6–12 Months*. London: HMSO; 1992.

7. www.organix.com/Our-Foods

8. www.cowandgate.co.uk/our_products/baby_food

9. www.heinzbaby.co.uk/products

10. Nielsen SB, Reilly JJ, Fewtrell MS, *et al.* Adequacy of milk intake during exclusive breastfeeding: a longitudinal study. *Pediatrics*. 2011; **128**(4): e907–14.

11. Department of Health. *Dietary Reference Values for Energy and Nutrients for the UK. Report of the Committee on Medical Aspects of Food Policy*. Report on Health and Social Subjects, 41. London: HMSO; 1991.

12. Uauy R, Castillo C. Lipid requirements of infants: implications for nutrient composition of fortified complementary foods. *J Nutr*. 2003; **133**(9): S2692–972.

13. Uauy R, Dangour AD. Fat and fatty acid requirements and recommendations for infants of 0–2 years and children of 2–18 years. *Ann Nutr Metab*. 2009; **55**(1–3): 76–96.

14. Royal College of Paediatrics and Child Health (RCPCH). *UK-WHO Growth Charts: early years*; London: RCPCH; 2011. Available at: www.rcpch.ac.uk/child-health/ research-projects/uk-who-growth-charts/uk-who-growth-charts (accessed 28 July 2011).

15. Schwartz J, Dube K, Alexy U, *et al.* PUFA and LC-PUFA intake during the first year of life: can dietary practice achieve a guideline diet? *Eur J Clin Nutr*. 2010; **64**(2): 124–30.

16. Brenna JT, Varamini B, Jensen RG, *et al.* Docosahexaenoic and arachidonic acid concentrations in human breast milk worldwide. *Am J Clin Nutr*. 2007; **85**(6): 1457–64.

17. Nielsen SB, Reilly JJ, Fewtrell MS, *et al.* Adequacy of milk intake during exclusive breastfeeding: a longitudinal study. *Pediatrics*. 2011; **128**(4): e907–14.

18. Ministry of Agriculture, Fisheries and Food (MAFF). *Fatty Acids. Supplement to McCance and Widdowson's The Composition of Foods*. London: MAFF; 1998.

19. European Commission. Commission Directive 96/4/EC/OJ, 28.2.96. *Official Journal of the European Union*. 1996; **L49**: 12. Available at: www.eur-lex.europa.eu/ LexUriServ/lexUriServ.do?uri=OJ:L:1996:049:0012:0016:EN:PDF (accessed 9 June 2011).

20. Crawley H, Westland S. *Infant Milks in the UK*. Abbots Langley, UK: The Caroline Walker Trust; 2011. Available at: www.cwt.org.uk/pdfs/infantsmilk_web.pdf (accessed 16 March 2012).

21. Scientific Advisory Committee on Nutrition and Committee on Toxicity. *Advice on Fish Consumption: benefits & risks*. London: The Stationery Office; 2004. Available at: www.sacn.gov.uk/pdfs/fics_sacn_advice_fish.pdf (accessed 12 June 2011).

22. Henderson L, Gregory J, Swan G. *National Diet and Nutrition Survey: adults aged 19 to 64 years. Volume 1: Types and quantities of foods consumed*. London: The Stationery Office; 2002.

23. Ruottinen S, Lagstrom HK, Niinikoski H, *et al*. Dietary fibre does not displace energy but is associated with decreased serum cholesterol concentrations in healthy children. *Am J Clin Nutr*. 2010; **91**(3): 651–61.

24. European Commission. Corrigendum to Regulation (EC) No 1924/2006 of the European Parliament and of the Council of 20 December 2006 on nutrition and health claims made on foods. *Official Journal of the European Union*. 2007; **L12**: 3–18. Available at: http://eur-lex.europa.eu/LexUriServ/LexUriServ.do?uri=OJ:L:2007:012:0003:0018:EN: (accessed 1 March 2010).

25. www.kallofoods.com

26. www.hipp.co.uk/products/our-baby-food-and-drinks

27. www.earthsbest.com

28. Scientific Advisory Committee on Nutrition. *Review of Dietary Advice on Vitamin A*. London: The Stationery Office; 2005. Available at: www.sacn.gov.uk/pdfs/sacn_vita_report.pdf (accessed 23 March 2011).

29. Department of Health. *Introducing Your Baby to Solid Food*. London: Department of Health; 2012. Available at: www.dh.gov.uk/prod_consum_dh/groups/dh_digitalassets/documents/digitalasset/dh_107710.pdf (accessed 16 July 2012).

30. The Caroline Walker Trust. *Eating Well: first year of life; a practical guide*. Abbots Langley, UK: The Caroline Walker Trust; 2011. Available at: www.firststepsnutrition.org/pdfs/First year of Life Practical Guide.pdf (accessed 2 August 2012).

31. Department of Health. *Infant Feeding Survey 2005*. London: Department of Health; 2007. Available at: www.ic.nhs.uk/statistics-and-data-collections/health-and-lifestyles-related-surveys/infant-feeding-survey (accessed 16 March 2011).

32. Infant Formula and follow-on formula regulations (England); 2007. Available at: www.legislation.gov.uk/uksi/2007/3521/contents/made (accessed 9 March 2011).

33. Codex Alimentarius Commission. Joint Food and Agriculture Organization of the United Nations/World Health Organization Food Standards Programme. *Report of the 25th session of the codex committee on nutrition and foods for special dietary uses, 2003*; 2004. Available at: www.codexalimentarius.org/input/download/report/34/al04_26e.pdf (accessed 16 March 2011).

34. Ross JS, Harvey PW. Contribution of breastfeeding to vitamin A nutrition of infants: a simulation model. *Bull World Health Organ*. 2003; **81**(2):80-6.

35. Committee on Toxicity (COT). *Draft minutes TOX.MIN/2012/03, Annex 12*. London: COT: 2012. Available at: http://cot.food.gov.uk/pdfs/cot8maydraftminutes.pdf (accessed 1 July 2012).

36. Abrams SA. Calcium absorption in infants and small children: methods of determination and recent findings. *Nutrients*. 2010; **2**(4): 474–80.

37. World Health Organization/United Nations Children's Fund/International Council for the Control of Iodine Deficiency Disorders. *Assessment of Iodine Deficiency Disorders and Monitoring their Elimination.* 3rd ed. Geneva, Switzerland: WHO; 2007. Available at: www.unicef.org/ukraine/2_Guide_for_IDD_managers_eng.pdf (accessed 10 July 2011).

38. Food Standards Agency (FSA). *Retail Survey of Iodine in UK Produced Dairy Foods. Food Survey Information Sheet No. 02/08.* London: FSA; 2008 Available at: www.food.gov.uk/multimedia/pdfs/fsis0208.pdf (accessed 17 April 2011).

CHAPTER 5

Food intake: food groups and portion sizes

Key facts

1. There are limited nutritional guidelines for infants in both the United Kingdom and elsewhere. There appears to be no pictorial representation of food intake by food group for infants.

2. Responsive feeding is followed.

3. While Committee on the Medical Aspects of Food Policy (COMA) guidelines give five food groups for infants, four are suggested, 'occasional foods' (salty and sugary foods) being excluded. The four food groups are (1) milk, dairy products and alternatives; (2) cereals (bread, rice, potatoes and other starchy foods); (3) fruit and vegetables; and (4) meat and alternatives (fish, eggs, beans and other non-dairy sources of protein).

4. COMA food group frequency guidelines (number of daily servings), which were based on 'pragmatic decisions', at 9–12 months are as follows: no advice on dairy other than milk (minimum of 600 mL of breast or formula milk at 4–6 months and 500 mL at 7–12 months); three to four servings of starchy foods; three to four servings of fruit and vegetables; and one serving of meat, fish or eggs or two of non-meat sources of protein. No portion size was defined.

5. Suggested food group–based dietary guidelines formulated to meet current government recommendations for energy intake, iron, zinc, calcium, iodine and vitamin D and suggested recommendations for fat and fibre intake are similar to COMA guidelines except for meat and

alternatives, portion size being defined. Where one portion is defined as a tablespoon (20 g) for most foods, the suggested number of portions a day for infants is three to five portions of cereals and fruit and vegetables, two to five portions of meat and alternatives, and one to two portions of dairy products and alternatives, with 500–600 mL of milk.

6. A suggested pictorial representation of these suggested food group–based dietary guidelines is a simple pie chart divided into five sections, called the Balanced Infant Guide. There are two equally sized sections for cereals and for fruit and vegetables, a slightly smaller section for meat and alternatives, a smaller section for dairy products, plus the largest section for breast or formula milk. The pictorial representation can be used to show daily food intake by food group (number of portions) or average intake over several days or a week.

FOOD GROUPS

As described in Chapter 2, foods that have similar properties can be grouped together. Grouping foods makes it easier for people to see whether they are eating a balanced diet, as described for adults and children aged 5 years and over in *The Eatwell Plate*.[1] The five food groups in *The Eatwell Plate*[1] are (1) fruit and vegetables; (2) bread, rice, potatoes, pasta and other starchy foods; (3) milk and dairy foods; (4) meat, fish, eggs, beans and other non-dairy sources of protein; and (5) foods and drinks high in fat and/or sugar.

Food group guidelines may differ by country due to differences in dietary patterns and hence differences in nutritional deficiencies, but also due to different nutritional recommendations arising from interpretation of the same dietary evidence.[2]

NUMBER OF FOOD GROUPS FOR INFANTS

A balanced diet for infants is different to that for adults, since infants have different nutritional requirements to adults – for example, higher fat,[3] iron, zinc and iodine requirements[4,5] in terms of the energy density of the diet, as described in Chapters 1 and 3.

> A balanced diet for infants is different to that for adults, since infants have different nutritional requirements to adults.

The COMA report *Weaning and the Weaning Diet*[4] listed five food groups for infants:

1. 'milk, dairy products and substitutes' (listing the recommended amount of breast or formula milk, whole milk for mixing solids, hard cheese, yoghurt, custard and cheese sauce)
2. 'the starchy foods' (rice, bread and cereals including breakfast cereals, with some wholemeal cereals from 6 months)
3. 'vegetables and fruit'
4. 'meat and meat alternatives' (including meat, fish, pulses, hard cooked egg)
5. 'occasional foods' (containing a lot of salt, sugar, fat or energy, such as cakes, crisps and fried foods), the advice being not to use foods from this group every day, while 'moderate amounts' (not defined further) of butter and margarine are advised after 9 months).

It should be noted that for the group 'occasional foods', COMA[4] states that 'none of these foods are necessary in the diet'. 'Occasional foods' are not specified as a group in parent advice booklets (*see* Chapter 2) produced by the National Health Service (NHS),[6] the NHS, Unicef and the Department of Health (DH),[7] NHS Wales and the Welsh Government,[8] NHS Health Scotland and the Scottish Government,[9] the Health Promotion Agency in Northern Ireland[10] or the Food Standards Agency.[11] Similarly, advice from one of the COMA panel members,[12] and for parents from the British Dietetic Association Paediatric Group[13] does not give 'occasional foods' as a separate food group.

Since foods containing salt should be limited and there is no need for foods containing added sugar,[4] it seems sensible not to include these foods as a food group, since inclusion could lead to misinterpretation of advice and encourage usage, and to give advice regarding their exclusion. This may be particularly true for any diagrammatic representation of infant food groups.

As mentioned earlier, COMA[4] advises the inclusion of butter or margarine in moderate amounts after 9 months, under 'occasional foods'. Suggested advice regarding the use of butter, margarine and oils in the normal preparation of family foods, with preference to polyunsaturated oils such as rapeseed and sunflower oils,[14] is to use them occasionally rather than daily. These fats could be included as a separate food group, as in *The Eatwell Plate* for adults and children over 5 years of age,[1] where they are included under 'foods and drinks high in fat or sugar', or under 'dairy foods', since butter could be included under 'dairy', with rapeseed oil, sunflower oil and margarine being given as alternatives to butter.

While dairy foods such as cheese and yoghurt are good sources of fat, protein, calcium and iodine, butter contains a lot more fat than cheese or yoghurt, little calcium, virtually no protein, but approximately the same amount of iodine as cheese[15] and may be seen as a poor alternative to these foods. However, the benefit of grouping butter, margarine and oils under 'dairy foods' is that a suggested intake can be given (rather than 'use occasionally'), as they would be used as an alternative to other dairy fat sources, such as cheese. Rapeseed and sunflower oils are good sources of omega-3 and omega-6 polyunsaturated fats and lower in saturated fat than cheese.[15]

While five food groups are used to describe recommended adult food intake,[1] it is suggested that four food groups are used for infants, as shown in Table 5.1. Dairy foods may be referred to as 'dairy products and alternatives', bread, rice, potatoes, pasta and other starchy foods as 'cereals', and meat, fish, eggs, beans and other non-dairy sources of protein as 'meat and alternatives'.

> It is suggested that four food groups are used for infants, namely cereals, fruit and vegetables, meat and alternatives and dairy products and alternatives.

TABLE 5.1 Suggested food groups for infants

Food group	Foods in group
Bread, rice, potatoes, pasta and other starchy foods	Cereals (including wheat cereals after 6 months): pasta, bread, breakfast cereals, rice, potatoes
Fruit and vegetables	All vegetables and fruit except potatoes (which are included with cereals), beans, peas and avocado (which are included with meat)
Meat, fish, eggs, beans and other non-dairy sources of protein	Red meat such as lamb, beef, pork, meat products such as sausages (limited because of salt content), poultry such as chicken and turkey, fish (tinned after 6 months), eggs (after 6 months), nuts (after 6 months), beans and peas
Milk and dairy foods	Milk (breast milk or infant formula)
	Custard and cheese sauce (can use whole cow's milk), yoghurt, cheese, butter or alternatives (margarine, and oils such as rapeseed and sunflower oils)
N.B. Foods and drinks high in sugar or salt	*Fizzy and fruit drinks, sweets, chocolate, crisps, biscuits, cakes and sweet rusks are not advised, as they may displace more nutrient-dense foods*
	Fats (butter, margarine and oils) are included under 'dairy foods'

NUMBER OF PORTIONS FROM EACH FOOD GROUP

While the food groups are similar for adults and infants, the proportion of each food group needed to give a balanced diet may be different, as described in the previous section.

Milk and solids may supply the additional fat required by infants compared with adults,[3] as described in Chapter 4. Compared with adults, infants appear to obtain a much higher percentage of their total fat intake from milk. The UK survey of 6- to 12-month-old infants (where most infants were introduced to solids before 6 months) found that at 6–9 months, infants obtained 47% of their fat intake from milk, 36% at 10–12 months[16]; in comparison, the more recent rolling UK National Diet and Nutrition Survey[17] found that adults (aged 19–64 years) obtained only 4% of their total fat intake from milk. Good dietary sources of iron and zinc include meat and alternatives and fortified cereals, while good dietary sources of iodine include whole cow's milk and fresh fish, as described in Chapter 4.

> Compared with adults, infants obtain over ten times as much of their daily fat intake from milk.

TABLE 5.2 COMA guideline number of servings per day from five food groups for infants

Food group	4–6 months	6–9 months	9–12 months
Milk	Minimum 600 mL of breast or formula milk	500–600 mL of breast milk, formula or follow-on formula	500–600 mL of breast milk, formula or follow on formula
Dairy products and substitutes	No guideline	No guideline	No guideline
The starchy foods	No guideline	Two to three servings	Three to four servings
Vegetables and fruit	No guideline	Two servings	Three to four servings
Meat and meat alternatives	No guideline	One serving	Minimum one serving from animal source (two from vegetable sources)
Occasional foods	No guideline	No guideline	No guideline
	Choose low-sugar desserts; avoid high salt foods	Encourage savoury foods rather than sweet Fruit juices are not necessary	May use moderate amounts of butter or margarine

Note: Adapted from DH information.[4]

Infant guidelines for the frequency of consumption of foods from different food groups were given by COMA[4] and are shown in Table 5.2. No guidelines were given for infants at 4–6 months or for dairy products and occasional foods at 4–12 months. These guidelines were based on 'pragmatic decisions' and available research. Further research since these guidelines enables the formulation of newer evidence-based guidelines. Suggested guideline daily numbers of servings from food groups are given later (*see* Meeting nutritional requirements: number of portions and portion size, p. 155).

PORTION SIZE

The portion size of foods may differ between infants, depending on their energy requirements, and hence information on the relative number of servings of foods from different food groups may be more useful than actual portion sizes. However, the portion size should also be relative since the intake of food from a given food group equates to both the number of servings and the portion size. A UK survey of 6- to 12-month-old infants found that even though infants were having a reasonable number of servings of meat and meat products, the serving size was low and largely accounted for a low iron intake.[16]

> The intake of food from a given food group equates to both the number of servings and the portion size.

Among 6- to 12-month-old infants,[16] the median daily intake of foods (grams per day) by food group, based on consumers only was:
- 42 g of yoghurt and 4 g of cheese
- 22 g of potatoes, 17 g of breakfast cereals, 13 g each of pasta, rice and bread, and 11 g of instant infant cereals
- 24 g of fruit and 6 g of vegetables (carrots)
- 71 g of meat-based commercial infant meals; 20 g of meat, including meat products and dishes, 12 g of eggs, 10 g of baked beans, 8 g of fish, 6 g of poultry and 4 g of peas.

Thus, a tablespoon of food weighing 20 g would approximate to the observed median daily intake of several foods for infants, including breakfast cereal, potatoes, fruit and meat, although variability in intake between and within infants may be high.

A tablespoon of food weighing 20 g would approximate to the observed median daily intake of several foods for infants, including breakfast cereal, potatoes, fruit and meat, although variability in intake between and within infants may be high.

It is important to note that these median daily intakes do not necessarily equate to the amount or type of food that was most nutritionally advantageous to the infant, but rather to what was given. Following responsive feeding, offering more meat, fish and vegetables, for example, could have led to a higher consumption of these foods (displacing foods such as soft drinks and cakes) and higher intakes of omega-3 fatty acids, zinc, iron and iodine. Thus, in suggesting suitable portion sizes for infants, it is important to take into account not only the usual amount of foods that infants eat, but the amount of different types of food that they could eat and which could be nutritionally advantageous.

> In suggesting suitable portion sizes for infants, it is important to take into account not only the usual amount of foods that infants eat, but the amount of different types of food that they could eat and which could be nutritionally advantageous.

Food portion data for 1- to 3-year-old children,[18] based on median portion weights from the 1992–93 UK National Diet and Nutrition Survey for children aged 1½ to 4½ years,[19] shows that the lower values of the interquartile range are similar to the median intakes for infants[16] for breakfast cereals (18–21 g versus 20 g, respectively) and meat (24 g for roast meat, 28 g for chicken and turkey, versus 20 g, respectively), with infant median intakes of potatoes, fruit, pasta, rice and vegetables being only a third of the lower values of the interquartile range for 1- to 3-year-old children.

> Food portion data for 1- to 3-year-old children[18] shows that the lower values of the interquartile range are similar to the median intakes for infants[16] for breakfast cereals and meat, median intakes of potatoes, fruit, pasta, rice and vegetables being only a third of the lower values of the interquartile range.

The Infant and Toddler Forum in the United Kingdom has produced numerical and pictorial evidence-based portion sizes for 1- to 3-year-olds for a variety of foods,[20] similar to those produced by Wrieden et al.[18] Portion sizes were developed using portion sizes from the 1992–93 UK National Diet and

Nutrition Survey for children aged 1½ to 4½ years[19] in addition to portion sizes from the Avon Longitudinal Study of Parents and Children,[21] with 15 mL tablespoons and other measures being used to define portion size.

A US study[22] found that for young children aged 2–5 years, the assessment of portion size using 'a tablespoon per year' of age met most nutrient requirements (except for fat), similar to the US pictorial food guide, the authors commenting that parents could easily use such an age-graduated portion size approach. No similar assessment of portion size appears to have been made for infants.

> A US study[22] found that for young children aged 2–5 years, the assessment of portion size using 'a tablespoon per year' of age met most nutrient requirements.

The Caroline Walker Trust[23] publication on infant feeding gives a weekly menu for infants at 7–9 months and at 10–12 months, which meets energy and nutrient recommendations. These menus include 600 mL of breast milk or infant formula at 7–9 months, but only 400 mL at 10–12 months (rather than the guideline minimum of 500 mL[4]). The portion size of a given food is not uniform throughout the menu, as the amount needed to meet nutritional recommendations is calculated rather than taking average portion sizes.[23] While consumption of differing amounts of the same food over several days may relate to normal infant eating patterns, the proposed intake of some foods is higher than the median values consumed by 6- to 12-month-old infants.[16] For example, at 7–9 months, the amount of milk used with cereals and of pasta, rice, potatoes and baked beans corresponds to the amount consumed by 1- to 3-year-old children.[18] However, the portion size used for fruit, vegetables, meat, fish and cheese is similar to that used in the current publication.

> The Caroline Walker Trust[23] publication on infant feeding gives a weekly menu for infants at 7–9 months and at 10–12 months, which meets energy and nutrient recommendations. The portion size of a given food is not uniform throughout the menu, as the amount needed to meet nutritional recommendations is calculated rather than taking average portion sizes.

In formulating an appropriate portion size for infants, previous portion size information for infants and young children[16,18,20,22] was compared with portion size information from infant food manufacturers and from personal weighing of food (unpublished data). The suggested infant portion size for most foods is 20 g or 1 tablespoon (half a piece of bread, half a small hard-boiled egg, half a small banana, apple or orange), 10 g or 1 tablespoon for dry breakfast cereals and cheese, 10 g or ½ tablespoon for beans, lentils, peanut butter and ground nuts, and 5 g or half a teaspoon for butter or oil.

> The suggested infant portion size for most foods is 20 g or 1 tablespoon (half a piece of bread, half a small hard-boiled egg, half a small banana, apple or orange), 10 g or 1 tablespoon for dry breakfast cereals and cheese, 10 g or ½ tablespoon for beans, lentils, peanut butter and ground nuts, and 5 g or ½ teaspoon for butter or oil.

MEETING NUTRITIONAL REQUIREMENTS: NUMBER OF PORTIONS AND PORTION SIZE

If the portion size of food and the number of portions of food from the four food groups are appropriate, then nutritional requirements should be met. The nutritional requirements were discussed in Chapter 3, while advice on meeting these recommendations was discussed in Chapter 4. This advice can be summarised as follows.

1. *Energy*: with 600 mL of breast or formula milk at 6 months and 500 mL at 7–12 months, breast or formula milk will provide 67% of total energy intake at 6 months, 50% at 9 months and 45% at 12 months. A 543 mL amount of breast or formula milk at 7–12 months will provide 54% of total energy intake, based on the revised Estimated Average Requirements (EARs) for energy for a breastfed boy at 7–12 months,[24] equal to COMA's guidance on the proportion of energy provided by milk.

2. *Fat*: 500–600 mL of breast or formula milk will help ensure that fat intake is sufficient. With 500 mL of breast milk, 8–10 g of fat may be needed from solids at 7–12 months to obtain >35% of energy from fat; one portion of higher fat meat and alternatives (such as nuts) and one portion of higher fat dairy products and alternatives (such as cheese) per day can meet total fat requirements at 7–12 months, while two to five portions of meat and alternatives (no more than one higher fat option such as nuts or oil) and one to three dairy products (no more than one portion of cheese, three dairy products only if these are milk and two yoghurt portions) per day will realistically meet total daily fat requirements at 7–12 months. One

higher fat meat alternative such as nuts would not be sufficient to meet iron requirements.

3. *Saturated fat*: saturated fat can be limited by using lean meat instead of fatty meat, and limiting intake of butter and cheese to no more than one portion in total per day.

4. *Omega-3 and omega-6 polyunsaturated fatty acids*: 300 mL of breast milk will meet omega-3 and omega-6 UK adult recommendations. A 500 mL amount of breast milk per day will meet the omega-3 suggestion (0.5% of energy). A 500 mL amount of breast milk, one portion of dairy alternatives (sunflower or rapeseed oil) and one portion of meat alternatives (hummus, tinned sardines or tuna in oil) per day will meet the omega-6 suggestion (3%–4.5% of energy).

5. *Long-chain omega-3 polyunsaturated fatty acids*: to meet 0.5%–0.7% of energy adapting the adult recommendation, appropriate intakes may be 84 g of fish, two 40 g portions a week or four 20 g portions a week, for a 12-month-old infant and two 30 g portions a week or three 20 g portions for a 6-month-old infant, one of which should be oily (such as pilchards or mackerel).

6. *Fibre*: to meet fibre suggestions for infants aged 8–12 months, 9–12 servings per day of food containing 0.5 g of fibre per serving are required. This can be achieved with an average of four portions of cereals (three to five portions, including wholegrain cereals), plus an average of four portions of fruit and vegetables (three to five portions, dependent on the fibre content of the fruit or vegetable) with or without one portion of meat alternatives (nuts, beans, peas or avocado).

7. *Iron*: beef, sardines, fortified cereals, wholemeal bread and formula milk contain relatively high amounts of iron. With 500 mL of follow-on formula milk, three portions each of meat and alternatives, cereals and fruit and vegetables meets iron requirements. With 500 mL of breast milk, even ensuring that the highest iron containing foods are consumed from each food group, it is difficult to meet iron requirements with five portions each of meat and alternatives, cereals and fruit and vegetables.

8. *Zinc*: over half of daily zinc requirements can be met by 500 mL of infant formula per day. Other good dietary sources include meat (such as beef and lamb) and meat alternatives, cow's milk, breast milk, some infant cereals and breakfast cereals, plus brown and wholemeal bread. At 7–12 months, 500 mL of breast milk plus five portions of cereals, five portions of fruit and vegetables, four portions of meat and alternatives and one portion of dairy

products will meet zinc requirements, or four portions each of cereals, fruit and vegetables and meat and alternatives, plus two portions of dairy products.

9. *Calcium*: dietary sources include dairy products, oily fish, breakfast cereals and bread, milk being the main source of calcium (cow's milk and formula milk containing more than breast milk). The following intakes will meet requirements: 500 mL of breast milk, two portions of high calcium breakfast cereal or bread, and one portion each of dairy products, fruit and vegetables and meat and alternatives, or four portions of cereals on some days or two portions of dairy products on some days; 600 mL of breast milk and one portion from each food group or three portions of cereals on some days or two portions of dairy products on some days.

10. *Iodine*: the following intakes will meet requirements: 500 mL of breast milk, two portions of meat alternatives (fish or hard-boiled egg) and one portion of dairy products (whole milk or whole milk yoghurt), or one portion of meat alternatives and two portions of dairy products, on some days; 600 mL of breast milk, two portions of meat alternatives (fish or hard-boiled egg) or and two portions of dairy products (whole milk or whole milk yoghurt), or one portion of meat alternatives and one portion of dairy products (Recommended Nutrient Intake (RNI) achievable every day).

11. *Vitamin D*: good dietary sources include formula milk, fish, oil, margarine and fortified cereals. A 500 mL amount of formula milk will meet 79%–100% of vitamin D requirements. One meat alternative (rapeseed oil, sunflower oil, or oily fish) or two meat alternatives (a hard-boiled egg) and two fortified infant cereals (Wheaty Biscuits, Creamy Oat Porridge or baby rice) will supply half the RNI for vitamin D a day. A vitamin D supplement is recommended.

12. *Vitamin A*: Dietary sources of vitamin A include liver, carrots, formula milk, fortified infant cereals and breast milk. A 600 mL amount of breast or formula milk a day will achieve the RNI for vitamin A. With 500 mL of breast milk, an additional 60 µg of vitamin A is required. With 500 mL of formula milk, an additional 25 µg of vitamin A is required. Additional vitamin A can be obtained from one portion of liver per month, one to two portions of carrots per week, one or two portions of infant cereals or dairy products per day, or two or more daily portions of specific fruit and vegetables or meat alternatives. A vitamin A supplement is recommended.

VERIFYING FOOD GROUP SUGGESTIONS

The ability of this food group and portion size advice to meet nutritional recommendations could be tested by comparing the average daily intake of energy and major nutrients, calculated using the suggested number of food group portions plus the guideline volume of milk,[4] with the recommended intake of energy and major nutrients. If this comparison was, for example, within 10% of recommended intakes, then the suggested number of food group portions and portion size could be deemed appropriate. However, more detailed testing and linear modelling would be needed to validate these suggested food based dietary guidelines.[25-27]

The estimated nutrient value for each food group is taken as the median nutrient value of the main foods in the food group. The portion size for foods within food groups is generally a 20g portion (1 tablespoon), 10g for cheese and dry breakfast cereals (1 tablespoon), nuts, beans and peas (½ tablespoon), and 5g (½ teaspoon) for oil, butter and margarine (*see* Table 4.2). Estimated nutrient values (median values) for food groups plus calculated daily intake of nutrients for different food group combinations can be found in the Appendix.

Verifying food group suggestions: energy

The energy value from suggested food group combinations that was closest to the EAR for energy for a given age was within 2.6% of the EAR for energy at 6–12 months for both boys and girls. As shown in the Appendix, for boys, with 600mL of breast or formula milk at 6 months and 500mL at 7–12 months, the best estimate of the EAR for energy from the food group combinations was from:

- two portions from each food group at 6 months
- three portions of cereals, fruit and vegetables, and meat and alternatives, and two portions of dairy products and alternatives at 7 months
- four portions of cereals and fruit and vegetables at 8 months (five portions of cereals and fruit and vegetables was also very close)
- five portions of cereals and fruit and vegetables at 9 and 10 months (four portions of cereals and fruit and vegetables was also very close)
- five portions of cereals and fruit and vegetables at 11 and 12 months
- the following food group combinations (cereals, fruit and vegetables, meat and alternatives, dairy products and alternatives) were the best estimates of the EAR for energy at 6–12 months respectively: 2,2,2,2; 3,3,3,2; 4,4,4,1; 5,5,2,2; 5,5,3,2; 5,5,5,1; 5,5,4,2.

For girls, with 600 mL of breast or formula milk at 6 months and 500 mL at 7–12 months, the best estimate of the EAR for energy from the food group combinations was from:

- two portions from each food group at 6 months
- two or three portions of cereals and fruit and vegetables at 7 months
- three portions of cereals and fruit and vegetables at 8 months
- three or four portions of cereals and fruit and vegetables at 9 months
- four or five portions of cereals and fruit and vegetables at 10 and 11 months
- five portions of cereals and fruit and vegetables at 12 months
- the following food group combinations (cereals, fruit and vegetables, meat and alternatives, dairy products and alternatives) were the best estimates of the EAR for energy at 6–12 months respectively: 2,2,1,1; 2,2,2,2 and 3,3,2,1; 3,3,2,2; 3,3,3,2 and 4,4,3,1; 4,4,2,2 and 5,5,2,1; 4,4,3,2 and 5,5,3,1; 5,5,2,2.

> In order to meet energy requirements, boys will move more quickly to higher food group combinations than girls, suggesting that it is better not to suggest a specific number of food portions at a set age, but rather to indicate broad food group combinations to meet requirements.

Verifying food group suggestions: fat

As shown in the Appendix, with 600 mL of breast or formula milk per day for boys, fat intake with:

- one portion from each food group was within the 6-month suggested fat range
- two to three portions from different food groups was within the 7- to 8-month suggested fat range, except for three cereals, fruit and vegetables and meat and alternatives with two dairy products and alternatives (in the 10-month suggested fat range)
- four portions from most food groups was within the 9- to 10-month suggested fat range, except for four cereals, fruit and vegetables and meat and alternatives with two dairy products and alternatives (in the 12-month suggested fat range)
- five portions from most food group combinations was within the 11- to 12-month suggested fat range, except for five cereals, fruit and vegetables and meat and alternatives with two dairy products and alternatives (which was 0.8 g higher than the 12-month suggested fat range).

For boys with 600 mL of breast or formula milk, all suggested food group combinations are within the suggested fat intake range (based on >35% of energy from fat to 45% of energy from fat) for different ages, as long as only one dairy portion is consumed with five portions each of cereals, fruit and vegetables and meat and alternatives.

As shown in the Appendix, with 500 mL of breast or formula milk per day for boys (for two or more cereals and fruit and vegetables), all food group combinations were within the suggested fat range:

- all two to four portion food group combinations were within the 6- and 7-month range, except for four cereals, fruit and vegetables and meat and alternatives with two dairy products and alternatives (too high) and three cereals, fruit and vegetables, two meat and alternatives and one dairy products and alternatives (too low);
- all three to five portion food group combinations were within the 8- to 10-month range, except for three, four or five cereals and fruit and vegetables, two meat and alternatives and one dairy products and alternatives (too low);
- all four to five portion food group combinations were within the 11- to 12-month range, except for four or five cereals and fruit and vegetables, two meat and alternatives and one dairy products and alternatives (too low).

For boys with 500 mL of breast or formula milk plus three to five portions of cereals and fruit and vegetables: three portions of meat and alternatives and one portion of dairy products and alternatives are required, or two portions of meat and alternatives and two portions of dairy products and alternatives, to meet the age-specific suggested fat intake ranges (>35% of energy from fat to 45% of energy from fat).

As shown in the Appendix, with 600 mL of breast or formula milk per day for girls and one, two or three portions of cereals and fruit and vegetables, fat intake was within the suggested range. However:

- with four or five portions of cereals and fruit and vegetables, only one dairy portion could be consumed for food group combinations to be within the suggested fat intake range, except for five portions of meat and alternatives with one portion of dairy products, which was still slightly too high.

With 500 mL of breast or formula milk per day for girls with two or more portions of cereals and fruit and vegetables, all food group combinations were
within the suggested fat intake range:

- all food group combinations with two or three portions of cereals and
  fruit and vegetables were in the 7- to 8-month suggested fat intake range
- all food group combinations with four portions of cereals and fruit and
  vegetables were in the 9- to 10-month suggested fat intake range
- all five cereals and fruit and vegetables food group combinations were in
  the 11- to 12-month suggested fat intake range.

> With 500 mL of breast or formula milk per day for boys and girls, all suggested
> food group combinations (with two or more portions of cereal and fruit and
> vegetables) are within the suggested fat ranges (>35% of energy from fat to
> 45% of energy from fat).

Verifying food group suggestions: fibre

As shown in the Appendix, with the same number of portions of cereals
and fruit and vegetables being consumed, and with zero to three portions of
cereals being wholegrain, the 8-month fibre suggestion based on intakes in
13-month-old Finnish infants[28] is not met until four portions of cereals per day
for girls (three portions being wholegrain), and five portions per day for boys
(two being wholegrain). These findings indicate that to meet the suggested fibre
intake from 6 months of age, zero to three wholegrain cereals can be included,
intake increasing as intake of cereals and of fruit and vegetables increases from
one to five portions a day.

> To meet the suggested fibre intake from 6 months of age, zero to three who-
> legrain cereals can be included, intake increasing as intake of cereals and of
> fruit and vegetables increases from one to five portions a day.

The 9-month fibre suggestion for girls (4.8 g per day) is attained at four portions
of cereals (three being wholegrain) and four portions of fruit and vegetables,
and for boys at five portions of cereals (two being wholegrain) and five portions of fruit and vegetables per day.

Based on suggested fibre intakes at 12 months (5.8 g a day for boys and 5.3 g
for girls; see Chapter 4), maximum intake of fibre is reached for boys and girls
at five portions of cereals, two being wholegrain, with five portions of fruit and

vegetables per day. Additional fibre intake will be provided by specific meat alternatives, namely peas, beans, lentils, avocado and hummus.

> The 12-month fibre suggestion is reached for boys and girls at five portions of cereals and fruit and vegetables per day. Two to three portions of cereals need to be wholegrain to meet the fibre suggestions.

Verifying food group suggestions: energy, fat and fibre

Good food-based dietary guidelines should enable the provision of adequate nutrient-to-energy density of the diet, not just provide adequate nutrients.[29] For example, the required amount of fibre and fat should be provided within appropriate energy limits. Examining the previous sections on energy, fat and fibre (with suggested fibre recommendations from eight months) shows that food group combinations to meet energy requirements are similar to those required to meet suggested fat and fibre requirements.

> Food group combinations to meet energy requirements are similar to those required to meet suggested fat and fibre requirements.

For boys:
- five portions of cereals and fruit and vegetables will meet energy requirements at 9–12 months
- four to five portions of cereals and fruit and vegetables will meet fat requirements at 9–12 months
- five portions of cereals and fruit and vegetables will meet fibre requirements at 8–12 months.

For girls:
- three to five portions of cereals and fruit and vegetables will meet energy requirements at 9–11 months
- four to five portions of cereals and fruit and vegetables will meet fat requirements at 9–11 months
- four portions of cereals and fruit and vegetables will meet fibre requirements at 8–12 months.

These findings infer that the suggested food group combinations may result in the adequate provision of energy as well as fat and fibre.

Verifying food group suggestions: iron

As shown in the Appendix, with the same number of portions of cereals being consumed as portions of fruit and vegetables, at one to two portions of cereals, with no wholegrain or iron-fortified cereals (since wholegrain cereals are not recommended until 6 months of age), 28%–42% of the 4- to 6-month RNI for iron is met with 600 mL of breast milk per day, and 100% of the RNI with 600 mL of infant formula. Consumption of one to two portions of iron-fortified breakfast cereals (such as Hipp Creamy porridge, which contains dried infant formula) would increase iron intake by 33%–53% among breastfed infants, so that 61%–95% of the RNI for iron is met at 4–6 months, and by 10%–18% among formula-fed infants compared with consuming no fortified cereals.

> Consumption of one to two portions of iron-fortified breakfast cereals by breastfed infants would enable 61%–95%, respectively, of the RNI for iron at 4–6 months to be met, a respective 33%–53% higher iron intake than when iron-fortified cereals are not consumed.

When three, four or five portions of cereals are eaten per day, including some wholegrain or iron-fortified breakfast cereals and bread, up to 33%, 47% and 58%, respectively, of the 7- to 12-month RNI is achieved with 500 mL of breast milk, and up to 65%, 79% and 90%, respectively, of the RNI with 500 mL per day of infant formula.

> When three, four or five portions of cereals are eaten per day, including some wholegrain or iron-fortified breakfast cereals and bread, up to 33%, 47% and 58%, respectively, of the 7- to 12-month RNI is achieved with 500 mL of breast milk, and up to 65%, 79% and 90%, respectively, of the RNI with 500 mL per day of infant formula.

With breast milk or infant formula, when all wholegrain or iron-fortified breakfast cereals and bread are eaten, iron intake is approximately 10% closer to the RNI than when only some wholegrain or iron-fortified cereals are eaten, and approximately 20% closer to the RNI than when no wholegrain or iron-fortified cereals are eaten (15% with three cereals per day and 26% with five cereals per day).

> Iron intake is approximately 20% closer to the RNI when all wholegrain or fortified breakfast cereals and bread are eaten than when no wholegrain or fortified cereals are eaten.

With 600 mL per day of breast milk, together with one to two portions from each of the four food groups, median daily iron intakes are well below the 4- to 6-month Lower Recommended Nutrient Intake (LRNI). At three portions of cereals and fruit and vegetables per day and 500 mL of breast milk, median iron intake is below the 7- to 12-month LRNI. Similarly, with four portions of cereals per day, some being wholegrain or fortified, median iron intake is below the LRNI. However, with 500 mL of breast milk, when four portions of cereals per day are eaten, all breakfast cereals and bread being wholegrain or fortified, plus three portions of meat, the median iron intake is above the LRNI. Further, with 500 mL of breast milk, when five portions of cereals are consumed per day, including some wholegrain or fortified or all wholegrain or fortified breakfast cereals and bread, median iron intake is above the LRNI.

> With 500 mL of breast milk, iron intake is above the LRNI only when four portions of cereals per day are eaten (all breakfast cereals and bread being wholegrain or fortified) plus three portions of meat, or when five portions of cereals are consumed per day, including some wholegrain or iron-fortified bread or breakfast cereals.

In comparison, with 500 mL of infant formula per day, median iron intake is above the LRNI at three to five portions of cereals and fruit and vegetables per day and two or more portions of meat and alternatives. When three to five portions of wholegrain or fortified breakfast cereals and breads are eaten, plus three portions of meat and alternatives per day, median iron intake is above the EAR; similarly, when five portions of cereals are eaten per day, including some wholegrain or fortified, median iron intake is above the EAR for iron.

Iron intake could be increased further (by a maximum of 1.5 g a day) if high iron containing meat and alternatives were eaten, such as beef, tinned sardines or pilchards, lentils or ground cashews or sunflower seeds, rather than lower iron containing meat and alternatives, such as chicken, turkey, salmon and pork. Higher fortification of infant foods or fortification of a wider range of foods, would also lead to higher iron intakes if these foods were consumed frequently.

The calculated median daily iron intake for formula-fed infants using the suggested food group combinations (three or more cereals) is higher than the median daily iron intake of 5.8 mg among UK infants aged 9–12 months,[16] the majority of whom were formula fed; this implies that the suggested food group combinations would lead to improved iron intake for infants.

It appears that the suggested food group combinations would lead to improved iron intake for infants compared with previous food group intakes.[16]

Calculated iron intakes, based on the suggested food group combinations and portion sizes, compare well with those generated by linear programming for complementary feeding in a developed country,[30] where 51% of the World Health Organization (WHO) RNI for iron was met by the optimal diet, 12% in the worst-case scenario and 65% in the best-case scenario with 616 mL of breast milk. With the current suggested food group combinations and portion sizes and 600 mL of breast milk, with one to two portions of iron-fortified breakfast cereals, 95% of the UK RNI was met (the best-case scenario), and 28% in the worst-case scenario (one to two portions of non-fortified cereals).

Iron intakes based on suggested food group combinations and portion sizes compare well with iron intakes generated by linear programming.[30]

Verifying food group suggestions: zinc

As shown in the Appendix, all food group combinations led to zinc intakes above the LRNI with breast milk (600 mL of breast milk at one or two portions of cereals per day, and 500 mL at three to five portions of cereals per day). At one or two portions of cereals per day with 600 mL of breast milk, and at three portions of cereals per day with 500 mL of breast milk, zinc intakes were below the EAR for zinc. Zinc intakes above the RNI were only achieved with 500 mL of breast milk when five portions of cereals, fruit and vegetables and meat or alternatives were consumed with one or two portions of dairy products, or when five portions of cereals and fruit and vegetables were consumed with four portions of meat and alternatives and two portions of dairy products.

With 500 mL of breast milk, some breastfed infants may not obtain the recommended amount of zinc until they are consuming five portions a day of cereals and fruit and vegetables and four to five portions of meat and alternatives.

With 600 mL of breast milk per day, 68% of the RNI for zinc is achieved with one portion of food from each food group and 75%–90% of the RNI for zinc is achieved with two portions of cereals and fruit and vegetables and one to two portions of meat and alternatives and dairy products and alternatives.

With 500 mL of breast milk per day three, four or five portions of cereals and fruit and vegetables, 68%–80% of the RNI, 74%–94% of the RNI, and 80%–108% of the RNI, respectively, is achieved.

The percentages of RNI achievement for zinc with the suggested food group combinations and breast milk compare well with linear programming models for complementary feeding in a developing country,[30] which produced an optimal model meeting 65% of the WHO RNI for zinc, while best and worst case models led to 83% and 36% of the WHO RNI for zinc.

> At least 68% of the RNI for zinc is achieved with three, four or five portions of cereals and fruit and vegetables and 500 or 600 mL of breast milk per day.

Zinc intake is above the RNI with 600 mL of infant formula a day and one or two portions of cereals and fruit and vegetables, and also with 500 mL of infant formula a day and all three to five portion food group combinations.

> With 500 and 600 mL of infant formula a day, zinc intake is above the RNI for all suggested food group combinations.

With 500 mL of infant formula and three to five portion food group combinations, median zinc intakes range between 4.9 and 6.9 mg per day; this is greater than the median zinc intake in a UK study of 6- to 12-month-old infants,[16] where the median zinc intake was 4.4 mg per day, infants receiving mainly infant formula and whole cow's milk.

> 500 mL of infant formula and three to five portion food group combinations lead to a greater median zinc intake than in the UK study of 6- to 12-month-old infants.[16]

Verifying food group suggestions: vitamin A, vitamin D, calcium and iodine

Verification of the suggested food group combinations could be undertaken based on vitamin A and vitamin D, calcium and iodine; however, these verifications are not included.

SUMMARY OF FOOD GROUP COMBINATION INFORMATION

Simplification of this information on meeting nutritional requirements with the different food group combinations is required to formulate comprehensible food based dietary guidelines for the public, although simplification can reduce the accuracy of information. A simplified summary of the suggested food group–based guidelines is given in Table 5.3.

TABLE 5.3 Suggested daily food group-based guidelines to meet nutritional requirements[*]

Nutritional requirement	Food group			
	Cereals	Fruit and vegetables	Meat and alternatives	Dairy products and alternatives
Fat			2+[a]	1–2 (3[b])
Saturated fat			Lean meat	Maximum 1 cheese or butter
Omega-6[**]			1 meat alternative[c]	1[d]
Long chain Omega-3			¾ fish a week at ⁶/₁₂ months	
Fibre	4 (3–5,[e] 2–3 wholegrain)	3–5		
Iron	3[f]	3[f]	3[f]	
	5[g]	5[g]	5[g]	
Zinc[h]	5	5	4	1
	4	4	4	2
Calcium	2–4[i]	0–1	0–1	1–2
Iodine			1–2 (fish/egg)[j]	1–2[j]
Vitamin D[k]	2 (fortified infant cereal)		1[l]	
Vitamin A[m]	1–2 infant cereals		1 liver per month, 1–2 carrots per week	1–2

Notes: *With 500 mL of breast milk, portion sizes 20 g for most foods (10 g for cheese, dry breakfast cereal, nuts, beans, peas and lentils, 5 g for butter, margarine and oil); **500 mL of breast milk will meet the omega-3 suggestion; [a]including zero or one higher fat meat alternative (nuts, oil, butter, margarine, two portions of egg); [b]three if one milk and two yoghurt only; [c]eggs, hummus, tinned sardines or tuna in oil; [d]sunflower or rapeseed oil; [e]maximum of two wholegrain cereals for girls with five portions of cereals; [f]with 500 mL infant follow-on formula; [g]with breast milk still difficult to meet RNI; [h]500 mL of infant formula meets half zinc RNI; [i]bread or fortified breakfast cereal; [j]two meat alternatives and one dairy product on some days or one meat alternative and two dairy products on some days; [k]with 500 mL of infant formula, amount of vitamin D from breast milk dependent on level of maternal vitamin D supplementation; [l]oily fish, rapeseed oil, sunflower oil or two portions of egg gives half vitamin D RNI; [m]with 500 mL of breast milk or infant formula, amount from breast milk dependent upon maternal vitamin A intake and status.

From Table 5.3 we can surmise that with 600 mL of breast or formula milk initially (with one to two meals or one or two servings of cereals and fruit and vegetables a day) and later 500 mL of breast or formula milk, the optimal food based dietary guidelines to meet nutritional requirements appear to be three to five portions of cereals (two to three wholegrain) and fruit and vegetables, two to five portions of meat and alternatives, and one to two portions of dairy products and alternatives.

> With 500 mL of breast or formula milk per day, the optimal food based dietary guidelines to meet nutritional requirements appear to be three to five portions of cereals and fruit and vegetables, two to five portions of meat and alternatives, and one to two portions of dairy products.

That is:

- three to five portions of cereals and of fruit and vegetables, dependent upon the fibre content of a portion – to meet iron, zinc and suggested fibre requirements
- two to five portions of meat and alternatives – one portion of meat and alternatives a day to meet suggested omega-6, long-chain omega-3 and fibre requirements and iodine and vitamin D requirements, plus one to four additional meat and alternatives to meet iron and zinc requirements and suggested fat requirements
- one to two portions of dairy products and alternatives – one portion to meet suggested omega-6 requirements, and two portions to meet zinc and suggested fat requirements.

In addition, the following constraints are required:

- two to three portions of cereals a day being wholegrain to meet suggested fibre recommendations
- two to four portions of cereals a day being bread or fortified breakfast cereals to meet calcium recommendations
- four portions of meat and alternatives a week being fish (two portions of oily fish and two portions of white fish per week) to meet the long-chain polyunsaturated fatty acids suggestion
- one meat alternative per day being egg, hummus, or tinned sardines or tuna in oil to meet the suggested omega-6 requirements (not achievable every day)

- one dairy alternative per day being sunflower or rapeseed oil to meet the suggested omega-6 requirements (not achievable every day).

PROGRESSION OF COMPLEMENTARY FEEDING BY FOOD GROUP COMBINATION

It is suggested that complementary feeding based on these food group combinations could progress as follows.

- With 600 mL of breast or formula milk:
  - ➤ increase to one portion from each food group initially
  - ➤ increase to two portions from each food group, except for dairy products (one or two portions).
- With 500 mL of breast or formula milk and the number of portions of dairy products staying at one to two portions:
  - ➤ increase to three portions of cereals and fruit and vegetables and two to three portions of meat and alternatives
  - ➤ increase to four portions of cereals and fruit and vegetables, two to four portions of meat and alternatives
  - ➤ increase to five portions of cereals and fruit and vegetables, two to five portions of meat and alternatives.

That is, one portion a day can be offered from each food group at the start of complementary feeding (the order is unimportant), then two portions from each food group except for dairy products and alternatives (where one to two portions are offered). As complementary feeding progresses, one to two portions of dairy products and alternatives a day can be maintained, plus three, four and then five portions of cereals and fruit and vegetables a day, with corresponding two to three, two to four and two to five portions of meat and alternatives, respectively.

This simplified increase in intake of foods by food group is shown in Table 5.4. To assist comprehension, the suggested balance between food groups is given per day. However, the balance does not need to be achieved on a daily basis, and could be achieved over a longer period – for example, a week.

TABLE 5.4 Increase in intake of food by food group*

Food groups	Cereals[a]	Fruit and vegetables[b]	Meat and alternatives[c]	Dairy products and alternatives[d]
Comparative number of portions a day[e]	1	1	1	1
	2	2	2	1–2
	3	3	2–3	1–2
	4	4	2–4	1–2
	5	5	2–5	1–2

Notes: * With 600 mL of breast or formula milk at 1,1,1,1 and 2,2,2,1-2 food group combinations and 500 mL for other food group combinations; [a]includes bread, rice, potatoes, pasta and other starchy foods (the eatwell plate); [b]excluding potatoes, avocado, beans and peas; [c]includes fish, eggs, beans and other non-dairy sources of protein (*The Eatwell Plate*[1]), plus peas,[4] avocado, nuts, peanut butter, hummus and tofu; [d]includes cheese, yoghurt, custard,[4] plus butter, margarine and oils; [e]a portion is typically 1 tablespoon (20 g) of most foods, half a small boiled egg (22 g), 10 g of dry breakfast cereals, cheese, ground nuts and peanut butter, 5 g of butter, margarine and oils, 50 mL of whole milk.

Note that the portion size is:
- 20 g (1 tablespoon) of most foods, such as pasta, rice, potatoes, meat, fish, fruit and vegetables and yoghurt
- 10 g (1 tablespoon) of dry breakfast cereals and cheese
- 10 g (½ a tablespoon) of ground nuts, peanut butter, beans, peas and lentils
- 5 g (½ a teaspoon) of butter, margarine and oils
- 50 mL of whole cow's milk
- half a small hard-boiled egg (22 g), half a slice of bread or pitta bread, half a Weetabix or Wheaty Biscuit, half an apple, orange or banana.

Note that the foods in each food group are:
- Cereals – including bread, rice, potatoes, pasta, rice cakes, infant cereals and breakfast cereals
- Fruit and vegetables – excluding potatoes, avocado, peas and beans
- Meat and alternatives – including beef, lamb, pork, fish (oily and white, tinned and fresh), egg, ground nuts, peanut butter, hummus, tofu, avocado, peas, beans and lentils
- Dairy products and alternatives – including cheese, yoghurt, cow's milk, butter, margarine, and oils such as sunflower and rapeseed oils.

PICTORIAL REPRESENTATION OF INFANT FOOD GROUPS

A pictorial representation of the proportion of foods that an infant needs from different food groups in order to meet their nutritional requirements could help parents to provide a healthy diet for infants, the infant being free to choose what he eats. There is no pictorial representation of a healthy balanced diet to meet nutritional requirements for infants in the United Kingdom, or elsewhere, owing to a lack of formulated dietary recommendations for infants.

Pictorial representation of food intake for adults and children: frequency and portion size

The UK 'eatwell plate',[1] described at the beginning of this chapter, only gives frequency of intake for fruit and vegetables (to eat at least five portions of a variety a day) and for fish (eat two portions a week, one of which should be oily), while portion sizes are also only defined for these foods (*see* Figure 5.1). In some countries, such as Australia, the number of servings of food from different food groups required to meet adult recommendations is given and their development clearly described in the literature.[30]

FIGURE 5.1 The eatwell plate (Department of Health in association with the Welsh Government, the Scottish Government and the Food Standards Agency in Northern Ireland) © Crown copyright

The US 'MyPlate',[31] which pictorially describes daily intake from food groups for children from 2 years of age in the form of a plate and circle, includes no frequency of intake of foods or portion sizes (*see* Figure 5.2).

FIGURE 5.2 MyPlate (US Department of Agriculture)

As shown in Figure 5.2, the plate is divided into four sections, two sections (fruits and protein) being marginally smaller than the other two (vegetables and grains), and includes a smaller circle for dairy. Similarly, Ireland gives pictorial food guidelines in the form of a pyramid for young children, while few other countries give guidance on proportional intake of food from food groups for young children.[32]

Infant guidelines on the frequency of intake of food from different food groups

The United Kingdom, unlike most countries, has guidelines for the frequency of intake of food from different food groups for infants.[4] However, these guidelines were formulated from 'pragmatic decisions', based on the available research at the time. Additional research is now available, as described in Chapter 3, which could be used to update these guidelines. Further research would improve the validity of future guidelines.

Updating guidelines on food group frequencies

Updating of food based dietary guidelines for infants in the United Kingdom should be based on diet and health-related concerns (e.g. iron intake and iron deficiency anaemia), critical nutrients (e.g. iron, zinc and iodine), and food consumption patterns (e.g. intake of meat and milk),[32] which are described in Chapter 3. A computer-generated diet could then be produced, for example, using linear programming[26] to meet infant guidelines, which could be represented pictorially[32]; guidelines could be included on the number of portions of food to be consumed from each food group, and on the portion size.

Suggested pictorial representation of proportional intake from food groups for infants

As the plate model[1] is used in the United Kingdom to represent the balance of different food groups that make up a healthy diet for adults, a circle or plate may be a good starting point in developing a representation of proportional intake from food groups for infants, although parents might confuse the two representations because of their similarity. A plate may not illustrate food and milk intake as simply as a circle (with different sections for food and milk), since breast or formula milk intake would have to be shown by a breast or bottle of formula in addition to a plate, similar to the US MyPlate.[31] A picture of an infant could be included, which may also reduce confusion between the pictorial representation of an adult's intake and an infant's intake.

Pictorial representations of the proportional intake of food from food groups could show how proportional intake may change from 6–12 months, as the infant's energy intake increased. However, only one pictorial representation of food intake is suggested, at around 9 months of age, to simplify the message for the public (pictorially, there is negligible difference between the different food group proportions from around 9 months).

This suggested pictorial representation of the balance between food groups for infants aged 9–12 months is shown in Figure 5.3. This representation, with additional information on suggested food group combinations and portion size has been used with a small convenience sample of 25 mothers with infants aged 5–9 months, who reported finding the information easy to understand and useful in practice, although no alternative representation was made available (unpublished data). Much research is needed to determine whether a representation of food groups for infants is necessary, and, if so, to find the most suitable representation.

It is important to note that the calculations of the nutrient content of the diet based on the suggested food group combinations are based on *estimates* of the nutritional content of food groups; a computerised analysis may give more accurate guidance on the number of portions and portion sizes.

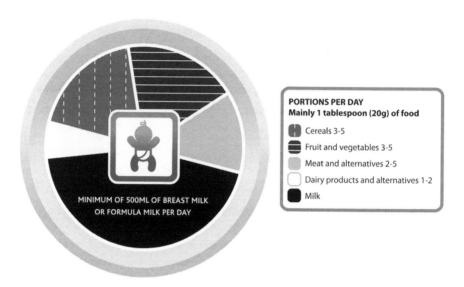

PORTIONS PER DAY
Mainly 1 tablespoon (20g) of food

Cereals 3-5

Fruit and vegetables 3-5

Meat and alternatives 2-5

Dairy products and alternatives 1-2

Milk

MINIMUM OF 500ML OF BREAST MILK
OR FORMULA MILK PER DAY

FIGURE 5.3 The Balanced Infant Guide to the number of daily portions from four food groups at 7–12 months of age (Tuck, 2012) ©Tuck and Davies, 2012

Revision of government recommendations for fat, fibre and additional nutrients for infants will lead to the production of authoritative food based dietary guidelines for infants. In the interim, it appears that the suggested number of portions and portion sizes may be appropriate and should be helpful to both health professionals and the public.

Revision of government recommendations for fat, fibre and additional nutrients for infants will lead to the production of authoritative food based dietary guidelines for infants. In the interim, it appears that the suggested number of portions and portion sizes may be appropriate and should be helpful to both health professionals and the public.

REFERENCES

1. Department of Health; Welsh Government; Scottish Government; Food Standards Agency in Northern Ireland. *The Eatwell Plate*. London: Department of Health; 2011. Available at: www.dh.gov.uk/en/Publicationsandstatistics/Publications/PublicationsPolicyAndGuidance/DH_126472 (accessed 16 March 2012).

2. Agostoni C, Decsi T, Fewtrell M, *et al.*; for ESPGHAN Committee on Nutrition. Complementary feeding: a commentary by the ESPGHAN Committee on Nutrition. *J Pediatr Gastroenterol Nutr*. 2008; **46**(1): 99–110.

3. Uauy R, Dangour AD. Fat and fatty acid requirements and recommendations for infants of 0–2 years and children of 2–18 years. *Ann Nutr Metab*. 2009; **55**(1–3): 76–96.

4. Department of Health. *Weaning and the Weaning Diet. Report of the Working Group on the Weaning Diet of the Committee on Medical Aspects of Food Policy*. Report on Health and Social Subjects, 45. London: The Stationery Office; 1994.

5. Department of Health. *Dietary Reference Values for Energy and Nutrients for the UK. Report of the Committee on Medical Aspects of Food Policy*. Report on Health and Social Subjects, 41. London: HMSO; 1991.

6. National Health Service (NHS). *Birth to Five*. London: NHS; 2011. Available at: http://webarchive.nationalarchives.gov.uk/+/www.dh.gov.uk/prod_consum_dh/groups/dh_digitalassets/@dh/@en/@ps/@sta/@perf/documents/digitalasset/dh_117167.pdf (accessed 28 May 2011).

7. National Health Service; Unicef; Department of Health. *Introducing Solid Foods*. London: Department of Health; 2011. Available at: www.dh.gov.uk/prod_consum_dh/groups/dh_digitalassets/documents/digitalasset/dh_125828.pdf (accessed 8 March 2012).

8. NHS Wales; Welsh Government. *Introducing Solid Foods: giving your baby a better start in life*. Cardiff: NHS Wales; 2011. Available at: www.wales.gov.uk/docs/healthchallenge/publications/110920solidsen.pdf (accessed 28 May 2012).

9. NHS Health Scotland; Scottish Government. *Fun First Foods: an easy guide to introducing solid foods*. Edinburgh: NHS Health Scotland; 2011. Available at: www.child-smile.org.uk/documents/303.aspx (accessed 21 May 2012).

10. Public Health Agency. *Weaning Made Easy: moving from milk to family meals*; 2012. Available at: www.publichealth.hscni.net/publications/weaning-made-easy-moving-milk-family-meals (accessed 12 June 2012).

11. Food Standards Agency (FSA). *Your Baby*. London: FSA; 2010 Available at: www.food.gov.uk/multimedia/pdfs/publication/yourbaby0210.pdf (accessed 19 April 2011). (accessed 19 April 2011).

12. Lawson M. Practical advice on food and nutrition for the mother, infant and child. In: Morgan JB, Dickerson JWT, editors. *Nutrition in Early Life*. Chichester: Wiley; 2003. pp. 325–63.

13. British Dietetic Association Paediatric Group. *Weaning Infants onto Solid Foods*. Birmingham: British Dietetic Association; 2009. Available at: www.bda.uk.com/publications (accessed 5 March 2011).

14. Brenna JT, Varamini B, Jensen RG, *et al.* Docosahexaenoic and arachidonic acid concentrations in human breast milk worldwide. *Am J Clin Nutr*. 2007; **85**(6): 1457–64.

15. Food Standards Agency. *McCance and Widdowson's The Composition of Foods*. 6th summary ed. Cambridge: Royal Society of Chemistry; 2002.

16. Mills A, Tyler HA. *Food and Nutrient Intakes of British Infants Aged 6–12 Months*. London: HMSO; 1992.

17. Pot GK, Prynne CJ, Roberts C, *et al*. National Diet and Nutrition Survey: fat and fatty acid intake from the first year of the rolling programme and comparison with previous surveys. *Br J Nutr*. 2012; **107**(3): 405–15. Epub 2011 Jul 18.

18. Wrieden WL, Longbottom PJ, Adamson AJ, *et al*. Estimation of typical food portion sizes for children of different ages in Great Britain. *Br J Nutr*. 2008; **99**(6): 1344–53.

19. Gregory JR, Collins DL, Davies PSW, *et al*. *National Diet and Nutrition Survey: children aged 1.5 to 4.5 years. Volume 1: Report of the Diet and Nutrition Survey*. London: HMSO; 1995.

20. More J. Evidence-based portion sizes for toddlers (aged 1–3 years). *Nutr Bull*. 2012; **37**(1): 64–6.

21. Golding J, Pembrey M, Jones R; for ALSPAC Study Team. ALSPAC: the Avon longitudinal study of parents and children. *Paediatr Perinat Epidemiol*. 2001; **15**(1): 74–87.

22. Ramsay SA, Branen LJ, Johnson SL. How much is enough? Tablespoon per year of age approach meets nutrient needs for children. *Appetite*. 2012; **58**(1): 163–7.

23. The Caroline Walker Trust. *Eating Well: first year of life; practical guide*. Abbots Langley: The Caroline Walker Trust; 2011. Available at: www.firststepsnutrition.org/pdfs/First year of Life Practical Guide.pdf (accessed 2 June 2012).

24. Scientific Advisory Committee on Nutrition. *Dietary Reference Values for Energy 2011*. London: The Stationery Office; 2012. Available at:www.sacn.gov.uk/pdfs/sacn_dietary_reference_values_for_energy.pdf (accessed 10 June 2012).

25. Ferguson EL, Darmon N, Briend A, *et al*. Food-based dietary guidelines can be developed and tested using linear programming analysis. *J Nutr*. 2004; **134**(4): 951–7.

26. Ferguson EL, Darmon N, Fahmida U, *et al*. Design of optimal food-based complementary feeding recommendations and identification of key 'problem nutrients' using goal programming. *J Nutr*. 2006; **136**(9): 2399–404.

27. Maillot M, Vieux F, Amiot MJ, *et al*. Individual diet modelling translates nutrient recommendations into realistic and individual-specific food choices. *Am J Clin Nutr*. 2010; **91**(2): 421–30.

28. Ruottinen S, Lagström HK, Niinikoski H, *et al*. Dietary fiber does not displace energy but is associated with decreased serum cholesterol concentrations in healthy children. *Am J Clin Nutr*. 2010; **91**(3): 651–61.

29. Smitasiri S, Uauy R. Beyond recommendations: implementing food-based dietary guidelines for healthier populations. *Food Nutr Bull*. 2007; **28**(1 Suppl. International): S141–51.

30. Australian Government National Health and Medical Research Council. *Infant Feeding Guidelines for Health Workers. Draft for public consultation*. Canberra, Australia: National Health and Medical Research Council; 2011. Available at: www.nhmrc.gov.au/guidelines/publications/n20 (accessed 3 April 2012).

31. US Department of Agriculture. *MyPlate*; 2011. Available at: www.choosemyplate.gov (accessed 2 November 2011).

32. www.eufic.org

Appendix

TABLES

Chapter 4: Average daily Estimated Average Requirements (EARs) for energy for breastfed infants aged 6–12 months

Age (months)	Boys			Girls		
	Weight (kg)	EAR per kg	Average daily EAR	Weight (kg)	EAR per kg	Average daily EAR
6	7.9	79	624.1	7.3	79	576.7
7	8.3	78	647.4	7.6	77	585.2
8	8.6	78	670.8	8.0	77	616.0
9	8.9	78	694.2	8.2	77	631.4
10	9.2	78	717.6	8.5	77	654.5
11	9.4	78	733.2	8.7	77	670.0
12	9.7	78	756.6	9.0	77	693.0

Chapter 4: Average grams-of-fat-per-day requirements for breastfed infants based on suggested fat intake of >35% energy from fat and reasonable upper limit of 45% energy from fat

(i) Boys

Age (months)	>35% energy from fat (0.35 × daily EAR)/9.0*		45% energy from fat (0.45 × daily EAR)/9.0*	
6	(0.35 × 624.1)/9.0	>24.3	(0.45 × 624.1)/9.0	=31.2
7	(0.35 × 647.4)/9.0	>25.2	(0.45 × 647.4)/9.0	=32.4
8	(0.35 × 670.8)/9.0	>26.1	(0.45 × 670.8)/9.0	=33.5
9	(0.35 × 694.2)/9.0	>27.0	(0.45 × 694.2)/9.0	=34.7
10	(0.35 × 717.6)/9.0	>27.9	(0.45 × 717.6)/9.0	=35.9
11	(0.35 × 733.2)/9.0	>28.5	(0.45 × 733.2)/9.0	=36.7
12	(0.35 × 756.6)/9.0	>29.4	(0.45 × 756.6)/9.0	=37.8

(ii) Girls

Age (months)	>35% energy from fat (0.35 × daily EAR)/9.0*		45% energy from fat (0.45 × daily EAR)/9.0*	
6	(0.35 × 576.7)/9.0	>22.4	(0.45 × 576.7)/9.0	=28.8
7	(0.35 × 585.2)/9.0	>22.8	(0.45 × 585.2)/9.0	=29.3
8	(0.35 × 616.0)/9.0	>24.0	(0.45 × 616.0)/9.0	=30.8
9	(0.35 × 631.4)/9.0	>24.6	(0.45 × 631.4)/9.0	=31.6
10	(0.35 × 654.5)/9.0	>25.5	(0.45 × 654.5)/9.0	=32.7
11	(0.35 × 670.0)/9.0	>26.1	(0.45 × 670.0)/9.0	=33.5
12	(0.35 × 693.0)/9.0	>27.0	(0.45 × 693.0)/9.0	=34.7

Note: *9.0 = energy content (kilocalories) of 1 g of fat.

Chapter 4: Average daily kilocalories and grams per day of omega-3 and omega-6 polyunsaturated fats for breastfed infants aged 6–12 months[*]

(i) Boys

Age (months)	Weight (kg)	Omega-6 (kcal/day) @1%	Omega-6 (g/day) @1%[a]	Omega-6 (g/day) @3%	Omega-3 (g/day) @0.2%[b]	Omega-3 (g/day) @0.5%[c]
6	7.9	6.2	0.7	2.1	0.1	0.4
7	8.3	6.5	0.7	2.1	0.1	0.4
8	8.6	6.7	0.8	2.4	0.2	0.4
9	8.9	6.9	0.8	2.4	0.2	0.4
10	9.2	7.2	0.8	2.4	0.2	0.4
11	9.4	7.3	0.8	2.4	0.2	0.4
12	9.7	7.6	0.9	2.7	0.2	0.5

Notes: *EAR for energy is 79 for 6-month-old infants, 78 for 7- to 12-month-old boys and 77 for 7- to 12-month-old girls; [a]kilocalories/9; [b](1% omega-6) g × 0.2; [c](1% omega-6) g × 0.5.

(ii) Girls

Age (months)	Weight (kg)	Omega-6 (kcal/day) @1%	Omega-6 (g/day) @1%[a]	Omega-6 (g/day) @3%	Omega-3 (g/day) @0.2%[b]	Omega-3 (g/day) @0.5%[c]
6	7.9	5.8	0.6	1.8	0.1	0.3
7	8.3	5.9	0.7	2.1	0.1	0.4
8	8.6	6.2	0.7	2.1	0.1	0.4
9	8.9	6.3	0.7	2.1	0.1	0.4
10	9.2	6.5	0.8	2.4	0.1	0.4
11	9.4	6.7	0.8	2.4	0.1	0.4
12	9.7	6.9	0.8	2.4	0.2	0.4

Notes: [a]Kilocalories/9; [b](1% omega-6) g × 0.2; [c](1% omega-6) g × 0.5.

Chapter 5: Energy – food group combinations based on Table 5.2

Food group number of portions (energy)[a]				
Cereals	Fruit and vegetables	Meat and alternatives	Dairy and alternatives	Total energy (+600 mL/500 mL milk)*
1 (28)	1 (12)	1 (31)	1 (40)	111+414/345=525/456
2 (56)	2 (24)	1 (31)	1 (40)	151+414/345=565/496
2 (56)	2 (24)	2 (62)	1 (40)	182+414/345=596/527
2 (56)	2 (24)	2 (62)	2 (80)	222+414/345=636/567
3 (84)	3 (36)	2 (62)	1 (40)	222+414/345=636/567
3 (84)	3 (36)	2 (62)	2 (80)	262+414/345=676/607
3 (84)	3 (36)	3 (93)	1 (40)	253+414/345=667/598
3 (84)	3 (36)	3 (93)	2 (80)	293+414/345=707/638
4 (112)	4 (48)	2 (62)	1 (40)	262+414/345=676/607
4 (112)	4 (48)	2 (62)	2 (80)	302+414/345=716/647
4 (112)	4 (48)	3 (93)	1 (40)	293+414/345=707/638
4 (112)	4 (48)	3 (93)	2 (80)	333+414/345=747/678
4 (112)	4 (48)	4 (124)	1 (40)	324+414/345=738/669
4 (112)	4 (48)	4 (124)	2 (80)	364+414/345=778/709
5 (140)	5 (60)	2 (62)	1 (40)	302+414/345=716/647
5 (140)	5 (60)	2 (62)	2 (80)	342+414/345=756/687
5 (140)	5 (60)	3 (93)	1 (40)	333+414/345=747/678
5 (140)	5 (60)	3 (93)	2 (80)	373+414/345=787/718
5 (140)	5 (60)	4 (124)	1 (40)	364+414/345=778/709
5 (140)	5 (60)	4 (124)	2 (80)	404+414/345=818/749
5 (140)	5 (60)	5 (155)	1 (40)	395+414/345=809/740
5 (140)	5 (60)	5 (155)	2 (80)	435+414/345=849/780

Notes: *Energy value of 600 mL of breast milk is 414 kcal and that of 500 mL of breast milk is 345 kcal – likely to have 600 mL of breast or formula milk with one or two meals, 500 mL otherwise; [a]energy value is median energy value of food group – energy range: cereals, 17–73; fruit and vegetables, 5–19; meat and alternatives, 25–59; dairy and alternatives, 16–45.

Note that total energy based on one to two portions of cereals and of fruit and vegetables is shown to illustrate possible food combinations from the start of complementary feeding; 24 or 48 more combinations are possible if the number of portions of cereals and of fruit and vegetables are not identical, with the number of dairy portions being one or two, respectively. However, a simpler message to the public would be to consume the same number of cereals as fruit and vegetables, and hence these additional possible combinations are not shown.

Chapter 5: Fat – food group combinations based on Table 5.2

Food group number of portions (fat)[a]				
Cereals	Fruit and vegetables	Meat and alternatives	Dairy and alternatives	Total fat (+600 mL/500 mL milk)*
1 (0.3)	1 (0)	1 (1.5)	1 (2.5)	4.3+24.6/20.5=28.9/24.8
2 (0.6)	2 (0)	1 (1.5)	1 (2.5)	4.6+24.6/20.5=29.2/25.1
2 (0.6)	2 (0)	2 (3)	1 (2.5)	6.1+24.6/20.5=30.7/26.6
2 (0.6)	2 (0)	2 (3)	2 (5)	8.6+24.6/20.5=33.2/29.1
3 (0.9)	3 (0)	2 (3)	1 (2.5)	6.4+24.6/20.5=31/26.9
3 (0.9)	3 (0)	2 (3)	2 (5)	8.9+24.6/20.5=33.5/29.4
3 (0.9)	3 (0)	3 (4.5)	1 (2.5)	7.9+24.6/20.5=32.5/28.4
3 (0.9)	3 (0)	3 (4.5)	2 (5)	10.4+24.6/20.5=35/30.9
4 (1.2)	4 (0)	2 (3)	1 (2.5)	6.7+24.6/20.5=31.3/27.2
4 (1.2)	4 (0)	2 (3)	2 (5)	9.2+24.6/20.5=33.8/29.7
4 (1.2)	4 (0)	3 (4.5)	1 (2.5)	8.2+24.6/20.5=32.8/28.7
4 (1.2)	4 (0)	3 (4.5)	2 (5)	10.7+24.6/20.5=35.3/31.2
4 (1.2)	4 (0)	4 (6)	1 (2.5)	9.7+24.6/20.5=34.3/30.2
4 (1.2)	4 (0)	4 (6)	2 (5)	12.2+24.6/20.5=36.8/32.7
5 (1.5)	5 (0)	2 (3)	1 (2.5)	7+24.6/20.5=31.6/27.5
5 (1.5)	5 (0)	2 (3)	2 (5)	9.5+24.6/20.5=34.1/30
5 (1.5)	5 (0)	3 (4.5)	1 (2.5)	8.5+24.6/20.5=33.1/29
5 (1.5)	5 (0)	3 (4.5)	2 (5)	11+24.6/20.5=35.6/31.5
5 (1.5)	5 (0)	4 (6)	1 (2.5)	10+24.6/20.5=34.6/30.5
5 (1.5)	5 (0)	4 (6)	2 (5)	12.5+24.6/20.5=37.1/33
5 (1.5)	5 (0)	5 (7.5)	1 (2.5)	11.5+24.6/20.5=36.1/32
5 (1.5)	5 (0)	5 (7.5)	2 (5)	14+24.6/20.5=38.6/34.5

Notes: *Fat content of 600 mL of breast milk is 24.6 g and that of 500 mL of breast milk is 20.5 g – likely to have 600 mL of breast milk or formula milk with one or two meals, 500 mL otherwise; [a]fat value is median fat value of food group – fat range: cereals, 0.1-1.0; fruit and vegetables, 0; meat and alternatives, 0.1-5.4; dairy and alternatives, 0.6-5.0.

Chapter 5: Fibre – food group combinations based on Table 5.2

Food group number of portions (fat)[a]		
Cereals[b]	Fruit and vegetables	Total fibre[c]
1[d] (0.4)	1 (0.5)	0.9
1[e] (0.8)	1 (0.5)	1.3
2[d] (0.8)	2 (1)	1.8
2[e] (1.2)	2 (1)	2.2
2[f] (1.6)	2 (1)	2.6
3[d] (1.2)	3 (1.5)	2.7
3[e] (1.6)	3 (1.5)	3.1
3[f] (2)	3 (1.5)	3.5
3[g] (2.4)	3 (1.5)	3.9
4[d] (1.6)	4 (2)	3.6
4[e] (2)	4 (2)	4.0
4[f] (2.4)	4 (2)	4.4
4[g] (2.8)	4 (2)	4.8
4[h] (3.2)	4 (2)	5.2
5[d] (2.0)	5 (2.5)	4.5
5[e] (2.4)	5 (2.5)	4.9
5[f] (2.8)	5 (2.5)	5.3
5[g] (3.2)	5 (2.5)	5.7
5[h] (3.6)	5 (2.5)	6.1
5[i] (4.0)	5 (2.5)	6.5

Notes: [a]Fibre value is the median fibre value of the food group – fibre range: cereals, 0–1; fruit and vegetables, 0.1–0.9; meat and alternatives, 0–1; dairy and alternatives, 0; [b]while the median fibre value for cereals is 0.4, at three portions, two wholegrain cereals (0.8) are consumed, two to three wholegrains at four or five portions of cereals (up to five wholegrain shown); [c]fibre content of breast milk is zero; the fibre content of meat alternatives (nuts, beans, lentils, peas, avocado and hummus) is 0.6, and zero for other meat and alternatives (red meat, poultry, fish and eggs). Since these meat alternatives are not consumed on a daily basis, the fibre value for meat and alternatives is taken as zero, while additional fibre will be provided from these meat alternatives when consumed; [d–i]zero to five wholegrain cereals, respectively.

Chapter 5: Iron – food group combinations based on Table 5.2

Food group number of portions (iron)[a]				
Cereals	Fruit and vegetables	Meat[*] and alternatives	Milk (breast/ formula)[**]	Total iron (breast/ formula)
1 (0.2)[b]	1 (0.1)[c]	1 (0.3)	(0.6/3.6)	1.2/4.2
2 (0.4)[b]	2 (0.2)	1 (0.3)	(0.6/3.6)	1.5/4.4
2 (0.4)[b]	2 (0.2)	2 (0.6)	(0.6/3.6)	1.8/4.8
3 (1.2[d]/1.8[e])	3 (0.3)	2 (0.6)	(0.5/3)	2.6/5.1,[d] 3.2/5.7[e]
3 (1.2[d]/1.8[e])	3 (0.3)	3 (0.9)	(0.5/3)	2.9/5.4,[d] 3.5/6[e]
4 (1.6[d]/2.4[e])	4 (0.4)	2 (0.6)	(0.5/3)	3.1/5.6,[d] 3.9/6.4[e]
4 (1.6[d]/2.4[e])	4 (0.4)	3 (0.9)	(0.5/3)	3.4/5.9,[d] 4.2/6.7[e]
4 (1.6[d]/2.4[e])	4 (0.4)	4 (1.2)	(0.5/3)	3.7/6.2,[d] 4.5/7[e]
5 (2[d]/3[e])	5 (0.5)	2 (0.6)	(0.5/3)	3.6/6.1,[d] 4.6/7.1[e]
5 (2[d]/3[e])	5 (0.5)	3 (0.9)	(0.5/3)	3.9/6.4,[d] 4.9/7.4[e]
5 (2[d]/3[e])	5 (0.5)	4 (1.2)	(0.5/3)	4.2/6.7,[d] 5.2/7.7[e]
5 (2[d]/3[e])	5 (0.5)	5 (1.5)	(0.5/3)	4.5/7,[d] 5.5/8[e]

Notes: *Iron from meat is better absorbed than from other sources; **iron content of 600 mL of breast milk is 0.6 (3.6 for formula milk) and that of 500 mL of breast milk is 0.5 (3.0 for formula milk) – likely to have 600 mL of breast or formula milk with one or two meals, 500 mL otherwise, breast/ formula shown; [a]iron value is median iron value of food group – iron range: cereals, 0–1.2; fruit and vegetables, 0–0.3; meat and alternatives, 0–0.6; dairy and alternatives, 0 (median 0); [b]no wholegrain (0.2); [c]with or without apricots; [d]including wholegrain bread and wholegrain/fortified breakfast cereal (0.4); [e]all wholegrain bread or wholegrain/fortified breakfast cereal (0.6).

Chapter 5: Zinc – food group combinations based on Table 5.2

Cereals	Fruit and vegetables	Meat and alternatives	Dairy and alternatives	Total zinc (+breast milk/ formula milk)*
1 (0.2)	1 (0.1)	1 (0.4)	1 (0.2)	0.9+1.8/3.6=2.7/4.5
2 (0.4)	2 (0.2)	1 (0.4)	1 (0.2)	1.2+1.8/3.6=3/4.8
2 (0.4)	2 (0.2)	2 (0.8)	1 (0.2)	1.6+1.8/3.6=3.4/5.2
2 (0.4)	2 (0.2)	2 (0.8)	2 (0.4)	1.8+1.8/3.6=3.6/5.4
3 (0.6)	3 (0.3)	2 (0.8)	1 (0.2)	1.9+1.5/3=3.4/4.9
3 (0.6)	3 (0.3)	2 (0.8)	2 (0.4)	2.1+1.5/3=3.6/5.1
3 (0.6)	3 (0.3)	3 (1.2)	1 (0.2)	2.3+1.5/3=3.8/5.3
3 (0.6)	3 (0.3)	3 (1.2)	2 (0.4)	2.5+1.5/3=4/5.5
4 (0.8)	4 (0.4)	2 (0.8)	1 (0.2)	2.2+1.5/3=3.7/5.2
4 (0.8)	4 (0.4)	2 (0.8)	2 (0.4)	2.4+1.5/3=3.9/5.4
4 (0.8)	4 (0.4)	3 (0.8)	1 (0.2)	2.2+1.5/3=3.7/5.2
4 (0.8)	4 (0.4)	3 (1.2)	2 (0.4)	2.8+1.5/3=4.3/5.8
4 (0.8)	4 (0.4)	4 (1.6)	1 (0.2)	3+1.5/3=4.5/6
4 (0.8)	4 (0.4)	4 (1.6)	2 (0.4)	3.2+1.5/3=4.7/6.2
5 (1)	5 (0.5)	2 (0.8)	1 (0.2)	2.5+1.5/3=4/5.5
5 (1)	5 (0.5)	2 (0.8)	2 (0.4)	2.7+1.5/3=4.2/5.7
5 (1)	5 (0.5)	3 (1.2)	1 (0.2)	2.9+1.5/3=4.4/5.9
5 (1)	5 (0.5)	3 (1.2)	2 (0.4)	3.1+1.5/3=4.6/6.1
5 (1)	5 (0.5)	4 (1.6)	1 (0.2)	3.3+1.5/3=4.8/6.3
5 (1)	5 (0.5)	4 (1.6)	2 (0.4)	3.5+1.5/3=5/6.5
5 (1)	5 (0.5)	5 (2)	1 (0.2)	3.7+1.5/3=5.2/6.7
5 (1)	5 (0.5)	5 (2)	2 (0.4)	3.9+1.5/3=5.4/6.9

Notes: *Zinc content of 600 mL of breast milk is 1.8 mg, that of formula milk is 3.6 mg, that of 500 mL of breast milk is 1.5 mg, and that of formula milk is 3 mg – likely to have 600 mL of breast or formula milk with one or two meals, 500 mL otherwise; [a] zinc value is median zinc value of food group – zinc range: cereals, 0.1–0.4; fruit and vegetables, 0–0.1; meat and alternatives, 0.1–0.8; dairy and alternatives, 0.1–0.4; zinc value for wholegrain or fortified cereals, 0.3, range 0.2–0.4 (zinc values from Table 4.14, Chapter 4).

WEBSITES

www.ars.usda.gov   US Department of Agriculture Agricultural Research Service; national nutrient database

www.babyledweaning.com   Baby-led weaning advice, run by a mother

www.bda.uk.com/foodfacts/   The British Dietetic Association; infant feeding

www.child-smile.org.uk   NHS Health Scotland; programme to improve dental health in Scotland; infant feeding

www.choosemyplate.gov   US Department of Agriculture pictorial representation of food intake for children aged 2 years and over

www.codexalimentarius.org   Codex Alimentarius; international food standards, guidelines and codes of practice

http://cot.food.gov.uk   The Committee on Toxicity of Chemicals in Food, Consumer Products and the Environment; advice on fish consumption

www.cowandgate.co.uk   Cow & Gate; infant food and milk manufacturer

www.cwt.org.uk   The Caroline Walker Trust; *Eating Well: First Year of Life* resource and *Infant Milks in the UK*

www.dh.gov.uk   Department of Health; UK National Diet and Nutrition Survey, infant feeding booklet and advice; the eatwell plate

www.early-nutrition.org   Early Nutrition Academy; early nutrition and metabolic programming research and training

www.eufic.org   The European Food Information Council; food-based dietary guidelines in Europe

www.eurreca.org   EURRECA (EURopean micronutrient RECommendations Aligned) European network; develop methodologies to standardise micronutrient recommendations

www.firststepsnutrition.org   First Steps Nutrition Trust; provides information and resources on nutrition from pre-conception to 5 years, by members of the 'First years' team of the Caroline Walker Trust; *Eating Well: First Year of Life* (2011) resource

www.food.gov.uk   Food Standards Agency; infant feeding booklet and advice

www.healthscotland.com   Scottish Health Improvement Agency (NHS Health Scotland); complementary feeding booklet and advice

www.healthvisitors.com   Health visitors' advice to the public

www.healthystart.nhs.uk   Information on free vitamins and free weekly vouchers (to spend on milk, fruit and vegetables and infant formula) www.heinzbaby.co.uk   Heinz infant food manufacturer

www.hipp.co.uk   HiPP infant food and milk manufacturer

www.ic.nhs.uk   NHS Information Centre; Infant Feeding Survey results

www.iccidd.org   International Council for the Control of Iodine Deficiency Disorders; iodine deficiency

www.infantandtoddlerforum.org   Infant & Toddler Forum; advice on healthy eating (toddlers), includes portion sizes for toddlers

www.iodinenetwork.net   The Network For Sustained Elimination of Iodine Deficiency newsletter; iodine deficiency

www.linkagesproject.org   Linkages, a worldwide project improving infant and young child feeding

www.mrc-hnr.cam.ac.uk   Medical Research Council, part of the research team for the National Infant Diet and Health Study

www.mumsnet.com   Parent advice and information in the UK; infant feeding advice

www.nhs.uk   National Health Service; the eatwell plate

www.noo.org.uk   The National Obesity Observatory (National Health Service; National Diet and Nutrition Survey)

www.organix.com   Organix infant food and milk manufacturer

www.publichealth.hscni.net   Northern Ireland Public Health Agency; infant complementary feeding booklet and advice

www.rapleyweaning.com   Baby-led weaning site by Gill Rapley

www.unitetheunion.org/cphva   Community Practitioners' and Health Visitors' Association

www.wales.gov.uk   Welsh Government; infant feeding booklet and advice

www.weetabix.co.uk   Weetabix, food manufacturer

Index

Entries in *italics* refer to figures; entries in **bold** refer to tables.

CPD with Radcliffe

You can now use a selection of our books to achieve CPD (Continuing Professional Development) points through directed reading.

We provide a free online form and downloadable certificate for your appraisal portfolio. Look for the CPD logo and register with us at: www.radcliffehealth.com/cpd